THE ITALIAN-AMERICANS

THE ITALIAN-AMERICANS

by **GARY NULL** and **CARL STONE**

in cooperation with

The Italian-American Civil Rights League

Stackpole Books

THE ITALIAN-AMERICANS

Copyright © 1976 by
Gary Null and Carl Stone

Published by
STACKPOLE BOOKS
Cameron and Kelker Streets
Harrisburg, Pa. 17105

Printed in the U.S.A.

Library of Congress Cataloging in Publication Data
Null, Gary.
  The Italian-Americans.

  Bibliography: p.
  Includes index.
  1. Italian Americans—Biography. 2. United States—Biography. I. Stone, Carl, joint author. II. Title.
E184.I8N84   973' .04'51 [B]   75-42436
ISBN 0-8117-0930-2

CONTENTS

PREFACE

ITALIAN-AMERICANS does not begin to include all of the significant Italian-American figures of the past and present. It is limited to about six hundred outstanding men and women who, through their creativity and energy, have contributed to the progress of an emerging American civilization. Their influence upon those who followed has been profound and unmistakable.

The Italians played a leading role in American scientific development, in the progress of medicine, and in our national life. Their creative genius and intellectuality have introduced new elements, new temperaments and new tones to art, literature and music.

In many ways the Italian-American has been a pioneer of the modern world. His ideas, revolutionary in thought and expression, helped shape this nation's development.

The following chapters will show how Italian influence has been distinctive in the building of America from the beginning. An impressive array of Italian-Americans have put their stamp on the forging of a great democracy.

From the days of the founding fathers, Italian-Americans have preserved their individuality and inherited characteristics while simultaneously integrating themselves into the American lifestyle and uniting with their neighbors in building, enriching and cherishing their new homeland.

In the preparation of this book we consulted many librarians and scholars, who gave of their time and knowledge with unstinting generosity. We also sought and received valuable assistance from several Italian organizations—Sons of Italy, Italian Civil Liberties Union, and the Italian Historical Society, to name only three. To this was added the enthusiasm and inspiration of our research staff: Norma Brizzi, David Handelberger, John Petrigac and Dave Barger. Our editor James Dawson added the finishing touches with his keen criticism and blue pencil.

The exigencies of publishing deadlines kept this book from being as up-to-date as the authors would like it to be but, under the best of circumstances, it is well nigh impossible to keep abreast of the accomplishments of the several hundred energetic and creative Italian-Americans whose careers are touched upon in these pages. We trust the reader will understand.

It is hoped that ITALIAN-AMERICANS will prove valuable for enjoyable general reading and reference, and that it will reveal the impact Italians have made on American life.

Like all minorities in the United States, Italian-Americans are a

vii

unique group within the nation, as well as an integral part of the nation itself. To know and understand their story, the early Italian settlers, the outstanding Italian-American citizen and the proud Italian-American individual who is so much a part of this country, is to know and understand the melting pot that is America.

INTRODUCTION:
From Columbus to Columbus Circle

The history of the Italian in America begins in 1492. On Friday, August third of that year, a little before sunrise, Christopher Columbus sailed out of Palos, Spain in the service of Queen Isabella. At length, after three months of wandering an uncharted sea, Columbus and his three ships reached the island of San Salvadore in the Bahamas on October 12. Without realizing it, he was on America's doorstep.

Cristoforo Columbo was born at Genoa, Italy in 1451. His name meant "Christ Bearer," which may have been a factor in shaping his determination to be a traveller and carry his religious tidings to "heathen" lands. Christopher Columbus is the Latin form of his name.

A sailor since his early days, he swam ashore to Portugal when his ship was sunk in a naval battle and decided to cast his lot with that seafaring country.

After years of voyaging under the Portuguese flag, Columbus drew up a sea route that was supposed to lead him to India, and he presented this short-cut to Isabella and Ferdinand, the joint sovereigns of Spain. Impressed with Columbus and his ideas, they promoted him to Admiral of the Ocean Sea, a title that sounded more impressive than it was, and sent him on his merry way westward with a caravan of three ships to claim land for Spain.

At San Salvadore, Columbus and his crew were greeted by the wide-eyed natives. Thinking he had landed at an outpost of India, Columbus called them Indians, a name that has stuck with all the dark-skinned, indigenous Americans—South, Central and North.

Sailing on from San Salvadore, Columbus stopped at Cuba and Haiti, colonizing the latter (the colony was massacred months later). On a second journey the following year, after he had returned to Spain and had been equipped with seventeen ships and 1200 men, Columbus also explored the Virgin Islands, Puerto Rico and countless other islands, claiming them all as territory for the realm of Spain. And on his third and fourth trips (1498-1505), he set foot on the Lesser and Greater Antilles, and South and Central America.

Thus it was Christopher Columbus, an Italian, who began the

great European migration to the New World nearly 500 years ago; the European history books credit him with "discovering" America.

When he heard of the results of Columbus' New World enterprise, King Henry VII of England granted authority to John Cabot and his three sons to sail west from England and cash in on the glory. Cabot and his small crew of 18 men left the port of Bristol on May 20, 1497. Slightly over a month later, they arrived at Newfoundland and planted the banner of St. George, then sailed southward to reconnoiter much of the coast between Labrador and Delaware, claiming for England, though Cabot didn't realize it at the time, all of North America east of the Rockies and north of Florida.

John Cabot had arrived in Bristol seven years earlier from Venice, Italy. He was originally a Genoese named Giovanni Caboto (or Cabotto).

Around 1500, a Florentine banker who had settled in Seville, Spain, signed up for several voyages under Spaniard Alonso de Ojeda and explored the coast of Brazil. Two years later he led his own expedition to South America. Upon his return, the Italian Amerigo Vespucci boasted that he had discovered the New World continent in 1497, a year before Columbus landed there on his third expedition. Vespucci's story gained credence through papers printed in Florence and found its way to a German college instructor, Waldseemuller, who was compiling a fresh edition of Ptolemy, with a new map of the world. When the book came out in 1507, the introduction said, "Since Americus Vespucius (Latin form) has discovered a fourth part of the world, it should be called after him . . . America, since Europe and Asia got their names from women." Waldseemuller's idea spread, and by 1530 every European country except Spain and Portugal called the New World America.

In 1524, France decided to send an expedition to the New World. Since Spain and England had already made their claims through Italian navigators, King Francis I picked a Florentine explorer, Giovanni da Verrazzano, to represent French interests. This Italian adventurer reached the Cape Fear River in March 1524 and sailed along the coast of the future Carolinas, Virginia and New Jersey. He traveled up the Hudson River and led the first expedition into New York harbor. A Franciscan missionary, Friar Marco da Nizza, reached Mexico in 1531 shortly after the Spanish conquest. He traveled as far north as the Grand Canyon and returned with tales of riches that began a series of Spanish expeditions.

Three Italian military engineers accompanied Fernando De Soto in his adventurous exploration of the American Southeast in 1539-43.

The first European to describe Niagara Falls was Father Francesco Bressani, who was later captured by the Iroquois Indians, in

1644. Italian missionaries were reported killed by Indians in the 1670's. Fra Eusebio Chino left Genoa for the New World in 1678 and, with Father Salvaterra of Milan, was a missionary in northern New Spain—the American Southwest. Fra Chino later proved that lower California was a peninsula.

In 1679 Enrico Tonti, in the service of France, built the first large vessel ever to sail the Great Lakes. He was second in command to Robert LaSalle. Tonti reached Louisiana in 1682, and later founded the first European settlement in Arkansas.

A group of Piedmontese Waldensians settled in what is now Delaware, after fleeing religious persecution in Italy. Italians numbered among the settlers of the colonial period; one of them was William Paca (originally Pace or Paci), a governor of Maryland and a signer of the Declaration of Independence. Philip Mazzei, born near Florence, came to Virginia in 1773 and served as an agent of the Commonwealth in gaining European support for American independence (see profile). Italians composed a large part of three regiments of the expeditionary force sent by France to aid the Americans in the Revolutionary War, and many of them settled in the United States afterward. Bracco, Finizzi and three members of the Tagliaferro family were officers in the Continental Army under Washington.

Colonel Francesco Vigo, from Mondovi, came to America in 1774, fought in the Revolutionary War, and contributed to the victory over the French at Vincennes in 1779, which gave the new United States control of the Old Northwest as far as the Upper Mississippi.

Salvatore Catalano, from Sicily, was Stephen Decatur's pilot in 1804, during the United States' war against pirates at Tripoli. He remained in America after his return.

Philip Mazzei, mentioned above, was commissioned by President Thomas Jefferson to find competent Italian artists to work in Washington. At least seven Italian painters came to the capital between 1806 and 1810. Later in the century Constantino Brumidi (see profile) did the fresco paintings in the Capitol Building.

In the early nineteenth century the bishops of St. Louis, New Orleans and Savannah were Italians. Father Giovanni Grassi of the Society of Jesus was the head of the new Georgetown College near Washington, D.C. in 1812.

Another distinguished Italian was Lorenzo da Ponte, from Venezia. In his youth he wrote the librettos for Mozart's *Le Nozze di Figaro, Don Giovanni,* and *Cosi Fan Tutte.* He heralded direct Italian culture in North America. Ponte taught the first classes on Dante at Columbia University and promoted Italian opera by building New York's first opera house, supported by other Italian immigrants, in 1833.

Not long afterward, architect-sculptor Joseph Coletti was commissioned to do the high-relief structures in the Baltimore Cathedral.

The early Italian settlers had a wide variety of family-acquired trades, such as glass blowing, stonecutting, cobbling, weaving and farming. There were also merchants, a number of skilled doctors, lawyers, teachers, musicians, and portraitists. These people had generally come to America to escape religious or political persecution, and their backgrounds allowed them to assimilate into the American culture without great difficulty.

In 1860 there were estimated to be 50,000 Italians in the United States. Most of the recent arrivals were in the New York area, though many had gone west ten years later to California in the gold rush.

Then, in the 1870's, Italy experienced its first great permanent emigration. Nineteenth-century Italy had been a time of great political revolution, wars and repression. Austria and France were constantly invading the city-states. Finally, national unity came in 1861 when Garibaldi (who had worked in a Staten Island factory ten years earlier) declared the Kingdom of Italy.

Millions of uneducated or semieducated Italians saw unification as a broadening of horizons beyond the now obsolete, traditional borders of the city-states. They saw an offering of distant opportunities that couldn't be found at home. When centuries-old divisions ended with the unification of the Italian nation, most of Italy was a depressed area. What little economic expansion occurred could hardly keep up with the population growth. Consequently, over a million emigrants, mainly from Northern Italy, left their country, and a small number of this group came to the United States.

In the 1880's and 1890's the emigration current became a tidal wave—in twenty years nearly five million Italians from throughout the country emigrated. Approximately one in four of them came to the United States. Many settled in the Italian ghetto in East Harlem —a place of squalor and degradation. Between 1900 and 1920, another ten million left Italy. What was significant about this latest emigration were the sharp increases in (1) emigrants from the South of Italy and (2) immigrants arriving in America. By the time Benito Mussolini's Fascist regime came to power and halted the migration out of the country, nearly five million Italians had come to the United States.

According to American records, by 1970 the number of Italians who had migrated to the U.S. was over 5.1 million, constituting eleven percent of all European immigrants who have come to this country since 1820. Of this 5.1 million, over two-thirds became American citizens and raised their children as Americans. The

Italian population in the New York City metropolitan area is greater than the population of Rome.

Much has been written about the suffering and discrimination encountered by the Italian immigrants, but this must be seen against the suffering at home in Italy. Without making excuses for American prejudice, we must nevertheless concede a basic fact: the late-nineteenth-and-early-twentieth-century immigrant had abandoned Italy for one reason—poverty. In Italy there was only unemployment and underemployment, low wages, semi-starvation, high mortality (especially among infants), squalor, little or no schooling, hopelessly poor housing, no medical care, rigid class structure, and exploitation. For the average Italian migration was liberation.

Of the 1.6 million Italians who came to this country between 1900 and 1910, only 9,000 had the equivalent of a college degree. About 300,000 possessed some vocational or professional skills, but the remaining one million and nearly three hundred thousand people were totally unskilled. Most had been agricultural workers, four out of five were men, and seven out of eight were between the ages of 14 and 44. Most of them arrived on American soil as paupers, without a dime (or a lira) in their pockets. Given these facts alone, one can see that the prognosis for immediate success was not good.

Additional problems were to be faced by these immigrants, especially those who came from the South where conditions of life were almost inhuman. The remnants of a feudalistic society still existed in Italy at that time: a tiny minority of arrogant aristocratic families led opulent lives and lorded over the others who lived in abject poverty. In many townships water was a luxury. Roads and streets were impassable in bad weather. Winter was short but it was harsh, and the hovels had no heating. Summers were fiercely hot and accompanied by drought.

The Southerner was bound with ignorance and poverty. Raised in a stagnant and stratified society cut off from the rest of the world, he could barely relate to the turmoil of the dynamic and competitive (and ostensibly egalitarian) society that awaited him in the United States.

Discrimination became "official" in 1921 when Congress passed and President Harding signed the Johnson Act, which limited the number of aliens admitted annually to 3% of the number of foreign-born of that nationality already in the U.S., according to the 1910 census. In other words, the fewer the number of immigrants who were already settled in America, the smaller the number from that same country would be allowed thereafter. The total number of immigrants allowed annually was set at 358,000, of which only 155,000 could come from southern and eastern Europe.

Some "racist" critics felt that the different folkways and traditions of southern and eastern Europe (from which most of the recent immigrants had come) were a menace to American society; others, like author Kenneth Roberts, feared a "hybrid race of good-for-nothing mongrels."

Perhaps more valid was the American concern over the new labor force from Italy, Greece and the Slavic countries. Coming from poverty, these laborers demanded little from the American market, and their presence kept wages low and hampered the attempt of unions to organize workers. Labor leaders were particularly afraid that they would lose their wage gains made during the World War.

There were also suspicions of importation of Sicilian crime and eastern European Communism, which spurred a more drastic, new Johnson Act of 1924. This act reduced the annual admittance to only 2% according to the 1890 census (prior to the great wave from southern and eastern Europe). This was a flagrant discriminatory move. Italian-American Congressman Fiorello LaGuardia was its staunchest, loudest critic.

In 1929 a third act fixed a quota of 20,000 to southern and eastern Europe *and Asia*. Africa was excluded altogether. Immigration policy was set clearly to keep America "white."

Fortunately, times have changed. In 1965 an enlightened immigration bill was passed. Though it retains the quota on entries, the discriminating national-origins restrictions have been discarded. The new bill does give preference, however, to the immigrant with special skills, or with established family connections in the United States.

But this does not change history. Regardless of the efforts of the immigrants to prove their intrinsic worth, American prejudice proliferated throughout the first half of this century and the latter decades of the last. Regardless of the amount and intensity of work accomplished by the Italian-Americans in this country, they were considered for many years as second-class citizens.

To the established American whose family had been here for awhile, the immigrants were trespassers to be looked down upon with distrust and dislike. Italians were given degrading "slang" names like "Wop," "Dago," and "Guinea," insults shared by all immigrants at one time or another. Every minority in this country has been tagged with derogatory names.

The term "Wop" supposedly originated in the Neapolitan dialect word *guappo*, which means a flashy, show-off type. It was used by southern Italians to describe their own dandies.

"Dago" originated from the Spanish word *Diego*, which Americans trimmed and adapted to refer prejoratively to anyone of Latin or Mediterranean origin. "Guinea" or "Ginney" is derived from the early American reference to the dark-skinned natives of British Guiana. It was later bestowed upon the swarthy, dark-eyed Italian immigrants.

The Italian-American fared no better than the American Negro in being stereotyped. Most Americans considered the strange Italian as a "dark foreigner," ignorant, dirty, loud-mouthed, and smelling of garlic and cheap wine. His pidgin English with its terminal vowels was comically unpalatable to their ears. Because of his explosive temper, he was feared. He worked at jobs which elicited no respect: organ-grinder, fishmonger, bootblack, stevedore, pushcart vendor, etc. A good many Americans attributed these "lowly" pursuits to racial inferiority, with which Italian children could supposedly never become acceptable American citizens.

The Italians themselves often worsened their own positions out of frustration, importing old regional prejudices from Italy. Northern and southern Italians constantly feuded and cast aspersions on each other.

It became necessary, then, for Italian-Americans to form fraternal organizations, like the Order of the Sons of Italy in America, to protect themselves against attacks of intolerance and its effects upon their self-esteem.

Not only the general American, but the Italian immigrant himself needed to be told about such great Italians as St. Thomas Aquinas, Michelangelo, Da Vinci, Raphael, Dante, Galileo, Garibaldi and Verdi. There was a need for pride and education of Italian culture, something these immigrants had not been familiar with, even in Italy. They had to learn that American culture and heritage paled before the glorious history of the Roman Empire that, twenty centuries ago, exercised a powerful civilizing force that would shape the Western world.

Roman civilization, along with that of the ancient Greeks, permeates every part of our lives today. Latin, in its classical form, has survived and flourished in jurisprudence, literature and the Catholic Church; and the Latin spoken by the common people is the root of French, Italian, Spanish, Portuguese and Rumanian. Though the English language is Germanic in origin, at least one-third of its words are Latin derivatives.

Roman architecture is still in use today in churches, commercial buildings and bridges. Roman writers like Cicero, Caesar and Tacitus have had a lasting influence in Western literature. The Roman Senate, symbol of a constitutional and democratic government, is the prototype of the government of the United States.

After the decline of the Roman Empire, Italy continued to have an effect on Western civilization. Fifteenth-century Italy witnessed a revival of "the grandeur that was Rome," and gave birth to the creative spirit. The Renaissance, a flowering of the arts, sciences and philosophy, began in Italy, and for two centuries it swept the cobwebs of the Dark Ages out of Europe and ushered in the modern Western world.

It was the Italy of this enlightened period that produced the great inventor and artist, Leonardo Da Vinci. The discoveries of astronomer, mathematician and inventor (telescope, microscope, thermometer) Galilei Galileo had a profound effect upon science. Niccolo Machiavelli shaped a new political thinking; Michelangelo, Giotto and Raphael set the standards for art, sculpture and beauty; Dante and Boccaccio produced great writings (Dante's works in the Italian vernacular established it as a literary language); Marco Polo opened up travel and international exchange; Antonio Pigafetta was one of Magellan's 18-man crew that first circumnavigated the Earth in 1522; Girolama Fracastoro founded modern medical pathology; Vannoccio Biringucci began the serious science of chemistry; other great Italians translated the works of the ancient Greeks, opening up new, or rather old, avenues of philosophy and science. Renaissance Italy was the greatest peak of human civilization since the Golden Age of ancient Greece. It was this Italy that sent explorers and adventurers all over the world, that produced Columbus and Cabot, that set the standards for the coming Age of Seapower, which would bring the entire world together and reshape civilization until it no longer resembled the yesterday of centuries before.

It is this proud heritage that Italian-Americans can claim. Italy has been called "the cradle of civilization." It is also the land of civilization's re-birth.

Today, in 1976, about one-third of all Italian-Americans live in New York State, forming a large segment of all urban communities. Another third of the population can be found in the neighboring states of New Jersey, Connecticut, Pennsylvania and Massachusetts. Sizable Italian-American communities are located in the Midwest belt between Chicago and Cleveland, in California, Florida, Louisiana and Colorado.

Presently, most Italian-Americans are second and third generation, with only a small percentage being foreign-born. Like the other large immigrant groups who preceded them to the ghettos of New York—the Irish, Jews and Germans—Italians have pushed up and out and mingled with the general population.

Italian-Americans have very strong feelings on most topics and rarely hide or dissimulate expression of their interests, their affections or their grief. They have an open and consuming love for children, parents, friends and country and all other things they consider beautiful. They have an intense pride in their work and craftsmanship and are ardently loyal to whatever cause or person they support. Body and soul seem to merge both in work and pleasure. They live life to the hilt. Few nationals work harder or more diligently than Italian-Americans. Perhaps it is significant that they suffer far less than most groups from heart disease, alcoholism, mental illness and suicide.

Examine the English language today and you will find a great many Italian (not Latin) words that are commonly known and used. Paesano—fellow countryman—has become synonymous with 'pal.' Vino is an affectionate term for wine shared among friends. Bambino is well-known as 'baby.' Other Italian-derived words include quota, motto, ballot, propaganda, fiasco, replica, incognito, contraband, gusto, virtuoso, confetti, manifesto, dilettante, altruism, ballerina, scenario, umbrella, malaria, influenza, lava, extravaganza, volcano and inferno.

The international language of music was given its orderly seven-tone scale by the Italians, who also contributed opera, coloratura, soprano, basso, falsetto, oratorio, solo, libretto, finale and tempo. Musical instruments such as the piano, viola, piccolo, trombone and timpani have Italian names. Sonnet comes from sonnetta; stanza, simile and terza rima (a verse form popularized by Dante's poetry) date back to the Renaissance. Italy, the cradle of art, gave us studio, fresco, tempera, torso, mural, cameo, terra cotta, portico, cupola, campanile and stucco. Even our military is influenced by Italian: battalion, brigade, cavalry, regiment, artillery, corporal, infantry, captain and general.

Bravo! is a universal exclamation. Pantaloons and pants come from *pantalone*. The slanting printing type used here is known as *italic,* originated by a Venetian printer. Jeans were first manufactured for wear in Genoa. Milliners were the hatmakers of Milan. Venetian blinds come from Venice, Roman candles from Rome, baloney from Bologna, and Neapolitan ice cream from Naples. Sardines were first caught commercially off the coast of Sardinia and cantaloupe was grown in and near the town of Cantalupo.

Most American housewives and restaurants serve pasta, macaroni, ravioli and lasagna. They use parmesan cheese, romano, gorgonzola, ricotta, mozzarella, rovolone, bel paese and salami. The popularity of dinner wine is a direct Italian-American influence. And nowadays who doesn't like those "all-American" dishes—spaghetti and pizza?

It is rather easy to see how deeply entrenched the Italian-Americans are in the life and culture of the United States. Indeed, we owe a great deal to them.

In the pages ahead Gary Null and Carl Stone have dealt extensively with many significant Italian-Americans who helped shape the destinies of their communities. The accomplishments of these people, you'll find, are nothing short of miraculous.

Carl Cecora, President
Italian-American Civil Rights League

Philip Mazzei

Philip Mazzei was born in 1730 near Florence in the Italian state of Tuscany, the son of a wealthy landowner and merchant. Philip's eldest brother became the head of the family upon the father's death and proved to be a tyrant. Later in his life, Philip Mazzei wrote that it was the deep hatred for his brother's tyranny that made him such a fighter, both physically and ideologically.

Mazzei's ability to discuss or debate on virtually any topic was practically matchless. Believing that everyone should be permitted freedom of thought and expression, he was noted for his candid remarks to people whom he thought were prejudiced and intolerant.

As a young man, Mazzei was a medical student at a Florence hospital, but when he protested against the manner in which poor students were treated he was expelled. Despite this dismissal, he continued to attend medical lectures. In his free time he voraciously read about art, politics and philosophy.

In 1753 he went to Turkey, where he lived with a Jewish doctor and helped him treat the poor. Three years later he returned to Europe and decided to go into practice in England, which at the time was considered to be one of the most philosophically and politically liberal countries in the world.

In London he gave Italian lessons to anyone who could afford them and attended medical lectures. When he discovered that the English wanted Italian products which were not available in England, Mazzei went into the business of importing wines, olive oil, cheese, fruits and candy.

In comparing governments throughout Europe he found England the most politically advanced and the others tyrannically reactionary. Nevertheless, he became painfully aware that many inequities existed in the English system and fervently became an advocate of complete democracy. He expressed sympathy for the American cause and he believed that the American colonies should achieve independence from England. After much consideration he decided to go to America and practice horticulture.

Thomas Adams, the noted Virginia statesman, had met Mazzei in London and written home about the young Italian to Thomas Jefferson, who was then a representative in Virginia's House of Burgesses. He told Jefferson that Mazzei was a man of exceptional qualities, that America needed men like him to contribute strength and zeal to America's fight for independence. Jefferson wrote Mazzei, invited him to come to America, and promised him full cooperation in his horticultural enterprise. Jefferson intimated that in America he could really be an innovator and plant the first wine grapes, olive and citrus trees, and mulberry trees for the production of silk. Benjamin Franklin, who had befriended Mazzei, also insisted that he come to America. So, in September 1773, Mazzei left England for Virginia and arrived three months later in Williamsburg, the colony's capital. Thomas Jefferson, George Wythe and George Washington gave him a warm welcome.

Jefferson and Mazzei became such good friends that Jefferson invited him to move into a large estate adjacent to his own Monticello. While his house was being built, he lived with Jefferson for two years. It was during this time just before the Revolution that Mazzei influenced much of Jefferson's political thinking.

Mazzei turned his efforts to writing articles urging complete political liberty and the formation of a militia that would be prepared to fight England at a moment's notice. One of the articles stated, "To attain our goal it is necessary, my dear citizens, to discuss the natural rights of man and the foundations of a free government. All men are by nature equally free and independent. This quality is essential to the establishment of a liberal government, a truly republican form of government cannot exist except where all men, from the very rich to the very poor, are perfectly equal in their natural rights."

During Jefferson's absences from Monticello, Mazzei was regarded as the leader of Albemarle County. As evidence of the confidence the local citizens had placed in him, he was one of twelve men elected to represent the county's voters, consult with the legislators at Williamsburg, and inform the citizen about significant proposals. His counterpart today would be a local congressman.

Jefferson now gave Mazzei an assignment. Since America needed financial support badly, Jefferson wrote John Hancock and John Adams requesting that Congress send Mazzei to France to represent Virginia in an attempt to borrow money. The measure was accepted and Mazzei left for France.

When he arrived in Paris early in 1780, he was met by Marquis de La Fayette and Benjamin Franklin. Franklin was there representing the Continental Congress in the same capacity that Mazzei was serving for Virginia—to enlist French support for a struggling American nation. La Fayette and Franklin gave Mazzei the names of influential persons who might be able to help him, and he dutifully went to these prospective supporters and tried to convince them that the new nation was a good risk and to inspire them with confidence in the unity and future prosperity of the United States. He published many articles throughout Europe in which he defended the War of Independence and told of the first struggles of a republican government, extolling its remarkable achievements.

Mazzei sent Jefferson progress reports that kept Virginia's new governor informed of European attitudes and events. He also contrived a plan, whereby the American land forces and French navy could together surround the British in New York. French officers were later to put this stratagem to use at Yorktown in 1783 and force Cornwallis' surrender, bringing the war to an end.

Mazzei's attachment to America was a thing of spirit, not of soil. He wrote Jefferson that his zeal was "not for the trees or the rivers or for the land of America, but for the asylum of liberty."

And so, with the Revolution over, this unusually talented man—a doctor, merchant, horticulturalist, pamphleteer and financial agent—left America in June 1785 and sailed for Paris. "I am leaving but my heart remains," he wrote James Madison. "America is my Jupiter, Virginia my Venus." Virginia Governor Benjamin Harrison wrote into the records that few Americans had made such "public exertions" for the colonies as did Philip Mazzei.

In Paris Mazzei became aroused over the unfair criticism which America was receiving in Europe. He decided to write a history of the new nation. For the next three years he labored over what was to be the first accurate history of America, and in 1788 the four-volumed *Studies of the Historical and Political Origins of the United States of North America* was published. Much of what Mazzei wrote in this work was later to be included in the United States Constitution.

He served briefly as an intelligence agent for the liberal King of Poland, Stanislaus, and in 1791 he was summoned to Warsaw as an advisor. However, when Poland was split up among Russia, Austria and Germany in 1792, he left for Italy.

Three years later, Jefferson, who was now Secretary of State under Washington, sent Mazzei a letter in which he described the conflict between the Federalists, headed by Alexander Hamilton and John Adams, and the Anti-federalists or Republicans, with Jefferson their leader. "The aspect of our politics has wonderfully changed since you left us," Jefferson wrote. "In place of that noble love of liberty and republican govt. which carried us triumphantly through the war, an Anglican, monarchical and aristocratic party has sprung up, whose avowed object is to draw over us the substance as they have already done the forms of the British govt. . . . In short, we are likely to preserve the liberty . . . only by unremitting labors and perils."

Mazzei thought it important to have a translation of the letter published in an Italian newspaper. The French followed suit, and then the English translated it from the French. Both France and England interpreted it as evidence of American political upheaval. It took nearly two years for the letter to reach America, but when it did in the spring of 1797, a political tempest erupted. The infamous "Mazzei Letter" discredited Jefferson in the eyes of many Americans. His relations with George Washington had been shaky; now they were severed and Washington never again spoke to Jefferson.

The letter could very well have caused Jefferson's complete political destruction had it not been that between the time of its writing and its appearance in America, he had become Vice President under John Adams.

Jefferson's future letters to Mazzei were of necessity more cautious, although Mazzei and Jefferson still remained the best of friends. In fact, Jefferson used segments of Mazzei's letter to him in the summer of 1776 in writing the Declaration of Independence. It was Philip Mazzei who first said "All men are by nature equally free and independent, and all men are created equal." In fact, many famous American sayings can be traced to Mazzei's early letters and his historic book.

In 1805, Benjamin Latrobe, the designer of the new American capital of Washington, D.C., asked Mazzei to find a gifted artist to work on the new public buildings. "The time is already approaching when our vines and our olives will spread your name and our gratitude over a great portion of the country," Latrobe wrote.

The elderly Mazzei supplied Latrobe with two talented sculptor-painters, Giuseppe Franzoni and Giovanni Andrei, and in their wake came several other Italian artists.

Mazzei wrote Jefferson frequently asking him to come to Europe, but the new President of the United States was too busy. Of Mazzei, Jefferson was later to write that "he was of solid worth, honest, able, zealous, had sound principles, moral and political, constant in friendship, and punctual in all his undertaking."

Philip Mazzei died at Pisa in 1816 at the age of eighty-five.

CONSTANTINO BRUMIDI

Each year hundreds of thousands of visitors touring the Capitol Building in Washington, D.C. marvel at the many beautiful murals on its walls. When they look up they see, some fifty feet high in the rotunda, a fresco frieze girdling the round room, painted in mute grays to imitate sculpture. It depicts landmarks in the settlement of the New World. Directly above, at the top of the dome, 180 feet from the floor, is the Capitol's largest painting, the famous fresco of the "Apotheosis of Washington," the glorification of the "Father of Our Country."

All of these murals and frescoes were painted a hundred years ago by Constantino Brumidi, one of the greatest and most gifted Italian artists.

Brumidi spent nearly twenty-five years of his life working on these murals, bringing the traditional mural art of his homeland to the walls of the Capitol of his new country. Soon after his arrival in

America, he was offered many commissions, but he declined them all, explaining that his "one ambition and . . . daily prayer is to make beautiful the Capitol of the one country on earth where there is liberty."

Brumidi was born in Rome on July 26, 1805. His mother was Italian, his father Greek. While still young, he showed exceptional talent for drawing and was sent to the Academy of Fine Arts in Rome. At the age of thirteen he entered the famed Academia di San Lucca, where he was tutored by the masters of his time. When his apprenticeship was completed, he was given regular work at the Vatican by the art-loving Pope Gregory XVI. Brumidi was also commissioned by Prince Alessandro Torlonia to do frescoes and sculptures for his palazzo, which later became Mussolini's residence in Rome.

Pope Pius IX commissioned Constantino Brumidi to restore the deteriorated Raphael frescoes in the loggia. The young artist also painted two portraits of the Pope and assisted in depicting the "Chronology of the Popes" in the new basilica at Saint Paul's.

During the Revolution of 1848, Brumidi was blacklisted by the Church and ordered to leave Rome forever because he had supported the ill-fated insurrection led by Garibaldi. Garibaldi, fearing for his life, had fled to America, and he urged Brumidi to join him in New York. Disgusted with the power-struggle going on in Italy at that time, Brumidi accepted his friend's advice and traveled to New York in 1852.

He was already well known among the leading artists in America; his reputation had preceded him to this country. He was quickly given an important commission to paint a huge altar-piece in New York's St. Stephen's Church. In November, he formally declared his intention to seek American citizenship.

Italian artists had already left their mark on Washington. The sculptors Giovanni Andrei and Giuseppe Franzoni had been sent over by Philip Mazzei earlier in the century to embellish the city's new public buildings, and other painters from Italy had followed them. Brumidi, therefore, felt that his desire to work in the Capitol was reasonable.

Captain Montgomery Meigs, an Army engineer heading a team of engineers and supervising new constructions for the Capitol, was interested in a muralist, especially one skilled in the technique of true fresco, which incorporates paintings into architecture itself. Americans were not experienced with murals in public buildings and none had ever used buono fresco. They were primarily easel painters who used oils and water colors and were restricted in their development because American art had been severely inhibited during the Puritan period.

Mural art was uniquely different from pictures on canvas.

Murals could not be moved around at the whim of the artist since walls were stationary. Americans were unfamiliar with them. Only Italians, with a long heritage enriched by Michelangelo and others, were schooled in the buono fresco technique. Thus when Captain Meigs heard about Constantino Brumidi, he commissioned him to work on the Capitol.

In 1854, the Capitol's two large extensions, or annexes, were nearly finished. The new marble extensions dwarfed the old copper-covered wooden dome at the center. Construction of a new dome, fashioned after St. Peter's in Rome and more than 300 feet high had just begun when Brumidi was given his first Government commission.

The Capitol provided acres of white walls that invited Brumidi's energetic imagination to paint every type of patriotic subject. Just as his native churches had glorified Christianity for centuries, the Capitol, he decided, would permanently preserve the spirit of American freedom and portray the men who had won it.

He began his new project in the age-old manner. First he made his working sketch, an oil painting on canvas highlighting the complete design of the mural. Then he drew life-size human figures on large sheets of stiff paper. While his assistant applied fresh plaster to the wall area to be painted, Brumidi prepared his paints by mixing dry tempera with water. He then pressed the figure outlines onto the fresh plaster by dusting powdered charcoal through perforations in the character figures or by etching lines on the wet surface with a stylus. After that, he painted the plaster, doing the flat surfaces first, and then the details and the light and shadow. Lastly, he painted the background.

At the end of each day he removed any unpainted plaster before it dried. On the following morning the entire process was repeated in an adjoining area of the fresco. While the plaster was drying, its lime combined with carbon dioxide and made a surface that resembled marble both in looks and durability. The paint lightened and gave a crystalline appearance.

Brumidi's first commission was completed in 1855. On the walls he had frescoed two scenes: "Cincinnatus Summoned from the Plow to Become the Dictator of Rome" and an American scene, "Putnam Summoned from the Plow to Fight for Independence." He also painted two murals in oil, depicting side by side the cutting of grain with a sickle, and harvesting with the more modern McCormick reaper. On the ceiling Brumidi painted frescoes with scenes of the four seasons.

He was also asked to design the ornate bronze railings which ran (and still run) down the four staircases leading from the House and Senate chambers. On them he sculpted beautiful cherubs, eagles and deer.

Many art experts consider Brumidi's finest work the President's Room in the Senate extension. This masterpiece of craftsmanship took him nearly five years. The room was opulently decorated with a gold-plated $25,000 chandelier, gold-edged mirrors, and elegant panels containing portraits of George Washington and the five members of his first cabinet. Above these were four vaulted corners on which he portrayed Americans from many walks of life and several early explorers and founders, including his Italian countrymen Columbus and Vespucci.

Brumidi's most praised painting was a large mural in the House of Representatives chamber depicting Cornwallis surrendering to Washington at Yorktown.

Life in Washington, D.C. had its difficulties for the Italian-American. Many American-born artists wanted to display their own talents upon the Capitol's walls, and when they found out that Brumidi had a mural scheduled, seemingly, for every inch of the building, they felt slighted. It seemed rather undemocratic that the work could not be done by many artists; but, American artists, as has been said, were not familiar with frescoes and did not have respect for the difficulty of the craftsmanship involved.

Fresco painting is so specialized that it usually takes five to ten years of apprenticeship. The artist has to work with extreme rapidity because of the drying plaster; he cannot afford the mistakes that an untrained artist might make. A change or erasure is difficult and the choice of colors is limited to pigments that safely combine with lime.

There were also physical problems for Brumidi. Most of the time he had to stand on high, often unsteady scaffolding; when he was painting a ceiling he had to lie flat on his back. Added to these burdens were the constant noise, distractions and drafts of the huge public building.

Still, Brumidi had many critics who were determined to have his work "whitewashed" and replaced with the paintings of American artists.

The dispute over Brumidi's work became public in 1858 when a petition of grievance was presented to Congress with the signatures of 127 prominent artists. In this petition they claimed that there was nothing in the design and execution of the ornamental work of the Capitol that represented America or the genius and talent of its artists. Instead of sheep, horses and cattle there were cupids, cherubs, Bacchus and other mythological characters.

Brumidi never once came forward to defend his cause. Instead, he continued his work as if nothing was happening, confident that his supporters—Gugleilmo Gajani of the *New York Daily Tribune,* and certain members of Congress—would come to his aid.

The controversy over his work was silenced when the Civil War began in 1861. However, his work was made more difficult. First there were the defense preparations for the Capitol. During the first year of the war it housed several thousand Union soldiers, who used the rotunda and several large rooms as barracks. Even so, Brumidi managed to continue painting. When he asked President Lincoln whether he should proceed with the work in the dome, the tall bearded man smiled at him and said, "If the world sees this Capitol going on, they will know that we intend the Union shall go on."

The 300-foot high Capitol dome consisted of two shells, one on top of the other, weighing nine million pounds. It is still appreciated for its engineering design. Its completion was officially celebrated on December 2, 1863, when a seven-ton statue of the Goddess of Freedom was placed upon the topmost lantern.

The Capitol architect, Edward Clark, called upon Brumidi to paint the mural on the circular canopy, the plaster-covered copper sheet covering the inside of the dome. It was a curved surface sixty-five feet in diameter, with a concavity of twenty-one feet. Brumidi was given $40,000 with which to begin work. His subject, he decided, would be "The Apotheosis of Washington."

The finished mural would show Washington seated amid celestial clouds, with Freedom and Victory at either side. They in turn were to be surrounded by thirteen pastel-garbed maidens, each representing one of the original states, holding a banner with the legend, "E Pluribus Unum." Encircled around these celebrants were to be six distinct groups of famous Americans and Roman gods and goddesses, who ruled or inspired specific areas of human interest. An armed Liberty, with a shield and a sword, driving out oppression, would stand sentry.

Brumidi began this work in 1865. He was raised by pulleys to a scaffold nearly 180 feet above the floor. In the first eleven months he completed frescoes on 4,664 square feet, an accomplishment never equaled. The design was complicated. Painting on a concave surface, he had to exaggerate many of the figures to give them normal proportions when viewed from far below.

By the end of the year he completed the work, and it was exhibited to the public in January 1866. The situation around him had much changed since he began the project in early 1865. The Civil War had ended, Lincoln had been assassinated, the slaves had been freed, and President Andrew Johnson was now in the White House.

In the post-war years, Brumidi occupied himself with less monumental tasks. Several blank walls still needed embellishment, especially those in the Senate extension. (Several of his works are in rooms occupied by Senators and cannot be viewed by the public normally). In the South and North Rooms he painted frescoes on the ceilings and walls, and in the Senate Reception Room he painted

General Washington conferring with Hamilton and Jefferson. The Senate corridor walls were covered with a profusion of oil paintings and frescoes—medallions or profiles of famous Americans, landscapes, studies of animals, birds and children, large dramatic scenes from history, and portraits in imitation sculpture.

It should be said now, perhaps, that not all of Brumidi's works are considered good art. The majority is beautiful by traditional, classical standards, and many of his portraits are accurate portrayals, but a few works are sentimental or merely ornate, dull or poor likenesses. However, one should appraise Brumidi's vast accomplishments as a whole. No other American artist has ever painted as many actual miles of decorations.

In the summer of 1877 Brumidi began to paint in chiaroscuro (light and shade) the nine-foot-wide panel that circles the rotunda walls, fifty-eight feet above the floor. He visualized the 300-foot long frieze as a "roll of history" recording fifteen important events in America since its discovery by Columbus.

Brumidi was 73 when he began this work. He was enthusiastic about continuing, but his income was insufficient. Congress had recently curtailed expenditures on the Capitol's remodeling. On several occasions he submitted petitions in hopes of being reinstated on a regular salary. Still, the security of a salary was denied him, but nonetheless he reported for work at the Capitol daily and painted from ten till three.

In October 1879, as he was working on the eighth section of the frieze, his chair on the scaffold tipped backwards. He managed to save himself by grabbing hold of a ladder rung, but the shock proved disturbing. He never returned to work on the scaffold.

At home he tried to complete his frieze designs so that a younger artist might complete them. But his devotion failed to sustain him. His health declined rapidly. On February 19, 1880 Constantino Brumidi died, having given the last third of his 75-year lifetime to painting the Capitol of the country he loved.

Shortly afterward, Senator Voorhees of Indiana, missing the figure who had almost become a fixture in the corridors and rooms, said of Constantino Brumidi, "How rich the inheritance he has left to the present and succeeding ages! During more than a quarter of a century, he has hovered along these walls from the basement to the dome, leaving creations of imperishable beauty on whatever he touched."

LUIGI PALMA DI CESNOLA

Luigi Palma di Cesnola began his fascinating American adventure in the Civil War, serving for the Union Army. Later, as a sideline to a brilliant diplomatic career, he became one of the most noted archeologists in America and headed the Metropolitan Museum of Art in New York City. Under his skillful guidance that institution became our country's outstanding art museum.

Cesnola's early life was spent under the disciplined military upbringing of his father, a Piedmontese nobleman who had served with Napoleon and fought in the 1821 Sardinian rebellion against Austria. For a time he was Minister of War for the Kingdom of Sardinia, the center of *Risorgimento,* the unification movement in Italy. Luigi, his second son, was born June 29, 1832, at Rivarolo, near Turin. A strong, spirited youth who wanted to follow in his father's footsteps, he attended the finest military schools. In 1848, when war again erupted between Austria and Sardinia, the young Luigi enlisted in the Sardinian Army. At the battle of Novara in 1849 he was field-commissioned to lieutenant, which made him the youngest officer in the army. When that war ended he went back to the Royal Military Academy to finish his education. Later, during the Crimean War, he was appointed to the staff of Sardinia's commanding general and played a major role in the fall of Sebastopol.

Cesnola went to America in early 1860 in hopes of finding something adventuresome to occupy his time, but he had to settle for a teaching position until the Civil War began. He offered his military experience to the Union Army; it commissioned him a lieutenant colonel with the 11th New York Cavalry Regiment. In 1862 he was made a brigade commander under General Judson Kilpatrick.

A year later, while fighting in the fierce battle at the Aldie gap in Virginia, Colonel Cesnola was wounded and taken prisoner by the Confederates. Along with the remainder of his brigade, he marched nearly a hundred miles to Richmond, where he was placed in the notorious Libby Prison to wait out the war.

After his release he was called to Washington for a meeting with President Lincoln, who gave him an honorary commission of Brigadier General and asked him to take the position of American consul on Cyprus. That island, an important strategic spot in the eastern Mediterranean, was in trouble with the Greek majority who were preparing war on their Turkish rulers. Cesnola was given his United States citizenship and shipped off on a new adventure.

On Christmas Day, General Cesnola entered the city of Larnaca, which was to be his new home for the next dozen years. After his arrival, he became interested in the study of Cypriot history, which, being so long, naturally led him into archeology. Before he realized it he was spending more time and energy digging in the remains of ancient tombs than at his office with diplomatic chores. He struck his first find less than a month after his arrival, a discovery of a handful of terra cotta figures that served to spark his interest in archeology to the point of frenzy.

Every day brought news of important discoveries in the long-lost sites of great cities in the classical world and in Asia Minor. This served to add fuel to his conviction that untold wealth of ancient artifacts lay beneath the soil of Cyprus. It is an old island, having been ruled or occupied at one time or another by the Phoenicians, Assyrians, Persians, Jews, Egyptians, Greeks, Romans, Arabs, medieval crusaders, Venetians and Turks. Yet very few finds had been made in Cyprus up to Cesnola's time; there was much to be discovered.

For two years his finds were interesting but not spectacular. But then one morning news reached his office that diggers had uncovered an enormous stone head and several smaller objects. Cesnola went immediately to the scene to supervise their recovery, fearing that if anything really valuable were uncovered, the police would confiscate it for the Sultan.

He hired twenty extra diggers to work through the night. By morning the area would be covered with peasants who would try to appropriate anything small enough for them to carry away. His diggers worked fast, and when the early streakings of dawn appeared on the horizon they had uncovered all of the objects in the dig: thirty-two statues showing Egyptian and Assyrian influence. All of them were broken, however.

Cesnola studied them and came to the conclusion that they were the artifacts that once surrounded a temple. He hurriedly purchased the adjacent land and began a careful search for the temple itself. After several days of digging a thick stone wall measuring thirty by sixty feet was uncovered. It was the historic Golgoi temple, dedicated to Venus.

When the Governor-General of Cyprus became aware of the fabulous discoveries being made by Cesnola, he ordered all digging stopped until official instructions came from Constantinople. Cesnola moved all of his newly unearthed relics to his home, where no foreign government could confiscate them.

In the meantime, he was busy stopping a possible war between the Greeks and Turks, sparked when the Turks ordered the entire Greek population on Cyprus to leave within twenty days. Cesnola spoke with the Governor-General in Nicosia, pointing out that if the Greeks left there would be no one left to harvest the crop. Also, there was a good chance that the European powers and America would intercede; Cesnola managed to have several European governments send him letters to that effect. Consequently, the Turks revoked their exodus order and averted both intervention and war.

With this matter out of the way, he returned to his archeology, a task he preferred to international diplomacy. He continued to gather precious remnants from past centuries at a phenomenal rate until, soon, both his house and warehouse were filled with hundreds of relics. A problem of what to do with them arose. The longer they remained on Cyprus, the greater the chance of their being stolen, confiscated or accidentally broken. And he was forbidden to ship any of his relics out of the country.

As a token of respect for the Sultan, and a bid for continuance of his archeological work, Cesnola sent two large selections of antiquities to the Turkish Ottoman Museum. However, greedy Turkish officials divided the bounty among themselves without letting one piece get through to the museum.

Angry, Cesnola called in a naval man-of-war vessel to remove his artifacts, and with the assistance of a few Greek diplomats, he managed to ship all them to England. He accompanied his valuable shipment of 10,000 objects with the hope of selling it to museums.

Only two museums—the Louvre and the British Museum—were interested in his findings. The relatively new Metropolitan Museum in New York City could not meet the bids offered by the other two. Since Cesnola had financed six years of archeological digging out of his own pocket, he was not going to be charitable in his dealings. Nonetheless, an American millionaire, Cyrus W. Field underbid the British Museum by $40,000 (the museum had offered Cesnola $100,000) and argued that the new Metropolitan Museum needed his collection, while the British Museum was already filled with valuable collections. The Metropolitan Museum, Field claimed, could give his collection the care and display it deserved.

Cesnola finally agreed to sell his collection to the museum in his own adopted country, which had sent him to Cyprus in the first place. At the time, his relics were believed to be the world's oldest. They would prove to give the new museum an impressive reputation.

After a quick trip to New York to supervise the uncrating and classifying of the 10,000 items, he returned to Cyprus to resume his archeological digs. The year was 1874. For nearly three more years Cesnola searched the historic earth of Cyprus. Near the ancient city of Curium, he discovered a mosaic pavement which he recognized as a temple floor. He ordered his fifty diggers to excavate the entire area, and after two weeks he located four vaults twenty-five feet below the floor that had been hidden from mankind for thousands of years. The four interconnected rooms were filled with gold, silver, jewelry, bronze lamps, vases, sculpture and thousands of rare articles. It was the richest archeological finding up to that time, netting Cesnola over two million dollars.

He sent the entire collection to the Metropolitan Museum and began new diggings, but the Turkish government immediately stopped him. Prevented from further pursuing his favorite pastime, he resigned his post as American Consul and left Cyprus.

A number of historians and fellow archeologists asked him to write a book on his world-renowned discoveries. While he spent his days back in the United States working on his enormous collection at the Metropolitan Museum, classifying more than 35,000 items recovered from nearly a thousand Cyprus tombs, his nights were spent on writing, *Cyprus, Its Ancient Cities, Tombs, and Temples.* After its completion and release, it became the most widely read book on archeological exploration in his day.

The trustees of the museum were so pleased and impressed with his work that they elected him Secretary of the Metropolitan Museum, a position he held for the remainder of his life. Within a month of this appointment he was asked to become the museum's first director. He gladly accepted, and the museum gave him a substantial salary and permitted him to run it as he saw fit.

Cesnola had a genius for organization and getting the most and best work out of his colleagues and subordinates. He approached every activity with a scholarship and enthusiastic devotion that impressed those who worked with him. Under this excellent direction, his museum became the third largest in the world.

But Cesnola had his problems, and his critics. Some of the latter were disturbed about his magisterial manner of getting things accomplished. One hostile article in the August 1880 issue of *Art Amateur* charged that many of the relics in Cesnola's collection were fakes. The General and the museum trustees invited art experts to examine the items in question, and when several came forward and conducted a lengthy investigation, they concluded and declared that the collection was completely authentic.

Still, another "expert" would come forward every six months or so and repeat the accusations against Cesnola and his large collection, which would usually result in Cesnola's personal expenditure of time and money to prove his innocence. He won every case but never succeeding in shaking the critics completely off his back.

In the last years of his life he was awarded many honors. Memberships in most of the world's literary and scientific societies were presented to him monthly. Princeton and Columbia Universities conferred honorary degrees upon him, and Italy struck two medals specially for him. In 1897 he received the Congressional Medal of Honor, the highest award given by the United States Government, for his performance thirty-five years earlier in the Civil War. He died peacefully on November 20, 1904, at the age of seventy-two.

Luigi Palma di Cesnola is best remembered as the man who made the Metropolitan Museum of New York what it is today—a display of the story of world civilization, as recorded for thousands of years in stone, clay, metal, cloth and paper.

Francesca Xavier Cabrini

It is said that the birth of every saint is accompanied by a flock of white doves. Naturally townspeople were happy and amazed when a flock of the beautiful birds flew over Saint Angelo Lodigiano in Lombardy, Italy on July 15, 1850, for that was the day their village grew by one. Francesca Cabrini was a frail infant at birth, which alarmed her parents even in the face of their optimistic neighbors who reported the doves, but she thrived and grew into a child of extraordinary perception and lively imagination.

As a child, Francesca seemed to possess an inner purpose. She constantly devoted her time to helping others in Saint Angelo Lodigiano, and as soon as she was of age she dedicated her life to serving God.

She attended the school of the Daughters of the Sacred Heart at Arluno for five years, at the end of which, in 1868, she received her teacher's certificate. She wished to enter a convent, but she was rejected because of poor health.

She lived and helped at home for several years until her parents died, then went to the town of Vidardo to teach. It was there she met Don Antonio Serrati, who would be her spiritual guide for many years. With improved health and experience as a teacher, Francesca again applied for admission to several convents, but again she was refused. When Serrati became a Monsignor in Codogno, he sent for her to come and work in the House of Province.

Monsignor Serrati, who knew her capabilities and her rapport with children, believed in her inner strength and gave her every opportunity to prove herself. In 1874 he allowed her to become a novice, and in 1877 she took her final vows.

Her first position as Mother Superior of an orphanage lasted less than a year before Serrati picked her to inaugurate a missionary order for nuns. She immediately converted an abandoned friary into her home and opened, with virtually no money, the institute of the Missionary Sisters of the Sacred Heart. With effort and work, however, it was soon operating an orphanage and a convent at Codogno.

Because of her success and her ability to work with children, Mother Cabrini was further asked to open schools and orphanages in other towns. In 1884 she founded the academy in Milan, Lombardy's capital, and by 1887 the Missionary Sisters were successfully operating seven schools.

Mother Cabrini went to the Vatican to make two requests: first, would it approve her flourishing institutions, and secondly, could she have permission to set up schools in America and elsewhere. She obtained an interview with Cardinal-Vicar Parocchi, also a native of Lombardy. He asked her why she wanted to compete with several older established orders at work in Rome. What could she offer that they couldn't. She answered him simply and to the point that she wanted to accomplish what was needed for mankind and not have to be restricted by a quota on who could work toward that aim. The Cardinal was moved by her determination and believed in her. Instead of giving her a school, he offered her two schools, both in poverty-ridden areas.

Within months her institute and constant efforts had gained the Vatican Council's favor. Cardinal Parocchi arranged for a private interview with the Holy Father, Pope Leo XIII, known for his own efforts to raise the standard of living of the poor. Her meeting with him was the beginning of a long and warm friendship.

The Pope was worried about the contadini, the peasants who had emigrated to America. He was receiving messages daily from the United States that the mass of immigrants arriving in America were not prepared for the radical changes in their lives. The Italians were living in congested, dirty slum areas of American cities, without doctors, teachers or priests. Since the government of the United States was not helping these immigrants, the Pope asked Mother Cabrini whether she would go to America to help the Italians there.

She agreed that she would go and bring security, ethics and consolation to the new Italian-Americans. She would also establish schools to bridge the wide gulf between the old culture and the new. With Pope Leo's blessings and six nuns, Mother Cabrini left Italy for New York in 1889.

Hardly resting from her long trip across the Atlantic, she immediately began teaching catechism classes to Italian children at St. Joachim's Church near Mulberry Street. After classes she went into the heart of the Italian slums to see what could be done. She found homeless children whose mothers had died or abandoned them, whose fathers were working in mines, logging camps or on railroads. These children were wearing rags, eating out of garbage cans and sleeping in cold hallways and tenements.

She went directly to Archbishop Corrigan for help in finding a suitable building for an orphanage for the children, and he in turn managed to find a spacious building on East 59th Street. Mother Cabrini and her nuns went out on the streets and into Italian shops asking for food, clothing and money for the orphans. With the new children, her catechism classes in the church basement grew into a regular parochial school.

Mother Cabrini realized that there were hundreds of "Little Italys" scattered throughout America, and that they needed help. She sensed a complete lack of joy in life among many Italian-Americans. And for good reason. They worked 16 to 18 hours each day for less than subsistence, or existence, wages, under the most deplorable working conditions.

When she had the orphanage and school functioning properly, Mother Cabrini returned to Italy to seek more nuns who could work in America. She explained the American situation to the Pope, telling him of the plight of the uneducated, socially unaware Italian immigrants. He agreed to help her in any way he could.

She returned to America with seven missionary sisters. Now, with the added teachers and supervisors and a growing flock of kids, the orphanage needed to expand. Mother Cabrini went at once to look at a large estate at Peekskill on the Hudson River, which she wanted to purchase to house her several hundred orphans, and where she could eventually establish a novitiate school for nuns. The estate had been offered for sale by the Jesuits at a low price because there was no water supply, except that which could be carried up the steep hill from the Hudson River far below.

Mother Cabrini begged relentlessly for funds among the rich until she raised enough money for a down payment on the estate. She named her new home West Park.

Two days after she had moved her orphanage into the estate, she discovered a natural spring while taking a walk. She had a well dug and ended the water problem.

In the fall of 1890 Mother Cabrini returned to Italy, this time to train sisters for a school to be opened in Nicaragua, the first of many she would found for the thousands of Italians living in the Central and South Americas.

By 1891, she had established fifty Missionary Sisters of the Sacred Heart in America, and now she responded to another important cause. When she returned to New York City, she went to Bishop Scalabrini, whose order was operating a hospital for Italians there. The Bishop was encountering many difficulties in keeping the hospital running, and on orders from the Pope he had requested Mother Cabrini's assistance. She not only sent him several of her nuns to be trained as nurses, but she herself volunteered to learn how to treat the sick.

After a few months, however, the difficulties of two orders working together presented themselves. She decided it would be in the best interests of everyone for her to open another Italian-American hospital under the directon of her own order. Renting two adjacent houses on 12th Street, she opened the hospital in September, 1892. Doctors were recruited from the other New York hospitals to donate their time, free of charge. Mother Cabrini managed to borrow medicine, equipment and furnishings, thus providing an efficient, clean and professional operation. Her nurses spoke Italian.

She named her new clinic Columbus Hospital.

Mother Cabrini began visiting Italian communities in other

American cities. She sent two nuns to New Orleans to buy a large tenement on St. Philip's Street and convert it into a convent with a chapel, and to start a parochial school and an orphanage.

Mother Cabrini also organized complex missionary ventures elsewhere. In every major community in Latin America and in every heavily populated city in America, she founded missions to help Italian-Americans. Within all this activity, she also found enough time to return to Italy and celebrate Pope Leo XIII's ninetieth birthday; and as always, when she left her homeland she brought more missionary sisters for her ever-expanding schools, missions, hospitals and orphanages.

At length, she was able to establish an American novitiate at West Park. Columbus Hospital grew so large that she relocated it in a building several times the size of the original one. New missions and hospitals were opened in Chicago, Newark and Arlington. For each, she had to raise funds, select the location and hire the staffs. Her ability for organization was remarkable. During her visits to Europe, she established missions and academies in Paris, Madrid, Turin and London.

In 1903, she was asked by the Archbishop of Chicago to establish a hospital there, and after months of fund-raising and strenuous effort she bought the once-fashionable North Shore Hotel. When word reached her in New York that the Chicago contractors were doing unnecessary demolition and were overcharging for labor and materials on remodeling the hotel into a hospital, she hurried back to the windy city, fired the contractor, and personally assumed supervision of the work.

In the American West, Italians were working in the mines under very difficult conditions. Mother Cabrini traveled out to see what she could do. Besides starting a school in sourthern California, an orphanage and sanatorium in Washington, and a hospital in Wyoming, she worked with many of the Italian families in Colorado living in the railroad tent camps and talked with the men as they worked. She wanted to instill in them a sense of respect for their fellow man. To assist the workers' wives and children, she established a mission in Denver.

Sadly and bitterly she observed the luckless fate of so many of her exploited countrymen in America. The Italian workers received the hardest and dirtiest jobs. Few, if any, regarded them as being human enough to be treated with understanding and sympathy. To the capitalists like John D. Rockefeller, John Jacob Astor and Andrew Carnegie, the Italian worker was a cheap, easily replaceable machine. Thousands died in the winter because Rockefeller did not supply adequate heating or clothing. On many occasions Mother Cabrini approached the bosses, the titans of American wealth, to plead for the Italian worker's cause. They told her to go back to

Italy. But with that and other insults, they sparked her to greater efforts and deeds in her battle for the poor.

By the time Mother Cabrini returned to Europe in 1906, she was internationally known and loved. It was the twenty-fifth anniversary of the founding of her order, which now had missions in eight countries, a total of fifty buildings, and a thousand sisters ministering in them. The Queen of Italy decorated her for her work. Even politicians attested to the amazing creative powers of this rare human being. The Italian Ambassador to the United States wrote of her, "I consider the illustrious Mother General of the Missionary Sisters a priceless collaborator, for while I work for the interest of Italy among the powerful, she succeeds in making it loved and esteemed by the humble, the infirm, and the children."

She contracted malaria while opening a new mission and hospital in Brazil in 1908, yet she continued to work ceaselessly. However, she never fully recovered. Her health from then on grew worse but she did not slow down in her projects and journeys.

Back in the United States she established a second hospital in Chicago. While in Seattle the following year, she became a naturalized American citizen. She sailed to Europe, inspected her missions and opened new ones. Returning to New York, she began construction on a new, larger Columbus Hospital. In Los Angeles she salvaged the wood, pipes and nails of an amusement park that was razed and used them in the building of an annex to a Los Angeles mission. She shipped the surplus to Denver for the building of an orphanage there.

Toward the end of 1916, she went to Chicago, where she established a farm to help feed her missions.

On December 22, 1917, while wrapping Christmas candy for school children in New York, the mighty heart of Mother Cabrini finally slowed down and stopped. She was sixty-seven years old. Her body was entombed in Mother Cabrini High School in New York.

A number of miraculous cures, occurring after supplications to Mother Cabrini and attested to by physicians on the cases, as well as other numerous, extraordinary events, caused the Vatican to waive the usual fifty-year period between the death of a candidate for sainthood and the beginning of the long process in which canonization by the Church is considered. In 1928, only eleven years after her death, Mother Cabrini's cause was undertaken. Ten years later she was declared Tuto in the ceremony of beatification, and on July 7, 1949, Pope Pius XII conferred the office of Sainthood on Mother Cabrini.

The first United States citizen to become a saint was an Italian-American.

AMADEO PETER GIANNINI

A.P. Giannini's contribution to American finance is an important one. He turned a tiny investment into the largest privately-owned bank in the world, because of faith and trust in the common man.

Unlike the Rockefellers, Mellons and Fisks, Giannini came from a poor family, which makes the story of his success that much more significant. It is said that he never once exploited another human being in the process of making money. No wonder he was the most beloved businessman in this country's history. The son of Italian immigrants, Giannini turned a hundred dollar investment into $15 billion in resources, more than seven-and-a-half million depositors, 28,500 employees and over 900 domestic and foreign bank branches. The Bank of America was his brainchild.

Amadeo Peter Giannini was born on May 6, 1870, in San Jose, California, where his parents ran a small boarding house. They eked out enough money from it to eventually make a down payment on a forty-acre ranch near Alviso, the busy port town on the south side of San Francisco Bay. When Giannini was seven years old his father was killed. His mother, used to hard work, continued to support the family on the meager earnings from produce grown on the ranch.

Lorenzo Scatena, a long-time friend of the family who was fond of the children, advised Mrs. Giannini on the running of the ranch. Two years later he married her. Realizing that the family needed more money than the ranch could bring, Scatena opened a small produce company in San Francisco.

Amadeo was fascinated by the small business and spent most of his time helping his step-father, and after his schooling was completed he was allowed to handle the buying of large quantities of perishable fruits and vegetables for resale to local merchants.

At the age of 15, Amadeo was already making buying trips to growers and shippers throughout California. He continually came up with new enterprising, bold ideas for increasing business, and within a year he had saved a hundred dollars, which he turned over to his step-father in exchange for half the business. His step-father agreed and Amadeo became a full partner in the young prospering business. As time went on, Amadeo took over more and more of the decision-making for the operation, and within ten years he had built it into the largest produce-commission house on the Pacific Coast.

By the time he reached his twenty-fifth birthday Amadeo was a millionaire and ready to retire from the produce business. He was not interested in merely collecting huge sums of money and hoarding it in a bank vault; he enjoyed the creative freedom money allowed him. The process of acquiring money and making it work fascinated him. He marvelled at what a large sum could do for a small town or an empty block. It could build a factory, hospital or office building. Above all, money gave him an opportunity to help others, for he believed in helping anyone who had a worthy, profitable cause.

He sold his interests in the produce business to concentrate on the management of various real-estate holdings. Among these holdings was a block of shares in the Columbus Savings and Loan Society, a bank created by prosperous Italian-Americans as a safe repository for their money. This is where Amadeo decided to narrow his interests. He began to suggest new ideas for the old, conservative bank, expressing his view to the directors that money should not be allowed to pile up in the vaults but should be loaned out to work for the people who badly needed it. The directors answered that the needy people were rarely able to pay back money they borrowed because they usually lost whatever they were given. They were bad risks, whereas the wealthy could be trusted since they deposited large sums of money regularly. Giannini countered by saying that in San Francisco there were many banks interested only in rich people, but not one bank willing to help hard-working immigrants. He maintained that there were thrifty and industrious Italians, who, with a little assistance from a bank could open a restaurant, barber shop, small farm, hotel, or simply buy a home for their families.

He urged the bank directors to have faith in the little man and lend him money at a reasonable rate of three percent.

Giannini tried every conceivable argument to gain the confidence and agreement of these directors, but after a year of listening to their negative replies the situation remained the same. Disgusted, Giannini quit his chairmanship and announced that he would open up his own private bank and follow through with his plans of subsidizing the little man who needed money.

Several wealthy Italian-Americans approached him and said they wanted to invest large sums of money in his new enterprise. Giannini refused. His bank, he maintained, would be financed, built and worked by the workingman. He then took to the streets and, for nearly three months, often spending ten or twelve hours a day, talking to the common man, the worker, explaining to him the purpose of his new bank. He sold shares at $100 apiece to finance construction, and when he had sold $300,000 worth of shares, he leased a building at the intersection of Columbus and Washington Avenues, remodeled the old saloon there into a one-room bank, and hired three employees.

The Bank of Italy was officially opened for business on October 17, 1904. Several hundred curious individuals, most of them never having been inside of a bank before, came into Giannini's bank on the first day. They were skeptical at first. They had a strong distrust of the rich who had always exploited them at every opportunity. But

Giannini, himself once poor, was able to relate to them. He went to peoples' homes and drank wine with them; he met them on the street and explained what he was trying to do. Each person who walked into his bank was met at the door by Giannini. He shook hands with and offered a glass of wine to every newcomer, asking him if there was anything he needed, if the family was doing well, and so on. He would allow none of the cold, subdued, impersonal approach from his personnel that was standard proceudre in other banks. When a father and son walked in, Giannini would often give the boy a five dollar gold piece and tell him to open a new savings account with it. In short, he offered his patrons a warm welcome in a bustling, disinterested city, and no one walked away from his bank without feeling that he had made a friend in Giannini.

Many of the people believed in him enough to be willing to place some of their savings in his little bank. On the first day, Giannini's bank had deposits totalling $8,780, and it was not long afterward that the Bank of Italy was able to provide small loans at reasonable interest rates. As its reputation spread, the people began taking their remaining savings out of their mattresses and bringing them to Giannini. Within a year the Bank of Italy showed one million dollars in assets.

Early in the morning of April 18, 1906, San Francisco was shaken by an earthquake that left the city in flames and destruction. The tremors rocked the home of Giannini twenty-five miles away. He immediately hitched a ride to the city and, upon arrival, found his bank untouched by the quake. In fact, his six employees had opened the bank and were waiting for his instructions. Although the quake itself had not damaged his bank, Giannini knew that the fires raging all over town could very well reach his old wooden building. He locked the bank and he and his employees withdrew all the money ($80,000) and put it into three canvas bags. He put the bags in the back of a produce cart and headed for his home, reaching it that night. Behind him, the fire spread and destroyed most of San Francisco, including the moneyless Bank of Italy.

The great fire lasted nearly a week, destroying more than 29,000 buildings and $500 million worth of property. Giannini's losses were minimal. As soon as it was safe to reenter the city, Giannini went to work rebuilding his bank. He sent several large ships upstate to bring back wood for his and other buildings. He also asked the other banks to lend anyone who needed money to rebuild their home, at no interest and with five years to repay the principal. Since most banks balked at his generosity with their money, it was again up to him to lead the way. He opened for business on the wharf with a counter made of a plank supported by two barrels, and placed posters and advertisements all over the city that said he would advance money to any residents who wished to rebuild. Withdrawals and loans were to be given for that purpose only.

At length, his energy and spirited enthusiasm, motivated by the enormous task laying ahead, inspired others. He possessed an uncanny knack for judging the characters of those who came requesting loans. Often he asked to see a man's hands; if they were calloused the man was not afraid of work. The Italians rallied to his support and the Italian-American community was the first to recover from the disaster. By the end of the year he had nearly 2,500 depositors and 2 million dollars in his vault.

At the beginning of the new year he traveled to the east coast to learn what he could from old established banking systems. It was a valuable trip in that it enabled him to see otherwise unforeseen troubled times ahead. Having not yet reached the West, these bad times were very real in Europe and certain areas of the East. He noted the dangerously low cash reserves eroded by stock investments and had enough insight to see that a financial crisis would soon grip all of America. Banks that were unable to supply cash to depositors demanding return of their savings would be ruined. Giannini returned to the west coast immediately and began to gather as much surplus cash as possible. He cut back all loans and launched a massive campaign for new accounts.

Giannini's prophecy turned out to be correct, for in the fall of 1907 the financial crash which he had prepared for began in New York and quickly spread across the country, reaching San Francisco in October. As panicky depositors hurriedly withdrew their money from banks, the cash supply dried up. Only Giannini's bank sat securely on a large pile of gold and silver. Long lines formed at other banks and Giannini went around telling these depositors that his Bank of Italy had plenty of money and that he would honor their passbooks. Thus he saved many other banks from the financial crisis.

The distress of 1907 convinced legislators that new effective legislation was needed to prevent similar panics from occurring in the future. New systems were developed, including the Federal Reserve Board. Giannini had many new ideas that he delivered to banking groups around the country.

While attending the 1908 banking convention at Denver, Giannini met another man whose views were similar to his. He was Woodrow Wilson, president of Princeton University, who said to the convention that, ''The banks of this country are remote from the people and the people regard them as not belonging to them but as belonging to some power hostile to them.''

Giannini agreed and added that a sturdy system of branch banks, simply and inexpensively run, could be developed by large, central banking facilities. He summed up by telling the convention that for too long banks had not been used to fertilize the country through investments in the people. It was only by helping the small man that the public's hostility toward banks and the men who controlled them could be assuaged and changed.

Soon after the bank convention, Giannini traveled to Europe and then to Canada to study their branch banking practicing. These banks were working well, and he was confident he could make them work in this country.

Upon his return to San Francisco, he opened a second bank. He explained to his investors that by offering small branch outlets they would be able to diversify their business and thus render better and broader service. Also, the giant produce industry was scattered up and down the state, but did its banking in San Francisco. It made sense to offer the local farmers and distributors the same convenient banking conditions as the retailers in the city.

In 1909, the California state legislature passed an act to regulate banking within the state. It was the first banking act in the state to sanction branch banks; it stated that for each new branch, a bank would have to add $24,000 to its capital. This was the spark that Giannini needed. Within a few months he opened his first branch bank outside San Francisco. Once again, he went on the fund-raising trail, selling stocks to local citizens, talking to farmers and making citizens aware of what his branch bank would offer and why they needed it.

Within two years, Giannini began his bank-buying campaign. He purchased many of the city banks and converted them into branch banks. In 1913, he opened banks in San Mateo and Los Angeles, the fastest-growing city in the state. He had a genius for developing eye-catching advertisements. Everywhere one looked there was a billboard announcing: THE BANK FOR JUST PLAIN FOLKS.

Naturally, he was disliked by the other bankers and businessmen who did not share either his creativity or success. He was a liberal among conservatives, all of whom labeled him a business exhibitionist and a "department store banker."

During the First World War, Giannini's banking operations were in a prime position to extend themselves to every part of California. As the war engulfed Europe, the demand for food was placed in the lap of the large agricultural state, and the Bank of Italy duly began opening branch banks in the booming farm communities. Giannini purchased faltering banks in the state and rescued depositors from losing their money.

By the time the United States entered the war, Giannini's banking empire had become the prime factor in establishing and financing new factories and business enterprises in California. He established special business consulting offices to instruct potential investors in the best operating techniques. His branches spread across the nation, along with his creed, "Our conception of a bank is that of a great public servant, an institution run in the interest and for the welfare of the people it serves."

Giannini also set up the first advisory farm and industrial service. At the time, the movie-making business was getting into full stride and making large loans from his bank to produce films. The automotive industry was also beginning, and people were needing auto loans. By 1921, both the Bank of Italy and Giannini were well-known throughout the United States and Europe. The bank had outgrown several locations and was now housed in the second largest bank building in the nation.

Giannini generated enthusiasm among those around him, especially his employees. He went to great lengths to make sure that his workers were the best paid, had the best working conditions and the most generous benefits of any employees in the country. He was the first employer to introduce profit-sharing for all of his employees.

His right hand man was his son, Mario, who had been raised in the doctrine of hard work. Mario worked in every department of the Bank of Italy until he became familiar with the entire operation, and by the time he became an executive he was ready to be an immense help to his father.

Unlike other banks that foreclosed on farms during the twenties and thirties, Giannini gave strict instructions that, if a farmer could not pay his mortgage payments, the bank would take over the farm but leave everything else as it was. The farmer could continue to work his land and when his luck returned he could pick up the payments. Never once did a farmer whose livelihood was mortgaged to Giannini's bank have to leave his property because of a business or crop failure. Few other banks showed such faith, as evidenced by the millions of homeless drifters during the depression years. Giannini's banking practices were continually under attack by the California Banking Department and the Federal Reserve Board. They tried every means to stop his bank's growth and to bring him into court on the claim that he was operating a monopoly. But Giannini wasn't about to let himself be pushed around. He hired the best lawyers in the country to set up holding companies and to make sure his enterprises stayed within the law. He formed Bancitaly, a holding company for his California banks, while his other banks retained their old names until 1927, when he was allowed to consolidate them into one large network called the Bank of Italy National Trust and Savings Association. It consisted of 276 branches, over 4,000 employees, and a million depositors, making it the third largest bank in the country.

Giannini had one major problem during the late twenties—he couldn't control the rush to buy stocks in his banking empire. He felt that purchases on margin were risky and that no corporation should accept less than fifty percent down payment on a share of stock. His intuition and good sense again proved accurate, for while vacationing in Italy in 1928, he was notified that the bottom had fallen out of the stock market and his banking empire was in trouble, mainly due to the huge amount of margin buying during the past few days. He returned to California immediately and tried to calm things down, but the country was panicking and there was little he could do. His depositors were withdrawing their money and his stockholders were rushing to sell their shares. Indeed, things looked decidedly bleak, but Giannini sought a way out. He removed Bank of Italy and Bancitaly stocks from direct contact with the fluctuating stock exchange by creating a gigantic holding company, the Transamerica Corporation, through which would flow his stocks, and the stocks of numerous other banks, major industrial, business and insurance companies in which Giannini had control. He also pumped nearly 60 million dollars from his own pocket into the corporation to build confidence and bring the panic sales of his stock to a stop.

To head his new corporation, Giannini went to Wall Street and hired Elisha Walker, who was head of a brokerage and investment house. This was Giannini's first step into J.P. Morgan's backyard and Morgan didn't like it. He told the Italian banker to go back to Sicily and pick fruit, to which Giannini replied that someday he would buy Morgan out.

Transamerica Corporation proceeded to buy still more banks and companies and the price of its stock soared. Giannini, on the verge of collapse from exhaustion, left for an extended rest in Italy, but no sooner had he departed that rumors of his bad health began a new round of stock selling. At first, his corporation weathered the sharp decline in values, but it soon ran into real difficulties. Its stock value took a deep plunge, causing frantic shareholders to sell at any price.

In September 1930, Giannini returned to California to survey the extent of the damage and to try putting the pieces together again. He changed the name of his bank to Bank of America National Trust and Savings Association. But he found the administration of his duties rough. When he went to Europe, he turned over the directorship of Transamerica Corporation to Walker, and now Walker and many of Giannini's old friends who were corporation officers were in disagreement with him on what was to be done. They opposed his every move. His nerves on edge, he was stricken with polyneuritis and sent to the hospital, where he lay gravely ill while Walker mishandled the crisis.

Walker was for liquidating, for selling outright at distress prices, most of Giannini's prized assets, among them the carefully built network of banks across the nation. At the news of this, Giannini rallied remarkably. He suspected that J.P. Morgan was backing Walker, and this made his blood boil. The doctors couldn't believe that this sick and aging man could muster the strength to get out of bed, rejoin his son Mario, and try to save his empire. He and Mario hid away to plan their battle strategy for a proxy fight. Word leaked out that the Gianninis were battling for control of TA and Bank of America.

With a proxy vote only weeks away, Giannini traveled across the country to rally support from the major stockholders, trying to convince them that the only way to regain the value of their stock was to give him back the control of the corporation he had created and not abandon it to Wall Street predators. He told them to look at his record. The selling price of the stock when he left the chairmanship was 46; now, with Walker at the helm, the price of the stock was down to 4 and falling. Giannini's budget for running the entire corporation was $300,000 a year, compared to $3 million under Walker. Giannini pointed out that he had been able to give millions of dollars of his own income to foundations and medical schools, and put the rest back into the business. In contrast, what had Walker done with his $100,000 a year salary?

Walker used every trick in his hat to keep proxy votes from going to Giannini. He went as far as to threaten all Bank of America employees with dismissal if they rallied to their old boss. Despite Walker's effort, however, on February 15, 1932, when the proxies were counted, Giannini had won by a landslide and was reinstated as chairman of Transamerica. Before him, only Henry Ford had ever won a proxy battle with Wall Street financiers.

Giannini went to work to put the faltering business back on its feet. He fired all of the executives and non-essential employees and spent the next two months trimming all expenses, launching a new accounts campaign, and urging everyone to work double-time. Before long, the stocks began to rise again.

As the Bank of America returned to normal, so did the State of California and businesses directly affected by the bank's condition. With the bank healthy again, hundreds of new jobs opened up. Giannini helped push through the contract to build the giant Golden Gate Bridge, which pumped $6 million into the economy. He put up a thousand large billboard posters which read, "Keep Your Dollars Moving. The Depression is a Product of Your Fear." Later, Roosevelt paid special tribute to Giannini, saying, "In my opinion, A.P. Giannini has done more to build California through his great bank and his personal efforts than any other Californian."

In an effort to gain closer control over the banks, the Federal Government declared a bank holiday in March of 1933. This allowed Congress time enough to pass the Emergency Banking Act and other legislation which could help the banks and the state of the country.

All of the banks which were solvent and capable of maintaining themselves were ordered to reopen on March 13. As the day drew near, the Bank of America had not yet received permission to reopen. If it failed to open, another panic would follow which would destroy it. Giannini made frantic calls to Washington to find out the cause for the delay. When he phoned Roosevelt, Giannini received the president's assurance that the matter would be looked into immediately. Roosevelt soon found out that the head of the Federal Reserve Bank in San Francisco, John U. Calking, a long-time enemy of Giannini's, had not filed a report on the condition of the Bank of America since Giannini's return as director of the bank.

Giannini had to work through the night with fifty staff members to compile a new up-to-date financial statement, showing that the bank had recovered and was solvent. The statement was wired off to Washington and the Bank of America received permission to open at ten o'clock in the morning of March 13.

As the country struggled back up the road to normalcy, Giannini found it difficult to expand his banking operations. The government's regulations of banking grew increasingly tighter. Nonetheless, the Bank of America continued to grow, and by the spring of 1945 had become the largest bank in the world.

Amadeo Peter Giannini, the man who made it all possible, died on June 3, 1949, just after his seventy-ninth birthday. Probably no other businessman had ever helped the working man as much as this great Italian-American.

FIORELLO H. LA GUARDIA

Fiorello La Guardia was the most famous and energetic mayor in New York City's history, or America's history, for that matter. His was a life-long fight against corruption, exploitation of the common man, injustice, intolerance and poverty. His style was flamboyant, occasionally bordering on the undignified and crass, but he was immensely popular with his constituents. He was an idealist who believed in the innate goodness of man and the intrinsic merit of democratic government.

Born in New York on December 11, 1882, Fiorello was the son of a U.S. Army band conductor, who had immigrated from Foggia (Fiorello's mother came from Trieste). Fiorello spent his early years traveling around the country with his family, getting a first-hand account of man's predatory instincts. He saw con-men and professional gamblers who swindled the gullible. He witnessed the long laboring of Italians who had been imported to work for starvation wages in mines and on railroads. And perhaps the greatest blow to his youthful idealism came during the Spanish-American War in 1898, when his father died as a result of improperly-processed beef.

This last episode occurred while he was working as a war correspondent for a Florida newspaper. Being only fifteen years old and measuring five feet, three inches, La Guardia was rejected when he tried to enlist in the Army, and he settled for the next best thing— reporting the conflict. No sooner had he begun, however, when he, along with several thousand soldiers, was poisoned by the "embalmed" beef that had been canned by profit-seeking meatpackers, who raked in large government contracts and produced their products cheaply and expediently, often unsafely, without regard for consumer welfare. The consumer in this case was the American soldier. Fiorello recovered from this food poisoning, but his father died.

Soon after the short war, La Guardia moved to Europe, where he became a filing clerk at the American consulate in Budapest. In his spare time he went to the local libraries and read world history, political and social science, and everything else that would broaden his limited knowledge of the world and its people. He also went to several speech and language classes to learn Italian, German, French and Yiddish. Every few months he would ask for a review of his work, hoping for a pay raise and promotion, but he was never given either because of his lack of formal education.

The aggressive, hard-working La Guardia refused to be put down, however, and soon left that consulate for a position in the American consulate in nearby Fiume. The office was a one-man operation with the twenty-one year old Fiorello as boss, clerk and handyman. He assumed authority and began to eliminate unnecessary protocol and formality and to mold the office into an efficient operation.

The Cunard Ship Lines carried on a bi-monthly shipping service from Fiume to America, jamming thousands of emigrants into steerage on each trip. With the return of every ship came hundreds of hapless passengers who had been rejected at Ellis Island for reasons of health and sent back.

La Guardia went into action to help spare these emigrants the discomforts and expense of a long, useless voyage. He refused to sign the requisite Bill of Health for all ship departures until every passenger had been given a complete checkup. The ship owner was furious at the brash young American, but fortunately, La Guardia had made life so easy and uncomplicated for the American Consul-General that he came to his defense and forced the owner to cooperate with him. As a result, Fiume had the lowest immigrant-rejection rate of any European port of embarkation. Regretfully, no other

European ports adopted his methods, although he continually bom-barbed the U.S. State Department and various embassies in an attempt to reform archaic, cruel immigration practices. Through the years he submitted hundreds of new proposals to Washington legislators, but the lawmakers considered him a young radical, too liberal for a conservative Congress. It would take nearly twenty years before his ideas were made into law and instituted throughout the world.

La Guardia realized that to get reforms accepted, he would have to take his ideas to the public. But the public, generally uninformed anyway, was only impressed by wealth or national accomplish-ments, neither of which he had. Determined to establish himself, he resigned from his government post and returned to the United States to attend evening classes at New York University's Law School. During the day he worked as an interpreter at Ellis Island, where he was able to observe the drama and disheartening treatment given to the nearly 5,000 immigrants who arrived daily.

Now more than ever, he was determined to help the poor and the uneducated who were constantly being intimidated and defrauded by immigration officials. Many officials would threaten to forbid them entry into this country unless they turned over all the money they had brought with them. This, of course, produced a dejected, penniless immigrant who, more often than not, had to become a public charge. Those who refused to pay were judged unacceptable for one reason or another and sent back to Europe.

La Guardia really became discouraged when he worked as an interpreter at Night Court in Manhattan. There he saw the wide-spread graft and corruption among policemen and judges. He saw how the law enforcers took advantage of the immigrants' naivete and helplessness. After six months of this, he quit in order to speed his studies in law so that he could graduate and begin doing some-thing to stop crime in the city.

In 1909, he received his degree from the New York University Law School and was admitted to the Bar. Although he set up in private practice, he admitted that the criminal elements in the law enforcement field and the corruption in the Bar Association itself prevented him from having any great pride in being a lawyer. La Guardia was a rarity among lawyers. He would not take a case, no matter how lucrative, if he thought the client guilty or wrong, and he generally offered his talents to the poor, often without a fee.

He was asked to represent a labor union in a strike against gar-ment industrial firms, notorious for exploiting Italian labor in almost unbearable sweatshops. Not only had the strikers' requests for bet-ter working conditions and higher hourly wages been refused, but the firms had several hundred of the strikers, including the leaders, thrown in jail.

La Guardia uncovered many of the tactics being used by the firms to break the strike and he raised such an uproar that the newspapers came on the scene. After a few days they began reporting which firms were doing what to whom. Within another week, the strikers had won, conditions were improved, the hourly wages increased and Fiorello H. La Guardia became widely known by both liberals and conservatives as a man who would take no nonsense and get the job done. The little lawyer was rapidly gaining himself a reputation.

He now turned his attention to Tammany (City) Hall, for which he had great dislike. He had become an active member in a local Republican club in the hope of using it as a springboard toward a seat in the House of Representatives. There was an open seat in the 14th District, a section of the Lower East Side of Manhattan with a large Italian-American population. Knowing the problems of the Italian community, La Guardia worked doubly hard to prove to the voters that he, not Tammany Hall, would represent them best.

Although La Guardia lost the election to established Congressman Michael Farley by a handful of votes, he proved himself a strong comer and racked up 15,000 more votes than anyone expected. This prompted Republican bigwigs to name him deputy attorney general for New York State.

He went to work at once at what he considered to be worthy causes, but he found it difficult or impossible to do anything because of political pressure and corrupt officials in high positions. He soon realized that his appointment to a powerless position had only been a token gesture.

Still, he fought for political reforms and painfully climbed the ladder of politics. Political bosses found it increasingly difficult to keep La Guardia from speaking out against other officials who were only interested in the fame, glamour, power and wealth of their positions. He wrote articles for the newspapers, exposing special privileges and political appointments to repay political debts, leaving these offices open to special interests.

Seeing that he could not work within the political system, La Guardia quit his post as Deputy Attorney General and went out to seek justice on his own.

He began spending all of his time giving lectures around the city, describing the widespread neglect of public services by the state legislators and explaining how a million dollar publicworks contract would never benefit the public because corrupt politicians put the money into their own pockets.

During the next (1916) election he campaigned in the same vibrant style he had two years before. However, this time everybody took him seriously, including Tammany Hall. La Guardia's new platform pledged improvement of living and working conditions for the people and a forceful and faithful representation in Congress. He also promised to expose those politicians who were not truly or honestly representing their constituency.

His forcefulness was rewarded. Fiorello La Guardia was elected to the House of Representatives with a plurality of 357 votes.

When he took his seat on March 5, 1917, he was the first Italian-American to serve in the Congress. And he didn't take just any seat. He chose a front seat in the chamber, something that simply wasn't done by a freshman. Several irate Congressmen approached to tell him to take a seat in the back of the House, in the last row, and keep his mouth shut for a year or so until he became known. With typical aplomb, La Guardia told them to go to hell!

Most of the representatives looked upon him as an oddity. Here was an unknown Republican who had won an upset victory in a Democratic stronghold. He had pledged his support to immigrant citizens and the urban masses, whom he alone was backing. The representatives neither welcomed nor approved of La Guardia. But still he was there, very visible and audible.

Soon after the opening of the 65th Congress, the country entered the First World War, an act which had been imminent for several months, due to Germany's attack on American ships. Again, La Guardia displayed his readiness to break precedent by taking the floor on his second day in Congress to propose a bill which would impose the death penalty on any manufacturer of defective military provisions. The bill was shunted off to a committee and forgotten.

During the first session of Congress he took strong stands on several important pieces of legislation. He objected to the Espionage Act, which he said would limit certain rights guaranteed to every American by the Constitution—the rights of free speech and assembly. His warnings went unheeded.

He also protested the escalation in food prices while food was still abundant, and the rise of rents and clothing costs while wages were stagnant. When he again took to the floor of the House of Representatives to argue for price controls, he told his audience that, "The right to food, shelter, and clothing at reasonable prices is as much an inalienable right as the right to life, liberty, and the pursuit of happiness."

La Guardia voted for the Selective Service Act, which caused ill-feelings in his strongly pacifist district, but he assured the young men of his district that he would fight in Europe alongside of them. In July 1917, he enlisted in the Air Division of the Signal Corps and was given a captain's commission.

He moved among the ranks boosting morale and made speeches in principal European cities, reassuring Italians and others of his country's assistance. He also participated in many Italian Air Force bombing raids over Austrian industrial and military sites.

In October 1918, two months after being promoted to major, La Guardia returned to New York to campaign for reelection. Petitions to unseat the absentee lawmaker had been circulating for months in his district. When he heard that many constituents did not seem to appreciate his taking on the extra duties of the front line at the expense of his office, he answered that if any signers of the petition would take his seat in his Caproni biplane, he would be only too happy to resume his seat in Congress.

Despite this sign of opposition, La Guardia, resplendent in uniform, won the election by a landslide. The Democrats, fearing a victory by the antiwar Socialist Party, had joined with the Republicans in throwing their support behind him. Since the war was nearly over, La Guardia resigned his commission and returned to Washington to resume his seat in Congress full time.

After the Armistice, the temper of the times changed abruptly. Peace became the word of the day, and La Guardia sought to bring the soldiers home as quickly as possible and switch government interest and emphasis to the many domestic problems. No longer considered an odd-man-out by his peers in Congress, he gathered support from liberal Congressmen and Senators for reforms on many issues.

In 1919, the Republican Party showed its faith in the little crusader by asking him to run for the office of President of the New York City Board of Aldermen, the second highest executive post in the city. He agreed, with two stipulations. First, if he won he would be the Republican mayoralty candidate in 1921, and secondly, that he would not afterward be asked for any special consideration or favors. The party agreed and put all its support behind him. As a consequence, he was elected to New York City's second highest post that same year, 1919.

Shortly after he began his work with the Board of Aldermen, La Guardia introduced reform legislation designed to clean up corruption in city hall. He made trouble for all vested interests in city government and went so far as to propose a law that could punish public servants taking bribes by cutting off their hands. He latter added an amendment that included those who offered the bribe in this harsh punishment. The public found these proposals rather amusing and good for newspaper copy in the human interest sections. Nonetheless, La Guardia came up with some good, workable ideas. One was a rent control program.

Everywhere one looked, there was Fiorello La Guardia, flamboyant, outspoken, uncompromising in his efforts to reform a corrupt city.

Despite its promise to him, the Republican Party leadership withdrew from supporting him in the 1921 mayoral race. He had ruffled the feathers of too many conservative Republicans who felt threatened by his reforming. When he was refused nomination, he entered the primary on his own with a platform calling for efficient municipal management.

La Guardia loved the spotlight, so he took every opportunity to get an interview with reporters. The press gave him good coverage, but it presented him as a picturesque, amusing showman. It should be noted, however, that this was generally his own doing. During interviews he took extreme stands on everything, projecting an image of a little man with grandiose schemes and quixotic ideas. He wouldn't heed the advice of friends who suggested that he restrain himself with the press and save his reforms for after the election.

When he lost the election his foes considered him over-the-hill. He left New York and took an extended vacation in Cuba to rest and contemplate his future and his past mistakes. Later, he returned to resume his law practice.

Several prominent Republicans felt that it would benefit their party if they brought La Guardia back into the fold, provided, of course, that they could keep him away from local politics. They offered to back him for Congress in the 20th District in east Harlem, and La Guardia accepted. Full of energy, he immediately dove into the race and campaigned in the slums of Harlem, the home of many Jewish and Italian families.

La Guardia won the election by a handful of votes and returned to Congress, where he fought many battles for the next decade. Through those ten years he proposed legislation which would benefit the American people, but it was either ignored, scorned or ridiculed by the majority of representatives. His humanitarian, socialistic ideas were too far ahead of his time. He was the first to suggest minimum wage laws, old age pensions, workmen's compensation, child-labor laws, the abolition of injunctions in labor disputes, publicly-owned utilities, and, above all, freedom of speech for minority groups. Had he made these same proposals a decade later, he would have been applauded, since only the Depression would force Congress to enact these solutions for the nation's economic ills.

La Guardia was also a persistent fighter against Prohibition. When the Volstead Act and the Eighteenth Amendment were enacted, he protested that the problems attending alcohol could never be legislated out of existence, and that prohibition would only beget worse problems. He was right—gangsters and corrupt public officials raked in millions of dollars from the illicit production, importation and illegal sale of liquor, and huge criminal empires were built that would still exist fifty years later.

His biggest battle in Congress came in 1924, over the passage of the National Origins Immigration Bill. Since the late 1800's, the country as a whole had been unhappy with immigration, feeling that there were already too many foreigners on American soil. They lived apart from the American mainstream, packing themselves into ghettoes and slums, speaking their own languages and following their own customs and beliefs. Many thousands of unemployed Americans bitterly resented the employment of immigrants, and labor unions were finding it difficult to establish higher hourly wages when unskilled immigrants were willing to work for low wages under deplorable factory conditions.

The situation moved both liberal and conservative politicians to support legislation against immigration from a number of countries, notably China and Japan, and to require literacy tests for immigrants from all other countries.

Congress had passed the first quota law—the Johnson Act—three years earlier (see introduction), which reduced the total number of immigrants allowed to enter the United States annually from 358,000 to 165,000. This law also rigged immigration quotas against the southern and eastern European countries, including Italy.

La Guardia called the Johnson Act absurd, loathsome and full of racial prejudice. He scathed his fellow representatives with accusations, forcefully reminding them that America owed much of what it had to immigrants, past and present. "In fact," he told them, "every American was once an immigrant."

Regardless of his efforts the restrictive act of 1924 was pushed through Congress by Harding and Coolidge. La Guardia was so angered by this that he refused to endorse Calvin Coolidge for reelection in 1924 and broke with the Republican Party, choosing to join the ranks of the Progressives, who were backing Senator Robert LaFollette for President. Although LaFollette was overwhelmingly defeated, La Guardia, who ran as a Progressive, was reelected by a strong plurality.

His next battle was with the Secretary of Treasury, Andrew Mellon. Mellon, one of the wealthiest men in the country, had proposed a tax cut for the rich, arguing that if they were allowed to keep all of their money, they would invest it in business projects that would provide employment. Mellon further proposed that whatever taxes were necessary should be placed on the purchase of basic commodities. La Guardia disagreed, pointing out that under such a taxation system only the poor would pay taxes, and they were the ones who could least afford it. In repeated debates with Mellon, La Guardia revealed that Mellon had no interest in the welfare of the working people. He was seeking only to benefit the members of his own class, the rich and powerful. After several weeks of debate, Congress moved toward La Guardia's side and imposed a tax only on luxury items that the poor did not buy.

In another instance, he rallied Congressmen to stop Henry Ford from buying Muscle Shoals in the Tennessee River for production of electricity and fertilizer. He proposed instead that the Federal Government develop hydroelectric plants to benefit the common people, instead of allowing them to be built and controlled by private industry. This is exactly what Roosevelt would later do with his Tennessee Valley Authority projects.

Another widely publicized La Guardia battle was for the Anti-injunction Bill, which forbade the use of force in settling labor disputes and stopped the practice of "yellow dog" contracting, used by employers who forced their employees to sign pledges not to join unions.

Encouraged by those successes in Congress, he threw his hat into the mayoralty race in New York City and managed to win the primaries, despite the Republican leaders' refusal to back him. But winning the election would be another matter. He was running against the city's most popular mayor, Jimmy Walker. La Guardia repeatedly exposed the vast network of graft, vice and inefficiency of the Walker administration, but New Yorkers didn't seem to care. They were too busy enjoying the bounty and excitement of the "Roaring twenties," and Walker typified this era. He was handsome, with a constant smile, always jesting, an extravert. La Guardia, on the other hand, was short, fat, homely, and always furiously serious. He seldom smiled or joked in public and appeared to have a rather severe disposition.

New Yorkers chose to laugh instead of heeding La Guardia's somber warnings of economic disaster, to which the nimblefooted Jimmy Walker was leading them. Walker easily won the election. One week later, the stock market crashed!

La Guardia was repeatedly told that most New Yorkers simply weren't interested in a reform mayor, but he refused to listen. He felt that if the charges of corruption were investigated by a higher court or an important political figure on the state or national level, then people would see that La Guardia was right, and Walker would be thrown out of office.

In line with this thinking, La Guardia went to several important Congressmen with his problem, but they told him it was a matter for the state courts. He then turned to Governor Franklin D. Roosevelt for assistance. Roosevelt listened to La Guardia's argument and called in Judge Samuel Seabury to look into his accusations.

Seabury began with the Magistrates' Court in New York City. After a few weeks, he uncovered agreements to fix trials made between city officials and prominent criminals. La Guardia took this evidence to the news media to inform all New Yorkers about the investigation. Governor Roosevelt then demanded that Mayor Walker go on the stand to answer the charges. Unable to handle his exposure, Walker resigned as mayor of New York City.

Meanwhile, the Depression, now in its third year, had sunk the country deeply into economic chaos, and Congress was now willing to take La Guardia's proposed legislation seriously. He was able to rush through a number of important measures—the government-sponsored public works act, which made thousands of new jobs available, federal insurance for bank savings accounts, unemployment insurance, and a shorter work week. Hoover's foot-dragging about signing these bills into law forced La Guardia to swing his strength behind Roosevelt, now a candidate for president, and a reformer like La Guardia.

The Democratic landslide, which gave the presidency to F.D.R., also caused the Republican La Guardia to lose his seat in Congress. But in the final few weeks of his term, in the lame duck session of Congress, Roosevelt called upon him to use his influence to push through the new bills on which he had been working. In effect, then, the new legislation which Roosevelt offered the country was also La Guardia's.

Fiorello La Guardia returned to New York City to resume his private law practice. Because of the exposures of the Walker administration, he saw that the city's political climate had changed and decided to again aim his sights on the upcoming mayoralty race.

The wealthy backers, the money-people behind politics, wanted a fusion-party of reform-minded Democrats, liberal Republicans and any independent groups who were for clean government. Their choice was Judge Seabury, who was looked upon as the hero of the Walker exposé. Seabury, disinterested in the mayoralty nomination, threw his influence behind La Guardia. President Roosevelt also split the Democratic vote by encouraging all reform Democrats to back La Guardia against incumbent Mayor O'Brien and his Tammany Hall machine.

On January 1, 1934, after his overwhelming victory, Fiorello La Guardia took over the office of Mayor of the City of New York, the first Italian-American to hold such a high political position.

Few people had foreseen the extent to which La Guardia would go to clean up the corruption in the city. Within a few days after taking his oath, he struck out at do-nothing bureaucrats, corrupt law enforcement officials, and known criminals. His new municipal government was a bold experiment revealing what a non-partisan, non-political, honest government could do.

A man of unassuming appearance, LaGuardia would walk into a Lower East Side relief office and stand in line, observing the slow-moving, condescending civil servants at work. When he had seen enough, he made his presence known, fired the worst offenders, and issued orders to the others to mend their inept ways.

There was no job so small that he wouldn't look into it. He inspected garbage trucks and dumps, read and answered most of the letters that poured into his office, and ordered his staff to inform him of every suggestion or complaint they received concerning the city. He shook the dust and dead weight out of every department and fired hundreds of lazy, lax city workers. He ruled with an iron hand and took to task commissioners or assistants who were doing a poor job.

His responsibilities as a Congressman were nothing compared to the enormous task of overseeing thousands of employees and seven million citizens. In some ways La Guardia was not a good mayor. He could have used a few lessons in winning friends and dealing with people. He expected too much from his staff and friends. He had little sense of humor and there was never a smiling face to be seen in his office. Outspoken, vividly human, hyperactive and temperamentally unsuited for his office, La Guardia became the chief subject of the newspaper political cartoonists and the topic of angry conversations across the country.

Yet he was something bigger and bolder than anything people had ever seen in public office. He worked sixteen to twenty hours a day and was constantly in motion. People hated, but respected him. He was a skilled politician with a very real sense of his people and their needs. Most importantly he got things done. He reduced every issue to the simple vernacular of the common people and distressed those who expected a metropolitan mayor to present a polished Jimmy Walker personality in public. He was blunt and to the point and usually at the center of any conflict. Certainly nobody was indifferent to him.

La Guardia lived life as a heavy drama. In his position of power with the entire city his stage, he exulted in a multitude of roles. He was often seen riding to fires on the back of a fire truck, then hurrying into burning buildings to make his own inspection. He rounded up thousands of gamblers' slot machines, personally smashed them with sledge hammers, then hurled the pieces into the East River. His antics, his earthy humanness endeared him to the people of New York, who soon called him, affectionately, "The Little Flower," which was a translation of his first name, Fiorello.

During the Depression he was given millions of dollars through government agencies, such as the Public Works Administration. He used his money to create thousands of new jobs.

He had a flair for the startling statement, like the one he made at his election victory party: "My first qualification for this great office is my monumental personal ingratitude. You can't be a good mayor and a good fellow."

He made every appointment on the basis of merit, not as a reward for political support or campaign backing. He notoriously offended Republican Party leaders by simply not speaking to them. Many powerful politicians labeled him a dangerous radical who had no party loyalty and could consequently only hurt party causes.

In the mayoralty election of 1937, the Republican-Fusion movement again refused to support him, until Judge Seabury and President Roosevelt again interceded in his behalf. Only the public seemed to want to support him, but that, of course, was all he needed. When the people reelected him, the second win made him the first reform mayor of New York City ever to win two terms.

When the 1940 presidential elections came round, it seemed likely that La Guardia would be tapped for the vice-presidential spot. He was, at the time, the second most important politician in the country. As mayor of New York City and a former long-time Congressman, he certainly had enough experience to handle the vice-presidency, but President Roosevelt felt that there was still too much prejudice in the country against anyone with a foreign name. When it also seemed possible that La Guardia would be appointed Secretary of War, again he was bypassed, this time because of political opposition. Indeed, the energetic, incorruptible mayor could have handled any of the cabinet positions with ease and honesty. Unfortunately, he never got the chance.

Thus, La Guardia saw his political future in continuing his office as mayor of New York City. In 1941 he campaigned for a third term. Always ready to excite the imagination of the voter, he campaigned with a large caged tiger, which symbolized municipal corruption. Whenever the tiger roared, the mayor exclaimed, "He's hungry, he's had no graft in years!" Again, Roosevelt supported his bid for office and made several speeches in his behalf. It was no surprise when La Guardia won third term by another landslide.

During the war La Guardia managed to keep the big city alive and well. When the New York newspapers went on strike, he went as far as to perform one of his most famous duties—reading the comic strips over radio for the kids, big and little. In 1941-42, he also served as director of the Office of Civilian Defense.

When the war came to an end, another New York mayoralty race was at hand, and again the Republican Party refused to endorse Fiorello La Guardia. When Judge Seabury again stepped forth to muster another fusion ticket, he supported La Guardia. And certainly the people of New York City were behind their mayor. But "The Little Flower" refused to run again. He had at last been worn down by the incredible pace at which he had been going for years. Wilted, he was too tired, mentally and physically, to be stimulated by another term in office.

The Democratic candidate, William O'Dwyer, won the election, and on New Year's Day, 1946, La Guardia drove away from the City Hall for the last time, after having been its greatest and most effective public servant for twelve years.

However, he was still not ready to retire. He kept six assistants busy in his law office in the RCA Building, worked on editorials for a local newspaper, appeared on radio, and attended neighborhood meetings. In 1946, he was appointed Director-General of the United Nations Rehabilitation and Relief Agency, in charge of feeding and resurrecting the war-ravaged countries of Europe, Africa and Asia.

In 1947, he returned from his world travels for the United Nations to accept the One World Award. Although he was dying of cancer, he continued to travel and perform his duties. When he became bed-ridden he dictated his memoirs, composed letters, described new reform measures, and advised district leaders on the best ways in which to help their constituencies. On September 20, 1947, the heart of Fiorello H. La Guardia, "The Little Flower," stopped beating. All the flags in New York were lowered half-mast to honor the little, flamboyant mayor and champion of the common man. Like other great men, this Italian-American now belonged to the ages.

ENRICO FERMI

In August 1945, when atomic bombs fell on Hiroshima and Nagasaki, the world saw the most destructive human invention ever devised. Yet, this tool of death could also be man's greatest servant. With the mushroom clouds still towering over Japan, scientists were already beginning to explore the endless peace-time possibilities of atomic energy. As with anything else, its value of good or evil depends solely upon the men using it. Whether atomic energy will truly be a great gift or a suicidal weapon for mankind remains to be seen.

The father of atomic energy was Enrico Fermi, an Italian-American. By leading the world into a new era, the Atomic Age, he radically altered the course of civilization. Fermi's genius transcended man's readily perceptible boundaries—land and ocean, wind and stars and that which we can appreciate through our senses. Fermi was a nuclear physicist whose world of theory and experimentation led him into uncharted intricate structures and complex behavior of atoms, the basic building blocks of matter, of which everything in the universe, including man, is made. Fermi epitomized the true nature of the explorer. He went where no man had gone before and charted the outer (inner, rather) regions, diligently pursuing the unknown, the abstruse, and emerging with knowledge that would change and improve human existence.

Enrico Fermi was born in Rome in September, 1901. His family farmed the land close to Piacenza in the Po Valley, but young Enrico did not share their agricultural interests. Instead, he showed a precocious, inquiring and inventive intelligence, with a particular interest in physics. A local professor gave him books on science and encouraged his interests, advising him to study at the Reale Scuole Normale Superiore at Pisa—a college for exceptionally bright students. Since Enrico did not have the necessary funds to enter this expensive school, he prepared and submitted to its staff a lucid and erudite report on the subject of vibrating strings. The college officials were overwhelmed by the youth's knowledge and gave him a special scholarship.

Though he was a brilliant student, Enrico also participated in sports, parties and other extra-curricular activities of college. He loved Pisa, since it was the city in which Galileo had experimented. He also developed a close friendship with Franco Rasetti, another outstanding physics student.

After the first year, it became evident that both Fermi and Rasetti were too advanced for the other students. The officials decided to give them freedom to pursue their own experiments. By the end of the following year, Fermi was teaching Rasetti and a few other students the new theoretical physics introduced recently by Albert Einstein which dealt with the theory of relativity and the quantum theory regarding the absorption or radiation of energy by matter.

Fermi received his Doctor of Physics degree in July, 1922 and graduated magna cum laude. His specialty was nuclear physics.

That Fall Fermi was invited to work at Gottingen under the guidance of the famous German physicist, Max Born. After a year's study with Born, he went to Rome to teach mathematics and physics at the university there, and moved to the University of Florence a year later. These two years of teaching allowed him time and facilities to carry on several experiments, and by the end of the year he had completed a paper called, "On the Quantization of a Perfect Monatomic Gas," which quickly established his reputation in the world of physics.

Meanwhile, Italian science was being tampered with. As Benito Mussolini and his Fascist Party rose to power, government control began to interfere with the institutions of higher learning. Laboratory experiments had to be approved by the Fascist leaders.

One of the few schools that was operating without any restrictions or intervention by the government was the physics department at the University of Rome, headed by an influential, non-Fascist senator, Professor Orso Mario Corbino. In 1926, Corbino was allowed to create a new chair in theoretical physics in his department, and Fermi won it over several other outstanding physicists. Franco Rasetti placed a close second and was also given a position, allowing him and his close friend to carry on their valuable experiments together.

Fermi was chosen as a member of the Royal Academy of Italy in 1929, the highest honor given to a scientist.

In the summer of 1930, Fermi visited America to spend a few semesters teaching at the University of Michigan. The trip proved to be one of new perspectives. In America, he was startled to read the news reports and listen to the heated discussions of what was happening in Italy, and from this new outside viewpoint he could see the damage being done in Italy by Mussolini's dictatorship. While living in Italy, Fermi had drawn a curtain around his life and had ignored everything except his experiments. America enabled him to open his eyes and give an objective glance around him. And when he returned to Italy, he could no longer be oblivious to the rest of the world, nor unaware of the conditions around him.

In 1932, he read of the noted British physicist James Chadwick's identification of the neutron—the particle within the atomic nucleus that, unlike the proton, carries no electric charge. A few years later, he learned of Frederick and Irene Joliot Curie, French scientists, producing the first artificial radioactivity by bombarding elements with alpha particles—the large, positive charged nuclear particles emitted in radiation. Fermi believed that if he could bombard elements with neutrons he would have a more effective nuclear projectile. Neutrons traveled faster and further than alpha particles and were not so easily halted. By hitting the nucleus of an atom, a neutron could dislodge protons, the result of which would be the creation of artificial radioactivity.

Fermi's determination intensified as he gathered samples of the ninety-two known elements. He had difficulty, though, in obtaining the proper amount of neutrons to work with. Radioactive particles spontaneously released alpha substances in huge amounts, but neutrons could only be obtained indirectly, through bombarding a substance like beryllium with alpha particles, and it took nearly 100,000 of these particles to obtain a single neutron.

The city health department supplied him with a gram of radium, from which he was able to use the alpha particles. Fermi then constructed a "neutron gun" by mixing radon with beryllium in a small gas tube.

His neutron experiments at first yielded nothing, but he persisted. One day, after he had exposed fluorine to his neutron gun, the Geiger counter chattered, showing that the material had become radioactive. Intensifying his efforts he created artificial radioactivity in a number of heavier elements, forming new radioactive forms or isotypes, or even changing the original element into neighboring elements on the periodic table. This latter accomplishment had been the life-long dream of alchemists throughout many centuries.

Fermi also uncovered another essential fact. If a "Moderator" rich in hydrogen, such as water or paraffin, was placed between the neutron source and the bombarded element, the radioactivity produced would be much greater than usual. Fermi demonstrated his new discovery in a simple goldfish pond, in which the neutron source and a chunk of silver were placed far from each other. When retrieved, the silver emitted at least a hundred-times greater radiation than the same element bombarded outside of water. This led him to conclude that the neutrons were more easily slowed when they hit protons in the hydrogen atoms, similar to a billiard ball decreasing in speed after striking another ball. These slow neutrons were then more easily captured by nuclei, creating increased displacement of protons in the bombarded element and causing the material to become radioactive.

Fermi finally began work on the most recently discovered element: uranium. A variety of radioactive substances was produced when uranium was bombarded by neutrons, many of which baffled him. Fermi was a physicist, not a chemist, so it was difficult for him to make chemical identification.

Of one thing he was certain. He had discovered element number 93. When Fermi made his announcement, it made world headlines, but since no one else was duplicating his work and could therefore not disprove his claim, most prominent scientists reserved judgement on his new, man-made element until further research could be carried out. Chemists and physicists everywhere began duplicating and varying Fermi's formula with uranium.

At the University of California, Ernest Lawrence was at work on the first cyclotron, a gigantic magnet that accelerated charged atomic particles. There his research team could use their much more powerful sources for neutrons, seeking further man-made elements. Other scientists, equipped with new, sophisticated resources, were also delving into the mystery of uranium bombardment.

In September 1938 Fermi won the Nobel Prize in physics. The citation read: "To Enrico Fermi of Rome for his identification of new radioactive elements produced by neutron bombardment and his discovery, made in connection with this work, of nuclear reactions effected by slow neutrons."

On the same day he was notified of his Nobel Prize, bad news reached him. A new law had been issued forbidding Jews to travel, and since Fermi's wife was Jewish, the Italian government revoked his passport. He was forced to plead with top Fascist officials to have it returned. Had he not won the Nobel Prize, which required his traveling to Stockholm to receive it, it is unlikely that he would have been allowed to leave the country. Even so, he was only allowed to take $50.00 out of Italy with him, not an extreme inconvenience considering that the $50,000 Nobel Prize money was waiting for him in Sweden. At the Nobel Prize ceremony Fermi demonstrated for Mussolini by neglecting to give the customary Fascist salute to the King of Sweden. He shook hands with him instead.

In December, 1938, the Fermis landed in New York. No sooner

had they unpacked their bags than Enrico was in a laboratory, furthering his experiments. The famous Danish physicist, Niels Bohr, arrived from Europe and announced to Fermi that German scientists had proved that the uranium atom could be split apart during neutron bombardment, a discovery that shattered the age-old belief that the atomic nucleus was indivisible. Fermi's unnamed element 93 turned out to be barium, with about half the atomic weight of uranium. It could be found mixed with other lighter elements in minute quantities after uranium atoms split.

This discovery had been made by the two German scientists, Hahn and Strassman, who sent their findings to a former colleague, Lise Meitner, a Jew who had to flee Nazi Germany for her life. Meitner theorized that a prodigious quantity of energy would be released during the splitting, which she named "fission." Knowing that such knowledge would be fatal to millions if Hitler was informed of these discoveries, she told only Bohr as he was leaving for the U.S.

Fermi had been the first to split the atom in his Rome laboratory in 1934, but he failed to recognize it at the time. It is possibly one of the most fortunate oversights in history, for had he known the significance of his discovery, he surely would have made his findings known to the public, and German scientists would have been far ahead of America in developing atomic energy and its lethal offspring, the Atomic Bomb.

Bohr's news caused Fermi to drop everything else and concentrate on studying neutrons again. Fermi advanced an original hypothesis that laid the foundation for the future development and use of atomic energy. He was convinced that the neutron entered and caused an instability in the uranium nucleus, splitting it apart. A great deal of energy would then be released, and neutrons would also be emitted. If these neutrons were emitted in greater number than other neutrons being absorbed, a chain reaction would be possible that would provide a new source of energy.

Fermi was thus suggesting the possibility of the chain reaction which is caused when an uranium atom, split by a neutron, divides in two and emits two neutrons, which in turn split two uranium atoms, which then emit four neutrons—a mounting, self-sustaining process that would halt only after all the uranium atoms have been split by, or have captured, the stray neutrons.

However, the complex nature of uranium posed a serious problem for Fermi. The element has two main isotopes, one containing a mass of 238, the other of 235. Uranium 238 makes up more than 99 percent of natural uranium, yet only U-235 is fissionable. It seemed an impossible task to separate them, to have enough U-235 quantities to test whether a chain reaction was possible.

Fermi felt that a chain reaction could occur in a large, specially constructed pile made up of chunks of natural uranium interspersed with a moderating material that would slow down the speed of neutrons released in the fission of the first U-235 atoms at the pile's nucleus. Slow neutrons, less easily captured by the nuclei of U-238 atoms, could split other U-235 atoms, emitting still more neutrons. It was hoped by Fermi that it would be possible to control a chain reaction within this pile and thus avoid a destructive explosion.

Fermi began work now on his "atomic pile." For his moderator, he selected graphite (almost pure carbon) as the material most likely to work. He then began to build graphite bricks in different arrangements around a neutron source, so that he could observe, on a lesser scale, different shapes for his atomic pile.

Many American scientists, fearing that the Germans were already ahead of them in atomic energy research, sent letters to scientists throughout the country, requesting that any further tests or research results with atomic energy be kept a secret. They also combined forces to work as a team, a brain trust, at Columbia University. Several high-ranking government officials were called in to inform Washington of valuable nuclear research and to request Federal funds for all future work on the project. Uranium and pure graphite were very expensive. The cost of just one chain reaction was more than any of the scientists could afford. Only the government would be able to finance a significant research program.

The government officials did not see the importance of the project until Fermi explained to them that if war came, one Atomic Bomb would be more powerful than a million of Hitler's conventional bombs, and even then they only obtained an initial funding that was so limited it would last no more than a few months. After a few more discouraging arguments with these officials, Fermi asked his good friend, Albert Einstein, a scientist with influence, to write a letter to President Roosevelt explaining the urgency of their needs.

The now-famous letter read: "Some recent work by E. Fermi and L. Szilard leads me to expect that the element uranium may be turned into a new and important source of energy in the immediate future. This new phenomenon would also lead to the construction of bombs." Einstein concluded the letter with a warning that the outcome of the world could hang in the balance because the Germans were pursuing the same work, but on a much faster scale, with unlimited financing from Hitler.

Roosevelt immediately appointed a Uranium Committee to investigate the situation. In the interim, the War Department allocated enough funds to Fermi to keep his staff busy with their experiments. Yet, little headway was being made. They needed more money, and time became essential. Hitler's war machine had overrun Czechoslovakia and now controlled the world's richest source of uranium. It had also captured the world's only heavy-water plant, in Norway. Time was running out for American scientists to develop something before the Germans did.

In December 1941, within a week after the attack on Pearl Harbor, Roosevelt appointed Arthur H. Compton, a Nobel Prize physicist from the University of Chicago, as head of the Uranium Project and gave him unlimited government financing. Compton was familiar with Fermi's work and was confident that a nuclear chain reaction could be achieved and an Atomic Bomb constructed. If Fermi's atomic pile worked, it might also produce a by-product, the newly discovered man-made element, plutonium. Formed in minute quantities from the fission of U-235, plutonium was also fissionable and could be used as an explosive.

During the summer of 1942, Fermi moved his atomic pile to the research center for atomic energy at the University of Chicago. Fermi could now work with a group of the most renowned scientists in America, without worrying about money or materials. He chose to use the squash court beneath the football field stands, because of the high ceilings. It took the scientists only six weeks to erect the bulky sphere of graphite bricks around chunks of natural uranium; then the entire structure was fortified by a wooden frame. Within a month Fermi proved his theory by achieving the first self-sustaining chain reaction, thereby initiating the controlled release of nuclear energy. The date was December 2, 1942.

Fermi's atomic pile had reached the point where it contained enough fissionable uranium to cause a chain reaction.

The news of Fermi's achievement was kept under wraps, except for a few discreet calls to important government officials. Dr. Compton telephoned Dr. James Conant, Roosevelt's top science adviser, and cryptically told him about the grand, historical display which he had just witnessed: "you'll be interested to know that the Italian navigator had just landed in the New World."

A casual observer would possibly wonder about all the excitement. Fermi had only produced enough energy, half a watt, to light a flashlight bulb. But to the trained scientific mind, it became instantly obvious that Fermi's discovery had taken mankind to the threshold of a phenomenal new source of power. It was obvious that atomic bombs could be built if the necessary quantities of U-235 or plutonium could be secured.

Roosevelt was excited about the new achievements and gave the go-ahead for the "Manhattan District Project," the code name for the uranium research and atomic bomb development. To speed up the work on the bomb, Roosevelt put the U.S. Army Corps of Engineers in control of the project. General Leslie R. Groves was placed in command of the Engineers with orders that work was to be done non-stop, twenty-four hours a day, until an atomic bomb was ready. Thousands of military personnel and scientists were put to work on the project, with its eventual cost running over two billion dollars; the Manhattan District Project became the biggest business in the country.

Fermi was constantly reminded of the unpleasant axiom that it was only the strife between nations which advanced the technology necessary for the development of atomic energy. Had it been peacetime, the practical applications of his research might have taken years to be developed.

Fermi's atomic pile was just the beginning stage for the actual construction of atomic bombs. A lesser amount of pure fissionable material would chain-react violently, but to obtain even miniscule quantities of the U-235 or plutonium 239 involved complex industrial processes which had not yet been systemized. At "Site X," an enormous series of plants were constructed to separate U-235 from U-238, which would give scientists enough uranium for a single bomb. Security was so tight that only a few of the 75,000 employees at the Clinton Engineering Works in Oak Ridge, Tennessee, actually knew what they were making.

Alongside the Columbia River at Hartford, Washington, the government built three large nuclear reactors, in which tons of uranium ore were converted into small quantities of plutonium 239. The third site, "Y," was located on a high, desolate mesa at Los Alamos, just south of Santa Fe, New Mexico. There, engineers and scientists designed the atomic bombs that would become operable as soon as enough fissionable material came from Oak Ridge and Hanford.

Fermi traveled between the three sites overseeing the work. In 1944 he moved his base of operations to Los Alamos, where he could work closely with J. Robert Oppenheimer, who had been busy at work on the advanced design of the atomic bombs, trying to calculate the "critical mass"—the precise amount of U-235 that would spontaneously explode when hit by a neutron. The same year Fermi received his American citizenship.

Hidden away from the world at Los Alamos were the greatest scientific minds in the world, including four Nobel Prize physicists. The neutron discoverer, James Chadwick, was present, as well as Niels Bohr. Everything was classified and given code names; Atom was called "top"; bomb became "boat"; uranium "tube alloy"; uranium fission "urchin fashion."

By July 1945, a sufficient amount of uranium 235 and plutonium 239 arrived at Los Alamos. The big Atomic Bomb using a gun-type detonator was nearing completion, though no one knew just how powerful the explosive force would be. The two plutonium bombs, with implosion mechanisms, were much more difficult to work with, and at least one of them would have to be tested to see what explosive force it contained.

The first atomic bomb test, code-named "Trinity," was scheduled for July 16, 1945 in the desert. The plutonium bomb, code-named "Fat Man," was set on top of a hundred-foot tower, with an automatic triggering device controlled by a detonator some five miles away. The hundreds of engineers, scientists, politicians and technicians were assembled ten miles from the blast site in concrete bunkers, most of them skeptical about the necessity of being a full ten miles away. Most of them guessed that the explosive force would be no more than a few tons of TNT, if indeed the bomb exploded at all.

At precisely 5:30 a.m., Dr. Oppenheimer ended everyone's guessing game. He gave the signal and the big bomb exploded with the incredible brightness of a man-made sun shattering earth and air. Within seconds, a gigantic fireball mushroomed up into the sky. A minute later came the roar of the blast .

The witnesses to this holocaust stared in disbelief—shaken, silent and awed—as they slowly began to comprehend the dimensions of this new weapon. Fermi quickly calculated that the blast had equalled 20,000 tons of TNT.

Within an hour, Fermi and Oppenheimer were on their way toward the blast site, Ground Zero, in a lead-lined tank protecting them from the deadly radiation fallout. At the site they saw the grim testament of the bomb's power. A wide crater had been ripped into the parched desert floor. The sand had been fused into shimmering green-glass particles by the blast's heat. There were no signs of life within three or four miles of the site.

In the weeks ahead, the major question for Fermi, his fellow scientists, the military brass and the political leaders was what to do with the bomb. Fermi and most of the other scientists immediately insisted that it not be dropped on any populated area. They chose either to hang it as a threat over Japan's head (Germany had already surrendered in April) like the sword of Damocles, or, if that didn't work, drop it on a military-industrial site.

President Truman, who had been completely unaware of the bomb's development until after he became President following Roosevelt's sudden death, appointed a special interim Committee to look into the arguments of both sides. This panel came to the conclusion that the only way to show the Japanese that continuing the war would be futile and to deter them from making a last-minute suicide attempt that would cost many American lives would be to drop the bomb on their most densely populated city.

Three weeks after the first test of the Atomic Bomb, the uranium and plutonium bomb was dropped on Hiroshima. When Japan made no response toward surrender, a second bomb leveled Nagasaki and the Second World War came to an abrupt end.

Since the atomic bomb and all of its research data were now no longer considered top secret, newspapers, magazines, radio and television told the world of the amazing work which had been going on for the past three years.

In every one of the feature stories the hero of the day was the Italian-American, Enrico Fermi. His contribution to the war effort especially pleased those Italian-Americans whose loyalty had been questioned during the war years.

With no more work to be done on the atomic bomb, Fermi left Los Alamos and returned to the quiet life of applied research at the University of Chicago. He concentrated his efforts on his specialty, the neutron.

On March 19, 1946, he was called to Washington D.C., and presented with the Congressional Medal of Merit, the highest award given to civilians. His citation read, in part, "To Enrico Fermi for exceptionally meritorious conduct in the performance of outstanding service to the War Department. A great experimental physicist, Dr. Fermi's sound scientific judgment, his initiative and resourcefulness, and his unswerving devotion to duty have contributed vitally to the success of the Atomic Bomb project." What they could also have mentioned was that he unlocked the door to limitless benefits for mankind in peacetime. For many years Fermi served on the General Advisory Committee of the Atomic Energy Commission, the blue-ribbon agency appointed to direct further nuclear research. A few of the off-shoots of his original creation were the radioisotopes, which were long-lasting and inexpensively created and gave hospitals and universities their own sources of radiation. They could also be used in medicine to diagnose and treat diseases, in biological research, agriculture, and industry in an ever-expanding variety of ways. Atomic energy also proved a valuable fuel for ships and for producing electricity. Meanwhile, scientists discovered element 100, which they named Fermium to honor Enrico Fermi.

During the early 1950's Fermi traveled extensively, lecturing at American and European universities, but in the summer of 1952 he became sick. Doctors diagnosed his illness as terminal cancer, the deadly disease which afflicted many who worked closely with radioactive materials.

In November 1954, Fermi was presented with the Atomic Energy Commission's first award for "especially meritorious contributions for the development, use, or control of atomic energy," an annual prize known today as the Enrico Fermi Award. Several weeks later, on November 28, Fermi died.

Samuel K. Allison, a long-time friend of Fermi's, summed up Fermi's life in a final tribute, "There is no doubt among those who knew him and could appreciate his accomplishments, that Enrico Fermi was one of the most brilliant intellects of our century. Here was a man who possessed a most extraordinary endowment of the highest human capabilities."

Arturo Toscanini

Although Arturo Toscanini never became a citizen of the United States, he was certainly one of our most creative and famous residents. For nearly fifty years his musical conducting in concert halls, opera houses, on recordings and over the radio brought America to the forefront of the music world. Today, he is ranked as one of the greatest orchestral conductors of all time.

He was born in Parma on March 25, 1867. As a youth, Arturo had an uncanny ear for tone. A single violin string that was out of tune in an orchestra of a hundred instruments, undetectable by anyone else, would tear at Toscanini's hearing. During school, he amazed his instructors with his comments on music. He told them that all the instruction in baton techniques and the intricacies of orchestral composition, all the experience in summoning music from other mens' instruments were useless and absurd if the conductor did not have the right head and heart for music. His friends and teachers agreed that whatever the reasons for his phenomenal skill and uncontrollable temperament, the two were apparently inborn and inseparable in Toscanini.

His early music teachers soon realized that his potential lay far beyond their scope and had the nine-year old Toscanini apply for entry into the Royal School of Music, where he was given a full scholarship. For the next nine years, Arturo lived and worked in the monastic atmosphere at the Parma conservatory. Although he preferred playing the piano, he specialized in the cello, and he astounded his instructors by committing entire scores to memory, knowing not just his own part but the other instrumental parts as well. They gave him the nickname of I Genietto—the little genius. He graduated from the conservatory with honors.

An opera company hired Toscanini as a cellist and assistant chorus master to tour with them to South America for the season. Their first stop was Rio de Janeiro, where, on the first night of the performance, the Brazilian conductor accused the Italian singers and musicians of conspiring against him and walked out. An unruly audience that was waiting to see *Aida* performed began to hiss and boo when the announcement was made that the conductor would not appear that night. The assistant conductor and choir master were brayed off the stage.

Then, to the laughter of the rest of the company, Toscanini, who had never conducted before, said that he would give it a try. He quickly dressed in a dark suit several sizes too large and walked onto the stage. The audience and orchestra were stunned to see the beardless youth standing before them. Yet, when Toscanini's baton descended sharply to start the overture to *Aida,* the choir and orchestra blended together into perfection and captured the audience. The boy wonder was given a five minute ovation at the end of the performance.

Upon his return to Italy in 1886, he was asked to meet with Catalani, who had just completed a new opera, *Edmea.* Word of Toscanini's triumph had preceded him by several months and all of Italy was talking of the new young genius. Catalani listened to Toscanini play through the score. (Arturo had never seen it before) and, impressed with the young man's musical intelligence and sensitivity, he offered Arturo the conductorship for the premiere.

Following his highly successful Italian debut, Toscanini knew that his future would be as a conductor and that only on occasion would he return to playing the cello. Even so, in 1887 he auditioned for and was accepted to a cellist chair at La Scala in Milan, so that he would be present at the world premiere of Otello, which was Verdi's first opera in sixteen years.

For the next ten years Toscanini traveled to all of the cities in Italy, conducting operas and symphonic concerts. He worked indefatigably against the poor quality and sensitivity in all areas of production in the provincial opera houses, although he realized that he would have to endure these conditions until he was established and could impose his own critical taste. Still, he drove himself and others and became outraged if the music did not reach the standard he desired. He never compromised when quality was in question, and he gained a reputation as a demanding, wild-tempered perfectionist. He was also noted for his extraordinary memory, acute hearing and a phenomenal sensitivity for the work he was conducting.

Respecting Verdi and Wagner above all others, Toscanini concentrated on Verdi's work for a few years, then began on Wagner's. He was impressed with Wagner's method for achieving the dynamic, giant-sized opera dramas. Beneath the powerful cataracts of Wagner's sound, Toscanini also found the touching, human-toned song that for him provided the common denominator for creative music.

Toscanini was the first composer to bring Wagner to the masses in Italy. Though many Italians did not care for Wagner's operas, he performed them anyway. In 1895, he introduced the first Italian performance of *Die Gotterdammerung,* an opera that, since he had never heard it played before, was conceived freshly and brilliantly. The work was a critical and popular success.

With every performance, Toscanini's prestige and following increased. At Turin he conducted the world premiere of *La Boheme* and *I Pagliacci*. Finally, in 1898, he was asked to take over the dictatorship of the 120 year-old Teatro alla Scala in Milan, Italy's foremost opera house. This was the highest honor possible for Toscanini.

Maestro Toscanini demanded absolute perfection from everyone —musicians, performers, set designers and lighting technicians. His word was first and last on all matters. He always wanted things to be done as they should, not as they usually were, and it was not uncommon for him to loudly curse at and berate his singers and musicians. He wanted them to bring to life the divinely inspired compositions, regardless of how complex and profound or light and gay. He resolved all questions by asking his musicians to fulfill faithfully the composer's intention.

It was under Toscanini's hand and baton that La Scala came into full flower. Many famous singers owe their success to the valuable training given them under Toscanini's strict, but inspirational, guidance. The incomparable tenor, Enrico Caruso, made his debut in *La Boheme* at La Scala in 1900, and it was under Toscanini that Caruso's career and worldwide fame commenced.

In 1908, Toscanini accepted an offer from the New York City Metropolitan Opera Company to bring his talent to America. Caruso and Antonio Scotti were already in America and doing impressively well.

Toscanini's first performance at the Metropolitan Opera House came on November 16, 1908, with *Aida*. It was the first performance of the season and everyone in society, including Caruso and Scotti, was on hand. That opening night would be the start of the Toscanini-Caruso collaboration which would last for many years.

Toscanini conducted with strenuous force, dominating power and potent artistry. His efforts created a revival of the Italian lyric opera, which was a pleasant contrast to the German-dominated earlier years at the Met. In the seven seasons Toscanini conducted at the Met, he prepared some eighty-five operas, fifty-nine of them being Italian. His tenure gave the Opera House a firm discipline and inspiration musical direction unlike anything it had ever known. Today, the Toscanini years at the Met are known as the Met's golden era.

It was Toscanini who brought Puccini's famous opera, *The Girl of the Golden West*, to the Met. He also premiered *Boris Godunov*, with the Russian basso Feodor Chaliapin, and he was responsible for taking the Metropolitan Opera Company to Europe in 1910.

Toscanini grew dissatisfied with the Met, especially its repertory system of rotating productions in performance rather than allowing a single opera to play as long as attendance permitted. This system presented constant problems of rehearsal tangles, scattered performances, and artists' schedules. Another of Toscanini's complaints was that the Met's business and production manager, Gatti-

Casazza, was limited to a small budget, precluding Toscanini's desire to get the best available artists. Therefore, it came as no surprise when, in the spring of 1915, Toscanini left for Italy without a word to anyone.

The World War was going on in Europe and Toscanini's son was in the Italian Army, so the conductor wanted to assist in the war effort. He gave many benefit concerts and occasionally traveled to the front lines to give encouragement and inspiration to the troops. Despite this patriotic gesture, he came under attack by Italian chauvinists who objected to his conducting programs by Haydn, Mozart, Brahms, Wagner and Beethoven. When Toscanini ignored them, his performances were boycotted. Yet, he never had had an empty seat in the house.

After the war, Toscanini startled everyone by entering politics. Feeling disenchanted by the war, he ran for a deputy post on the Socialist ticket. However he lost, along with fellow aspirant Benito Mussolini, and thus ended his political career.

When the owners of La Scala offered him a lucrative contract that gave him absolute authority, he accepted and returned to the famous opera house. He spent another eight seasons at La Scala, not all of them without conflict.

In 1922, Mussolini ruled Italy. All concert halls and opera houses were required to decorate their lobbies with pictures of Il Duce, but Arturo Toscanini openly defied the government decree by not allowing one picture in La Scala. The Fascist Black Shirts, recognizing Toscanini's enormous popularity, avoided an open conflict with him. Toscanini was possibly the only Italian free to denounce Mussolini and his government, and time and time again, he taunted the Black Shirts, telling them they would have to kill him to keep him from speaking out against them. He refused to play the two Italian anthems—the *Royal March* and the Fascist *Giovinezza* — which were required before all public performances. Toscanini called it childish foolery, saying that "La Scala is not a beer garden or Fascist propaganda territory."

Toscanini returned to New York in 1926 to make his conducting debut with the New York Philharmonic. For the next few years he became the Philharmonic's principal conductor. He traveled between New York and Milan in order to keep his commitment with La Scala, but in 1928, he was intimidated into leaving his country by the Fascists, who had decided he was causing more trouble than he was worth. This brought to an end his thirty-year period of opera conducting, during which the world's finest singers were guided under his direction.

Once again he returned to New York, where he appeared each season at Carnegie Hall. He was a box-office wonder, selling out every performance. It was a rare pleasure for New York music enthusiasts to listen, transfixed, to brilliantly interpreted Beethoven symphonies; to delicate Mozart concertos; to thundering Wagnerian overtures; to the mood music of Respighi. Toscanini became so popular that his concerts were carried over radio to all parts of the country.

Toscanini could not forget his beloved homeland, and on several occasions he tried to return to Italy to perform, but Mussolini's government forbade him to conduct anywhere unless he agreed to silence about the Fascists. He answered that his conscience would not allow him to compromise his freedom of speech, even if it meant giving up the one thing he cherished most, conducting.

In 1937, The National Broadcasting Company and its affiliated recording company, RCA Victor, offered Toscanini a special orchestra of virtuoso musicians and a specially-constructed sound studio in Rockefeller Center. He accepted their offer, for even at seventy years of age, he had not lost his dynamic energy; he seemed tireless, ageless.

Samuel Antek, a violinist with the NBC Symphony, called this time a period of "musical and spiritual regeneration . . . Music making became once more a hallowed calling and you felt musically reborn."

For the last sixteen years of his life, Toscanini gave the world the last full measure of his musical genius; there was an intense joy and at the same time a searing pain which music held for him. As his age advanced, his ardor, his memory, his perpetual persuit of the ever-elusive perfect symphony, passage or single note, never diminished.

Toscanini's effusive temperament during rehearsals became conservative gestures in performance. He did not believe that it was necessary for a maestro to conduct by mechanical gyrations or flail his arms, roll his head or display other podium pyrotechnics.

For weeks Toscanini would be quite content; then, without warning, he would go into one of his rages and break his baton, tear his score to shreds, upset his music stand and throw it at someone, or take his jacket off and rip it into pieces. He is estimated to have smashed at least twenty wrist watches and was sued on several occasions for attacking his musicians. In fact, if there was no fight or outrage for any length of time, a tenseness would settle over his orchestra and the musicians would begin to worry about him. Suddenly he would break into a fury, and everybody knew that he was still in good form.

Toscanini was asked to return to Italy after the war, but he refused, claiming that he would never return as long as the Fascist-supported king, Victor Emmanuel III, was still on the throne and would not let democratic rule be established. Still, he gave a million lire for the restoration of La Scala, which had nearly been destroyed in air raids during the war. In 1946, when Italy began to establish a democratic government, Toscanini returned to Milan and conducted his first concert in the rebuilt La Scala on May 11. Everywhere he traveled, the people hailed him as a champion of freedom. The new president conferred an honorary life senatorship upon him. Since the public wanted to see him conduct additional concerts, he arranged his schedule to spend the concert season in New York and his summers giving performances in Italy.

In March, 1948, Toscanini made his first television appearance, featuring an all-Wagner program, which allowed millions of Americans to see the great maestro, then eighty-one years old. In addition, he made a six-week tour throughout the country in 1950, playing in twenty cities.

In 1954, NBC decided to disband the Symphony because it felt that the pace was too much for the aged Toscanini; over the past two years his health had become precarious and a guard rail had to be placed around the podium because of his weakening legs. Still, Toscanini wanted one final concert before he retired.

His last performance was given on April 4, 1954, at Carnegie Hall. He launched vigorously into the Wagner program, but then, in the midst of orchestral music from Tannhauser, his baton faltered. He seemed dazed, his memory had fled. For several bars the orchestra continued without him but finally halted. He wiped his brow and continued, and the remainder of the concert was given without further embarrassment. At its conclusion Toscanini stepped down from the podium and was escorted offstage. He did not return for a standing ovation. The somber audience knew that this was the last time they would ever again see Arturo Toscanini perform. It was a melancholy, indelible conclusion to his sixty-eight years of conducting.

A few weeks after the concert, he left for Italy. His orchestra played a final tribute to him, facing a dramatically empty podium.

After two years of living in Milan, Toscanini returned to New York, where he could listen raptly to the music to which he had devoted his life. Nearly blind, his only remaining world was the glorious music of his past.

The great Maestro died at Villa Paulina in Riversdale, New York on January 16, 1957, at the age of eighty-nine. His body was returned to Italy for burial, but much of the incomparable music that was Arturo Toscanini's remained in America.

GUGLIELMO MARCONI

In the early 1890's the waves we call radio waves were already a subject of intense speculation and experiment. Because it was

Heinrich Hertz of Germany who, during the years 1886-89, had clearly demonstrated their nature, they were at the time called "Hertzian waves." He had shown how to set them in motion and how to detect them.

Scientists all over the world were working on Hertzian waves. They represented a new and astonishing world—unlike light waves, they could pass through a London fog. They revealed the possibilities of telegraph without wires or any costly appliances.

Guglielmo Marconi was currently a youth in his late teens, living with his family in a villa near Bologna. His mother was an Irish girl who had crossed the Channel against her parents' wishes and married his Italian father, who was older than her and a widower.

Guglielmo was a thin, intense youth who read all the scientific journals and books at the villa and revered Benjamin Franklin and other giants of electricity. Much of his education was provided by tutors.

In 1894, twenty-year-old Guglielmo and his half-brother Luigi took a vacation trip to the Italian Alps, where he picked up a periodical on Hertzian waves. From that time on he was like a man possessed, constantly sketching strange diagrams and making calculations. Returning to the villa, he practically confined himself in a third-floor room that had become his workshop.

His isolation disturbed his family, who thought he was wasting his time, and his first experiments were failures. But in due time he reached the point at which he could ring a bell downstairs by using Hertzian waves. His family began warming to his work, and his brother Alphonso became his helper.

Marconi introduced a Morse key into his circuit, aiming to break "the emission up into long and short periods so that Morse dots and dashes could be transmitted." He moved his experiments outdoors.

Using methods and devices developed by other scientists, he added several essential elements of his own—antennae, groundings and a receiver. In 1895, he sent his first signal across a large field outside the villa.

The elder Marconi consulted the parish priest and family doctor and they in turn wrote a letter to the Italian Minister of Post and Telegraph. When the government replied that it had no interest in Marconi's invention, he and his mother went to England. There, the British Empire was held together by ships and thin ocean cables and could use a new means of communication, such as Marconi promised.

The black box containing his invention immediately aroused the suspicion of British customs officials; two years earlier, the French President had been killed by an Italian anarchist. Not knowing what to do with the strange box of wires, batteries and dials, the officials smashed it.

As Marconi began rebuilding his box, he was put in touch with

Sir William Preece, chief engineer of telegraphs in the British Post Office system, who had also experimented in wireless, with some success. Together, they began testing, first in the London Post Office, then out on the Salisbury plain, reaching a hundred yards, then one mile, then six miles, then nine.

Marconi received his patent July 2, 1897, and in that same month a small, powerful British group joined with him to form Wireless Telegraph and Signal Company, Ltd., which later became Marconi's Wireless Telegraph Company, Ltd. At twenty three, Marconi received half the stock (the company was capitalized at 100,000 pounds) and 15,000 pounds in cash, and became one of the six directors and was put in charge of development.

His invention received world-wide excitement when he communicated over 18 miles of water, through rain and fog, with a ship. Naval and military observers came to England from everywhere. In 1898, the new company received its first revenue when wireless equipment was ordered for several lighthouses.

During 1899, Marconi equipment was being installed on three British battleships and was being used in naval maneuvers. Large-scale international rivalry and intrigue began, as Russian, French, German and other scientists were now trying to catch up with and surpass Marconi's achievements. Because these other scientists were beginning to patent their own equipment, Marconi moved fast.

He approached the United States armed forces on the subject of wireless and demonstrations for the navy. On September 11, 1899, Marconi arrived in New York. As the U. S. Navy began testing Marconi's invention, the Marconi Wireless Company of America was incorporated in New Jersey, on November 22. Twenty years later this would become the Radio Corporation of America—RCA.

On January 19, 1903, a greeting from President Theodore Roosevelt to King Edward VII was hurled out in noisy dots and dashes by a Marconi station at South Wellfleet on Cape Cod, and a reply was received—the first intercontinental, trans-Atlantic radio message.

The following years were not easy ones for Guglielmo Marconi —not only was he constantly battling with rivals and government, but a long, fierce battle began between his company and the other communications giants—AT&T, Bell Telephone, and others.

Because so many amateur scientists and inventors were working on wireless in many parts of the world and their inventions were often obscured for years, it would be presumptuous to call any one of them the original inventor of radio. Every one of them built upon the inventions and findings and theories of men before them.

However, Marconi can easily be called the Father of Radio.

Heaped with honors, and financially successful, Marconi lived the rest of his life in further research and in making wireless a universal communications medium.

Though he never became an American citizen, most of his work was done in this country. His greatest success and impact on science and business were distinctly American.

Returning to Italy in the twenties, he was appointed to the Italian senate by Mussolini in 1929 and became president of the Italian Academy in 1930. He died in 1937.

ENRICO CARUSO

He was a natural singer, with little or no formal education of any kind. Born of a peasant family in Naples on February 27, 1873, Caruso realized early that his voice was treasure.

In Italy he had lived like a king in his quiet, secluded villa Bellosguardo, built in the fifteenth century on the crest of a hill within a park of pools, statues, formal gardens and long avenues of ancient cypress trees.

He spent his mornings and afternoons rehearsing his singing and his evenings relaxing. He was often lonely but never alone. Twenty-one people lived with him; a few were guests, the rest relatives.

But now, in America, he had to change his lifestyle a bit. In New York, Caruso lived in a fourteen-room suite on the ninth floor of the Hotel Knickerbocker, overlooking the festive life on 42nd Street and Broadway, the heart of Manhattan.

Enrico traveled with his own blankets, sheets and special mattresses. His linen had to be changed every day, whether in hotels, ships or trains. A specially constructed trunk contained his perfumes, toilet waters and all the atomizers, inhalers and medicines he needed for his throat.

His day began at six o'clock with breakfast consisting of two eggs, cheese and a glass of wine. He exercised and prepared the music for Fucito, his lifetime accompanist, who arrived at nine and began to play at once. Enrico read the music criticism in the newspapers, studied the cartoons and read the news in *La Follia*. At nine, dressed in an enormous white robe, he went to his dressing room, while his bath was prepared with salts and his steam inhaler was turned on. Enrico did not sing in his bath. After his inhalation, which occupied half an hour, he set a mirror against the window, opened his mouth wide and thrust a little dentist's mirror far down his throat, to examine the reflection of his vocal cords. If he found them too pink he would paint them with a special solution. Dr. Holbrook Curtis always treated his nose and throat, but Enrico himself took care of the Caruso vocal cords.

An armchair was placed by the window and beside it a music

rack holding the score of the opera he was to perform. His personal secretary, Zirato, waited, notebook and pen ready for the day's orders.

After the bath Enrico came in like a Roman emperor, ready to greet his subjects. As the barber shaved him, Fucito played and Enrico followed the score on the music rack, but without beating time or humming. Occasionally he gave orders about engagements, letters and telephone messages to Zirato.

Meanwhile, Mario tiptoed about the room, noiselessly opening drawers and closets. He had to lay out the clothes very carefully; every piece had its place and had to be in exactly the same place every day. Enrico sang softly as he dressed, listening carefully to the music from the next room. He was able to dress automatically if his things were in their proper places; if not, his work was interrupted while he called for them. He was demanding, but never capricious.

When he dressed he joined Fucito at the piano in the studio, ready for the real work of the day. He never sang in full voice a role he was studying; he whistled, hummed or sang a phrase on the syllable "ah," explaining to Fucito what he intended to do and what he wanted him to do. Only when he was satisfied with his conception did he use his full voice.

Two hours of intensive work were enough. By this time Zirato had covered the desk with letters to be answered, photographs to be autographed and checks to be signed. Enrico attacked these tasks with the same intensity that he gave to singing. Many of the checks he signed were in answer to appeals for money which he received daily. He was never known to refuse anyone.

When he wanted a little exercise he drove up Riverside Drive, then got out and walked while the car followed behind him. If too many people gathered to look at him he got back into the car, drove on and got out again. Often he tried to walk on Fifth Avenue. He liked to window-shop, but it was difficult because people would stop him and ask to shake hands. He rarely went to public places, theaters or smart restaurants; the crowds became too great. He never took this attention as a personal tribute. "My face is easy to remember. They don't love me, they're just curious."

Enrico was warm and cordial, yet in some ways unapproachable. Affection was given to him, but he couldn't accept it. There was a vacuum around him in which it could not exist. He didn't want to be stared at and spoken to by strangers whenever he left the house; he wanted to be a private person when he was not singing. He wanted the right to walk in the streets, the right to look in shop windows, the right to buy one rose instead of a dozen. He was constantly questioning people as to why they couldn't leave him alone. Why did they feel his life belonged to everyone?

He was powerless against this menace to his peace of mind.

Since the quality of his work depended upon his emotional equilibrium, he found a way to protect his inner life: he put on a mask for the public - laughed, made faces, played the clown, shook the great tassels of the Metropolitan curtain as he took his final bows. He had learned never to take off his mask except when he was at home.

Enrico had no intimate friends, although a group of Italians came to the house every day, each one claiming to be the "closest friend of Caruso" and each intensely jealous of the others. They arrived separately and waited in Zirato's room until Enrico came to speak to them. Often he didn't choose to see them, in which case they picked up their hats and left, united for once in their common disappointment. They were Enrico's entourage, people for whom he cared nothing individually but who, collectively, were necessary to his life. They amused him, spoke Neapolitan with him, accompanied him to lunch and were self-appointed scouts for art objects to be added to his collections. In return they basked in reflected glory, received free tickets to the opera and huge commissions from the antique dealers. Enrico was completely aware of their motives, but concealed his opinion of them under a mask of jolly good-fellowship. They were harmless, speaking ill only of each other; they spread the legend of Caruso the lighthearted wherever they went.

Enrico's greatest friend among the artists at the Metropolitan was the baritone, Antonio Scotti. He lived at the Knickerbocker Hotel, in the apartment under Enrico's. Scotti was a bachelor, immensely popular, good-looking and full of charm. He and Caruso lunched together daily at the corner table in the restaurant of the hotel.

Enrico's nature was not only uncomplicated; it was elemental. He was made in large blocks of essentials. His humanity was deep, his humor was broad, his faith was high. He wasn't worn, he was fresh; he didn't need spices. He was able to taste bread - he knew the taste of bread. He didn't have to do anything to sharpen any of the human appetites. The simplicity of his design was too apparent to be readily believed. The public made a mystery of what in reality was a truly simple man.

He didn't know the difference between the different sects of Christianity any more than he knew the difference between our political parties; Christian and American were enough for him.

Although Enrico had no formal education, his instincts were educated. He knew that people's lives would be rich if they would only look into them and not keep looking at the lives of other people. He lived his own life so noiselessly, with such concentration, such intensity, such inner stillness, that he had no need to draw on the lives of others to replenish it. Being so full, so rich in himself, he could not absorb the kaleidoscopic life of other people. Caruso didn't think of his contemporaries—he greeted them. Only when their orbits crossed his, as on the stage, did he feel their proximity. He didn't speak of them except in relation to his work. Even then he neither praised nor criticized their singing; nor did he express a preference for singing with one artist rather than another. His complete absorption in his own work left him neither the time nor the desire to indulge in the usual commentaries on events and people.

Enrico didn't use his sympathetic nervous system for the enjoyment of his art; he used it only to vitalize his remarkable capacity for work. Because he wouldn't vitiate this power, he wasn't able to use his gift for his own enjoyment or for the recreation of others. In this respect he was different from other great artists like Rachmaninoff, Kreisler, John McCormack. They would entertain their friends and themselves for hours, playing with their music as children play with toys.

Instinctively Enrico avoided parties. When he did accept an invitation, when he had finally decided to go and have a good time, he went not as one anticipating a delightful evening but as one who had already entered a state of pleasure. He beamed at the butler who opened the door, at the footman who took his hat and coat and at all the smiling faces over the banisters as he mounted the stairs. He didn't greet his hostess with charming, untruthful and inconsequential words; he simply said, "So glad," and everyone who heard felt warmed and complimented. He never paid the small polite compliments; he didn't have to—his expectant eyes, his cordial hands, his vigorous back and impelling shoulders pulled and exhilarated the spirit of everyone in the room.

His manner was perfect and at the same time affable and impenetrable. He passed through events and people as if they were a landscape - they pleased him, he pleased them. If he didn't allow people to treat him as a public idol, if at first they were disappointed in finding only a man instead of the god they had expected, they soon forgot their disappointment, for Enrico's gift of making others shine brightly was equal to his own bright light. His stories were robust and not vulgar; his laughter was hearty and not loud. He listened attentively and talked sufficiently. He discussed but didn't argue, and melted away from conversation too heated or too personal. He had invented his own English idiom, and much that was said to him he didn't understand. Because Americans speak quickly and slur whole sentences, he often caught only the last three words of a phrase. He didn't ask what had been said; he would simply repeat the last three words in a tone of surprise, commiseration or delight, according to the expression on the speaker's face.

He beamed his way out as he had beamed his way in, and only when he said, "Tomorrow I must sing," did anyone know that he had left the state of pleasure for the state of work.

Enrico lived as he did, not to preserve his voice, but to preserve his life. He restored in his silences the life forces he had expended while singing. The quiet concentrated hours he spent were as necessary to him as water to a garden.

The source of his existence lay only in himself. This was true in every aspect of his life, even his singing. From babyhood he sang as birds sing, without instruction, from his heart; at the age of nine he sang alto in the little church of his parish; for one year, when he was nineteen, he listened to Maestro Vergine teach other young singers. That one year of listening was all the musical training he ever had. The full knowledge of his metier—his musicianship, his technique of voice production, his meticulous standards of quality and nuance, his formalization of his personal emotions—all came from within himself.

Nor did he depend on others to advise, amuse, comfort or inspire him, since he knew that his source was uniquely within himself. He was born with a voice; his perseverance, perceptions, courage and integrity made it a great voice. His knowledge of the nature of his aims accounted for his passion for perfection; his voice was the instrument to be perfected; his consciousness of being his own source was the force which, as in all geniuses, spurred him toward perfection. Genius is a self-sustaining fire. Whatever may be its mystery, these qualities are surely among its divine constituents.

Everything that Enrico did was as great as his singing because his vital force was expended on each task. As the public didn't know this, they regarded his singing as a huge outgrowth, overshadowing all else he did. But he always used his full emotional energy for any accomplishment - whether it was for singing a perfect song or making a perfect envelope.

He didn't preach tolerance, kindness, generosity, justice, resourcefulness, these requisites of wisdom were the elements of which he was made. He had no superknowledge, but he acted as if he had. His actions were the reflections of his thoughts.

When Enrico cared for people it was for their inner qualities, not for what they could give him.

Eleven decorations were given to Enrico: from Italy, the Order of the Chevalier, the Order of Commendatore, and the Order of Grande Ufficiale of the Crown of Italy; from Germany, the Order of the Red Eagle of Prussia and the Order of the Crown Eagle of Prussia; from Spain, the Order of St. James of Compostella; from Belgium, the Order of Leopold; from England, the Order of Michael and the Order of British Victoria; from France, the Legion of Honor and the Palm of the Academy.

America as a nation gives no medals for achievement in the arts, so he did not receive any honors here, yet the love the American people had for this man was undeniable. They supported his concerts and purchased his recordings by the millions.

Enrico's love for America was deeply rooted in his heart. During the four years of the First World War he not only raised twenty-one million dollars by singing at benefits, but gave immense sums to the Allied Relief Organizations and the American Red Cross; he also converted all his prewar securities into United States Government Bonds and invested his income, royalties and salary thereafter only in Liberty Loan Bonds.

He had his own art gallery on Fiftieth Street near Fifth Avenue, where he kept his collections of antiques, furniture, velvets, brocades, marbles and bronzes, enamels, tear bottles, snuffboxes and jeweled watches.

Enrico didn't like to discuss his singing and all the business connected with his singing he discussed only in the executive offices of the Metropolitan. He had no vanity about his voice, in fact, he regarded it almost objectively. When talking of his singing he spoke of himself in the third person rather than risk appearing proud. The magnitude of his humility made a deep impression upon his millions of admirers.

His comments about his fellow artists were almost never musical. Once after he had sung a duet with a celebrated soprano, more noted for her beauty than for her voice, he was asked how he liked her singing. "I don't know. I've never heard her." Many of his observations had to do with personal hygiene, since he himself had a fanaticism about cleanliness. If he wore a shirt even for an hour he never put it on again until it had been laundered; in the theater he changed between every act, and had himself sprayed with eau de cologne as he put on each fresh garment. In a certain opera he had to sing an impassioned love song to a large, dark and fat diva while clasping her in his arms. Backstage before the performance one night he said pathetically, "Ai me! It is terrible to sing with one who does not bathe, but to be emotional over one who breathes garlic is impossible. I hope the public observe not my lack of feeling. Tonight I must act better than I sing."

At another time a French tenor invited Caruso and his wife to sit in his box at a concert. Hardly had he seated before Enrico turned to him and said, "Monsieur, Madam cannot remain unless you go home and brush your teeth." The wretched man left at once, and returned gleaming. Enrico examined him, then said, "Bene, it is important to take care."

When the New York crowds celebrated the Armistice, Enrico had been in his dining room in the Knickerbocker, listening to the roar from the street, when Mr. Regan, the hotel manager, came to tell him that the crowd was shouting for Caruso. He went out on the balcony, where two huge flags, American and Italian, had been hung. When the crowds saw Enrico they went mad. He sang the national anthems of America, England, France and Italy; the crowds roared "More!" and he called to them to sing with him. Thousands of voices surged up at his, and Enrico's soared above them all. He asked the florist in the lobby to send all his flowers and he threw hundreds of red roses, white carnations and blue violets from the balcony.

Enrico never spoke boastfully of himself as the "greatest tenor in the world." He was more flattered by having a race horse named for him than by all the eulogies he received on his voice. He knew nothing whatever of racing, but every day he searched in the racing sheets for news of his namesake. This horse, whose career he followed with unflagging interest, never won a race; but Enrico placed a bet of ten dollars on him every time he ran. Enrico could never hear the lovely quality of his voice when he sang - he simply felt something inside when the notes came out well. Only by listening to his records could he hear what others heard. "That is good, it is a beautiful voice," he would say in astonishment. But he always added, a little sadly, "With a beautiful voice it is not hard to reach the top. But to stay there, that is hard."

It was more than hard, it was a form of slavery. The more he sang, the more people demanded of him. He could never let them down and he drove himself beyond endurance. He no longer sang because he loved it, but because it was something he had to do. And because he was a perfectionist he had no satisfaction within himself; perfect as he tried to be, he knew there was something beyond, a place better than his best. He got no comfort from music.

Enrico only enjoyed his lunch when he went to a little Italian restaurant on Forty-Seventh Street. People always recognized him, and he would respond, "Hello, good morning, thank you very much," while Zirato made a passage for him through the crowd. He ate simply in that dark little restaurant - boiled chicken or beef with vegetables, fruit, cheese and coffee. The linen was coarse, the silver dull, the plates were heavy. Pane, the restaurant keeper, served while his niece did the cooking. He was old and many years before, Enrico had helped him when he was in financial trouble. But the real reason for Enrico's daily visit there was, after lunch, Pane brought out a deck of Italian cards and played with Enrico for hours, no strangers to stare or whisper or speak, just two old friends in an old Italian restaurant, playing with an old deck of cards.

On the day of a performance there was never music in his house. Through the silent hours he played solitaire, drew caricatures, pasted clippings and sorted the collection of rare gold coins he had begun in 1907, when he was singing in Paris at the Theatre Sarah Bernhardt.

He often said that he would rather draw than sing, and although he had never had a drawing lesson he was an expert caricaturist. When he made sketches of himself he didn't look in a mirror; he only felt the contours of his face with his left hand as he drew. A book of his caricatures had been published and every day he made a new sketch for *La Follia*. Years before, Marziale Sisca, the publisher of the paper, had offered him an incredible sum for a daily cartoon, but he had answered, "I do not want money for what I enjoy so much to do. My work is singing - we are friends and I make you caricatures for nothing." Once when he was out walking he saw in the window of an autograph shop a caricature of President Wilson made by Enrico. He went in to inquire the price. When told that it was seventy-five dollars he was delighted. "That is good pay for work of ten minutes," he said, "Better I stop singing and draw."

He clipped all the war cartoons from the newspapers and pasted them in albums. As his hobby became known, artists sent him their original drawings and people from all over the world contributed to his collection. He was completely happy when he was cutting and pasting, drawing and tabulating. The only occupations that relaxed and amused him were those in which he could use his hands. He cared nothing for books, and was not known to have ever read one.

At the end of the silent day that always preceded a Metropolitan appearance, Fucito came and Enrico began a half-hour of exercises. He never sang scales except before a performance. He walked up and down, a cup of steaming coffee in his hand, as he sang the difficult exercises in full voice. At seven o'clock he left for the theatre with Mario and Zirato.

It has often been stated that Caruso was not nervous when he sang. This is absolutely untrue. He was always extremely nervous and didn't try to conceal it. He himself said: "Of course I am nervous. Each time I sing I feel there is someone waiting to destroy me, and I must fight like a bull to hold my own. The artist who boasts he is never nervous is not an artist - he is a liar."

Meticulous about his appearance on the stage, Enrico's make-up was always perfect to the smallest detail and he insisted that each of his period costumes be historically correct.

Before each performance he went to the washstand and filled his mouth with salt water, gargled it for several minutes then spat it out. Mario held out a box of Swedish snuff from which he took a pinch to clear his nostrils; then he took a wineglass of whisky, next a glass of charged water and finally a quarter of an apple. Into the pockets that were placed in every costume exectly where his hands dropped, he slipped two little bottles of warm salt water, in case he had to wash his throat on the stage. When all was ready Mario handed him his charms - a twisted coral horn, holy medals and old coins, all linked together on a fat little gold chain. Then came a knock on the door and Vivinai, the assistant stage manager, asked, "May we begin, Mr. Caruso?" Just before he left the dressing room he called upon his dead mother for help, since the thought of her gave him courage. No one ever wished him luck because, he said, that was sure to bring disaster.

Enrico was often asked about his favorite role. He answered that he had none. Even so, he especially loved to sing *La Juive* because it gave him an opportunity to prove that he was a great actor as well as a great singer. Undoubtedly his most popular role was Canio in *Pagliacci*. He became affected each time he sang *Vesti la Giubba* and sobbed for several minutes in his dressing room after the first act. On several occasions he fell on the stage, faint from emotion; but whatever his own emotions were, his audience was invariably overwhelmed. Asked to explain the secret of this power, he said, "I suffer so much in this life. That is what they feel when I sing, that is why they cry. People who felt nothing in this life cannot sing."

Earlier in his career, when he was twenty-four, he was singing the role of Rodolfo for the first time in *Livorno*. The soprano Giachetti was making her debut in the same opera. She was also young, and very beautiful. Enrico fell deeply in love with her, and she with him. They couldn't marry for many reasons, but they made a life together. In time a son was born, and, some time later, another. Enrico wasn't happy in this relationship, but even after ten years, in spite of many heartaches, he was as much in love with her as ever. He couldn't always be with his family. One year he went to sing in South America, leaving the devoted Martino in charge of the household. On his return he found only Martino - Giachetti had gone, taking the children with her. She left a note saying that she no longer cared for him, that she would never return. She didn't even tell him where she had gone.

Enrico was heartbroken. Nevertheless, he had to open the London season, and an ironical fate had chosen *Pagliacci* for the first performance. On that night Enrico didn't have to pretend to be Canio - he was in fact the betrayed lover, singing his own tragedy.

For the remainder of the season, he refused all invitations, received no one and stayed alone with his faithful servant, who never left him day or night. Martino ate all his meals with him, walked and talked with him and slept just outside his door.

When the London season was finished, Enrico had to go to Germany to sing. As in other years, a few days after his arrival he received a command invitation to dine at Potsdam. No one else was ever invited to these dinners, for the Kaiser wished to talk only about music and to hear Enrico's opinion of the operas to be given during the season.

Enrico refused to go because his servant Martino had not been invited also. The Kaiser immediately returned a note of apology and invited Martino.

The state dinner for two was served in the banquet hall of the palace and presided over by a major-domo who gave all his orders by moving only his eyes. Footmen in imperial livery passed elaborate dishes, and behind Enrico's chair stood Martino, with an unimpressed look on his face as to the magnificence surrounding him, for he was concerned only with Enrico's appetite. From time to time he leaned a little forward and looked into his plate.

The conversation took its usual form, a series of sharp questions. What new operas would be sung this season? Which had London liked?

At the end of the dinner the Kaiser raised his glass, "Mr. Caruso, I want you to drink a toast to me." Then for the first time he looked at Martino. "To your servant, Martino, and if I were not Emperor of Germany, I should like to be Martino."

Enrico read the music critics' reviews with great interest and preserved them in big scrapbooks because they showed him what the public liked about his singing and acting. In one of these old books there is this criticism, dated December 25, 1914: "Neither Geraldine Farrar nor Enrico Caruso were vocally at their best. Caruso sang with great emotional intensity despite the difficulties he had to contend with in his mezzo-voice." Across this notice Enrico had written the word LIAR, in huge letters with exclamation points.

Besides his rehearsals he had to make records in Camden, New Jersey for the Victor Company. This was his hardest work, far more difficult than singing an opera. He hated every minute of it. "My voice is cold and heavy in the morning, and I don't feel to sing."

The first records Enrico ever made were not for the Victor Company. He had already experimented in Italy in 1896 on wax cylinders and a recording machine that was sent down from Germany. In 1898 he made other recordings for a small Italian Company which was later taken over by Victor.

His first recordings for the Victor Company were made in 1903 in Carnegie Hall, where the recording laboratory was then situated, and since he had no contract he was paid in cash. Although he never spoke of the amount of money paid him for his early recording sessions, it was later found that he made the same amount as his fee at the Metropolitan. He sang twice a week and was paid $2,500 for each performance. Whenever he traveled around the country on tour the price was much more. In Mexico City, he performed for an entire summer at $15,000 a performance, the highest price ever paid to any singer. His first ten recordings were all operatic arias and included:"Vesti la giubba" (Pagliacci), "Celeste Aida" (Aida), "Una furtiva lagrima" (L'Elisir d'amore,) "La donna e mobile"

(Rigoletto), "E Lucevan le stelle" *(Tosca),* "Recondita armonia" *(Tosca),* "Le Reve" (Massenet's *Manon),* "Di quella pira" *(Il Trovatore),* and the "Siciliano" *(Cavalleria Rusticana).* The popularity of these recordings secured for Enrico his first Victor contract.

At the Victor studio in Camden, New Jersey, he sang into a short square horn connected with the recording machine. The operator, who was working the machine behind a partition, made signs to him through a little window. The musicians who accompanied Enrico sat on stools of graded heights at the back of the room. Their relative positions controlled the volume of sound, as there were no amplifiers in those days.

He began by singing with the orchestra. Then he told them any changes he wanted and sang the song again. Then he made the sign to the operator and sang the song. When he had finished the record was immediately played back to him and he discussed it with Mr. Child. If he disliked the way a certain tone of his voice had registered, he insisted on making still another recording. At last, after two hours, a satisfactory record might be achieved. This was used to make the copper master record from which the black rubber ones would be stamped. Each time he went to Camden he sang at most only two or three songs. Two days later when Mr. Child brought samples of the finished recordings to New York, he and Enrico listened to them once more. This was the most important test of all, for both men had to agree on the perfection of every note before the record could be offered to the public. If they didn't agree, it was destroyed and Enrico had to return to Camden and do it all over again.

Although Enrico denied having a favorite opera, he had favorites among his recordings. Of his Neapolitan songs he liked best "A vuchella," by Tosti, and he often sang it at his concerts as an encore. He considered "Rachel" from *La Juive* the best of his operatic arias, and "Solenne in quest' ora" from *La Forza del Destino,* with Scotti, the best of his duets. He liked both Victor Herbert and his songs. The grave magnificence of Handel's "Largo" moved him deeply. Simple songs like the "Campane a sera" carried him back to Italy and his home.

As a wedding present the Victor Company sent him a black and gold Chinese lacquer phonograph. On the inside of the red lid was attached a gold record of "La donna e mobile," because this was the first song he had recorded for them, in 1903.

Up to January, 1920, royalties amounting to $1,825,000 had been paid to Enrico by the Victor Company, for which he made most of his 234 recordings.

The Metropolitan Opera Company gave performances in Philadelphia every other Tuesday. They traveled in a special train, and on Caruso nights he traveled with them. Enrico was always silent on the journey, because he was going to sing, but after the performance, on the way back to New York, he was in high spirits and communicated his exhilaration to everyone. He took large baskets of chicken and veal cutlets, salad, quantities of fruit and wine and cheese, and sweet loaves of fresh Italian bread. He would invite his special friends, Scotti, Amato, De Luca, Rotheri, Didur and other members of the company to have supper with him while he told stories of his youth. He recalled the old days when he had to sing two operas on Sundays at the Teatro Mercadante in Naples, and the summer season in Salerno when he was so hungry that during the entr'actes he let down a little basket on a string from his dressing-room window for the sandwich vendor to fill. He told of the night in Brussels when there wasn't even standing room left and music-loving students of the university, unable to get into the theatre, gathered in the street and shouted up to his dressing room; he opened the window and sang his aria to them before going down to the stage. There was also his story of the first time he ever sang in a theatre in a little town near Naples when he was just nineteen. He was hissed off the stage because, not having expected to sing that night, he had drunk too much red wine with his supper. He returned to his little room, certain that his career was ended. But the following night the audience so disliked the substitute tenor that they called for "the little drunkard." Enrico was sent for in haste and made his first success that night. The next morning when photographers arrived to take pictures of the promising young singer, they found him naked in bed - he had sent his only shirt and pants to be washed. He draped the bedspread around his shoulders and posed for his photograph with a proud and stern expression. This picture was the first ever published of Caruso.

Enrico was a musician who had no time for music. He never went to hear opera, except those in which he himself sang; and even then he never stood in the wings to listen to the other singers. He never went to the symphony concerts either.

He didn't play the piano, he could strike only a few chords; but he never regretted not being able to play it because he only concentrated on one thing at a time.

No amateur accompanist ever played for him, nor did he ever sing "for fun" at parties.

The only person to whom Enrico ever gave a singing lesson was Ricardo Martin. He didn't like to teach, nor did he think he did it well. When he sang he never thought of his throat or the position of his tongue. He considered words to be of first importance in singing. "I think to the words of my aria, not to the music, because first is written the libretto and is the reason of the composer to put the melody, like the foundation for a house."

The cavities within Enrico's face were extraordinary. The depth, width and height of the roof of his mouth, the broad cheekbones and flat even teeth, the wide forehead above wideset eyes - this spacious architecture gave him his deep resonance of tone. His chest was enormous and he could expand it nine inches.

When he was asked what were the requisites of a great singer he said, "A big chest, a big mouth, ninety per cent memory, ten percent intelligence, lots of hard work and something in the heart."

His memory was phenomenal. He knew sixty-seven roles, and to his repertoire of more than five hundred songs he was continually adding more. He spoke and sang in seven languages.

As he grew older his voice became richer, heavier, darker, and this development gave him full mastery of great dramatic roles like Samson, Eleazar and John of Leyden, while he still excelled in lyric operas like *Martha* and *L'Elisir d'amore*. He sang in French, Italian, Spanish and English but never consented to sing in German even when so requested by the Kaiser. On that occasion he told the Berlin press: "Italian is the most simple language to sing. It has five vowels pure, and very few consonants. It is impossible for me to sing in German because the consonants repeat too often, and because the sharp accents stop me to phrase properly and take from my voice the brilliancy. Foreign artists who sing in German have better technique than me."

Although by the time he was twenty-one Enrico had sung publicly at some small theaters in the vicinity of Naples, he didn't consider that he had made his official debut until November 16, 1894, when he sang in the opera *L'Amico Francesco* at the Nuova in Naples. He received eighty lire a night and was engaged for four performances.

Twenty-five years later, on March 22, 1919, his jubilee was celebrated at the Metropolitan - his five hundred and fiftieth performance on that stage. Enrico sang an act from three different operas - *L'Elisir, Pagliacci* and *Le Prophete*.

Each time Enrico came in from the street he changed all his clothes, and unless he was receiving people he never wore a conventional suit in the house. He wore dark red, green or blue brocaded coats with sashes, slate-gray silk trousers and soft shirts. He had a variety of clothes in his wardrobe. One closet held eighty pairs of shoes, another fifty suits.

He dressed his wife on the same grand scale. He began by ordering sixty-nine costumes - fifteen evening gowns, twelve afternoon dresses, eight tailored suits, six topcoats, twelve evening wraps, four tea gowns, twelve house pajamas, and all this was just for one season. Every season, everything both of them had was thrown or given away and completely new wardrobes were purchased.

During his long career many legends grew up around the name of

Caruso. Some of them were fantastic, some were true. True or false, they have continued. Extensive research has thrown new light on some old legends.

Enrico was five feet nine inches tall and weighed 175 pounds.

His hair was black, coarse and straight.

His body was hard but not muscular.

He bathed his face with witch hazel only.

He weighed three pounds less after each performance.

He did not rest during the day.

He never ate five plates of spaghetti for lunch. His lunch was always vegetable soup with the meat of chicken left in and a green salad.

For dinner he usually had a minute steak, two green vegetables and ice cream.

When he was to sing, he ate only the white meat of chicken or two small lamb chops.

He did not drink beer, highballs, milk or tea; he drank two or three quarts of bottled mineral water a day.

He smoked two packages of Egyptian cigarettes a day, always in a holder.

He never shattered either a mirror or a wineglass with his voice.

He took no medicines of any kind except, the night before he sang, half a bottle of Henri's powdered magnesia in water.

He did not make his debut as a baritone.

In all his life he sang in only one amateur performance - *Cavalleria rusticana,* given in Naples in 1892.

He always retained his Italian citizenship.

Above all countries he preferred to sing in America.

The great Caruso pushed himself beyond endurance. In January 1920, he began to weaken and during one of his performances, he was forced to stop, due to blood forming in his mouth. A quack doctor told him he only had intercostal neuralgia, and that he could continue singing. Caruso's condition worsened, yet he still performed several more concerts. One night at the Metropolitan, the curtain rose a quarter of an hour late, something which had never happened before. The four long acts of gaiety began, as the audience applauded wildly when Enrico came onto the stage. Standing close to the footlights, he began at once to sing. When he finished he turned his back and reached for his handkerchief. He gave a little cough, but came in on his cue, finished the phrase and turned away again. When he faced the audience, the front of his smock was scarlet. A whisper blew through the house but stopped as he began to sing. This time it was an aria and he couldn't turn his back. From the wings Zirato's hand held out a towel. Enrico took it, wiped his lips and went on singing. Towel after towel was passed to him and still he sang on. All about him on the stage lay crimson towels. At last he finished the aria and ran off. The act was ended and the curtain came down.

For long moments the theater was as silent as an empty house. Then, as if a signal had been given, a thunder of sound and movement shook the audience. Shouts and screams, voices crying "Stop him!" "Don't let him go on!"

For the first time in his life he didn't protest but consented that the audience be dismissed.

His final performance in *La Juive,* was given on Christmas Eve 1920.

His intercostal neuralgia turned out to be acute pleurisy which had developed into bronchial pneumonia. But he had allowed the quack doctor to treat him too long and his illness had become irreversible. He died on August 2, 1921 at the age of forty-eight.

The name of Caruso is an intimate part of the proud Italian-American heritage. Often when listening to classical music on the radio you can hear his voice singing gloriously. He has been given many memorial programs over the radio. He would have liked these tributes and would have said, "So kind of them to remember, after so long."

NICOLA SACCO & BARTOLOMEO VANZETTI

After World War One and the Russian Revolution, this country witnessed a Red Scare. Aliens were plagued by mass arrests instigated by the U.S. Attorney General, A.M. Palmer. Homes were entered without warning in Palmer's Red Raids, and men were held in jail for long periods without hearings or trials. There were thousands of deportations and many suicides.

Sacco and Vanzetti were Italian anarchists who had come to the United States to continue their agitation among the Italian colony in eastern Massachusetts. In 1917, faced with the draft, they had fled to Mexico, returning to Massachusetts only after the Armistice.

Sacco was a factory worker. He had a wife and two children. Vanzetti, 41, was an eloquent factory worker, strike leader and fish peddler. During the Red Raids, they were prime targets for surveillance and arrest, and when the police picked them up on May 5, 1920, they had pistols in their possession.

The two were questioned about a robbery-murder that had occurred less than a month before, April 15, in South Braintree, Massachusetts. A five-man bandit band had seized a $15,776 payroll belonging to the Slater & Morrill shoe factory after killing paymaster Frederick Parmenter and guard Allessandro Berardelli.

They were also questioned about an earlier attempted payroll holdup. They denied both crimes.

Nevertheless, the two men went on trial in Dedham, Massachusetts, for the attempted holdup. Sacco had an ironclad alibi, but Vanzetti was found guilty after a week and sentenced to 12-15 years imprisonment, unheard of for a first offender.

On September 11, Sacco and Vanzetti were indicted for the South Braintree killings, and on May 31, 1921, their second trial opened. It was also held in Dedham and presided over by the same judge who had sentenced Vanzetti to jail, Honorable Webster Thayer, an aging pillar of the Back Bay aristocracy and a violent foe of all things radical. And Sacco and Vanzetti were definitely radical. Thayer said to the jury about Vanzetti, "This man, although he may not actually have committed the crime attributed to him, is nevertheless morally culpable, because he is the enemy of our existing institutions . . . the defendant's ideals are cognate with crime."

Despite insufficient evidence, both men were found guilty of murder and sentenced to death by electrocution.

The Sacco-Vanzetti trial received full national and international attention, creating much controversy because many liberals felt that more than an actual murder case was being tried. It was a lynching on general principles. Both men were immigrants and radicals and anarchists in a time of witchhunting. Also, they had not been proven guilty beyond a doubt; indeed, as the two men waited in the deathhouse at Boston's Charleston Prison, new evidence was turning up that pointed to the glaring errors in the prosecution's case. The doomed men waited—for seven years.

Radicals and labor leaders took to the cause of the defendants, followed by the intelligentsia—writers Sherwood Anderson, Dorothy Parker, John Dos Passos, Upton Sinclair, Thomas Mann, Sinclair Lewis, H.G. Wells, John Galsworthy; playwrights Maxwell Anderson and George Bernard Shaw; poetess Edna St. Vincent Millay; scientist Albert Einstein; humorist Robert Benchley, and many others, including Alfred Dreyfus, himself the victim of trial based more on anti-Semitism than any actual crime. All protested the injustice of Thayer's court.

It was at this point that Harvard law professor Felix Frankfurter entered the case and brought many neutrals with him. In an article for the *Atlantic Monthly,* Frankfurter coolly appraised the case as an indictment of American injustice and showed the prejudices and errors of Thayer, the absurdities and contradictions of the prosecutor's case, and the improbability of the prosecution's story.

A special advisory committee, the three-man Lowell Commission, found no miscarriage of injustice toward Sacco and Vanzetti. Massachusetts Governor Fuller accepted these findings, but on August 10, 1927, he granted a twelve-day reprieve for final legal moves; the stay of execution reached the deathhouse less than an hour before the two men were to be electrocuted.

This touched off bombings and demonstrations throughout the world. There were street fights in Paris (20 people killed) and disorders outside the American Consulate in Geneva. The American flag was burned outside the American Consulate in Casablanca. There were riots in London, Berlin, Warsaw, Buenos Aires, Mexico, Cuba, Japan, Milan, Turin, and elsewhere. Throngs marched in Boston and New York City.

Still, on August 23, 1927, seven years after their indictment, Nicola Sacco and Bartolomeo Vanzetti went to their scheduled deaths. The Commonwealth put an armed garrison around Charleston Prison so that the execution could proceed on time, since thousands of demonstrators besieged the gray walls.

One observer summed it up this way: "The tragedy of the Sacco-Vanzetti case is the tragedy of three men—Judge Thayer, Governor Fuller, and President (of Harvard) Lowell—and their inability to rise above the obscene battle that raged for seven long years around the heads of the shoemaker and the fish peddler."

The Sacco-Vanzetti case has been reinvestigated over and over and constantly subjected to new analysis and methods of detection. History has found the two men not guilty, but unfortunately they cannot be given the fair trial they were denied in the twenties.

Their legacy lies in many stories and poetry anthologies and works of art. World-famous sculptor Gutzon Borglum made a large bas-relief dedicated to Sacco and Vanzetti, which was offered by Einstein, Eleanor Roosevelt and others to the Commonwealth of Massachusetts, so that it may be placed on Boston Commons as a reminder of the injustices of yesteryear. Massachusetts refused it.

Vanzetti gave perhaps the best epitaph: "Never in our full life could we hope to do such work for tolerance, for justice, for man's understanding of man as now we do by accident."

RUDOLPH VALENTINO

When moviegoers, actors, and writers call to mind the great lovers of the screen, certain names inevitably come to the fore: John Barrymore, Greta Garbo, John Gilbert. But it is the name of Rudolph Valentino that always heads the list. Perhaps because he specialized in exotic romantic roles even more than they did; perhaps because, unlike them, he never appeared in a talking picture, he remained the symbol of glamour and romance on the silent screen, just as Chaplin represented laughter, and Fairbanks adventure. Still, after all these years, little is known of the events surrounding his career.

He was a man inordinately ill-served by everyone—the public, the press, the people who created and marketed his films, himself. His chief crime, in which all of these forces participated, was against the standard American concept of ideal manhood. He was too graceful and too beautiful—that was clear—but worse than that, he seemed weak. His weakness was merely sensed, sensed and commented upon by the American male, who did not like him, sensed and not admitted by women, who did like him.

In the still-lingering afterglow of the hysteria he generated he has become a kind of comic symbol of the excesses of his time and, indeed, there was much that was extremely funny about Valentino. There were, to begin with, the absurdly exotic settings in which his screen character was generally placed, not to mention the ludicrous costumes and decor with which they were freighted. But more important was the gap between the style he was forced to adopt in these films and the style that might have been natural to this rather shy and passive personality. The result was a terrible strain on him, and it is largely this strain which has been captured in the still photographs which are this generation's chief link with him. Adolph Zukor, who employed The Sheik, wrote that his acting "was largely confined to protruding his large, almost occult, eyes until vast areas of white were visible, drawing back the lips of his wide, sensuous mouth to bare his gleaming teeth, and flaring his nostrils." In other words, to indicate the outbursts of a smoldering flame that did not, in fact, exist, Valentino resorted to heroic thespian exertions, defying all the laws of successful screen performance. The miracle is that he triumphed despite this nonsense.

For this triumph he could thank the sensibilities of the women, who detected beneath the fakery, the real Valentino. If you are not distracted by the wildly flailing attempts to indicate a quality quite beyond him, you can still detect this essential Valentino at odd moments in his films. There is, to begin with, the softness of his mouth when he forgets to set it in a hard, determined line, when he is not forcing it to leer. There is, in addition, the withdrawn sadness of his eyes in their unpopped condition. Finally, and most important, there is the insinuating gracefulness of his movements when they are unencumbered by period costumes. It is not the grace of an athlete; it is quite un-Fairbanksian, it is the grace of, frankly, a seducer, perhaps even a gigolo. It is grace directed toward a single purpose, the smooth transfer of a woman from an upright to a reclining position. To waste such grace on a high jump or a pole vault would have been madness. To use it as he did was an insult to all the Anglo-Saxon traditions of male-female relations, refreshing to women, des-

picable to men. He was, in short, that infinitely attractive thing—a
boy in man's clothing and a boy, what's more, with an obvious talent for sensuality, a talent which any woman might wish first to test
and then to develop to a man's full-scale sexuality.

There has never been a movie star in whose presence women
more wanted to be, no star they more wanted to touch. There
seemed to spring in his fans an eternal hope that one of them would
awaken the real forces that slumbered within him. They could see
the strain which posing as a man of action caused him, they knew
the gap between the pretenses his scenarios forced upon him and the
real Valentino, and all of them thought they just might be the
women, if only he would just notice, through whom he could bridge
the gap.

Undoubtedly they sensed the truth about the real man, that he
was fatally attracted to women stronger than he was. The one he
chose as his wife very nearly succeeded in wrecking his career
before his sudden death in 1926 ended it. She was a Salt Lake City
girl named Winifred Shaunessy, stepdaughter of cosmetician Richard Hudnut. She was a designer and actress, and in pursuit of these
professions chose the name Natacha Rambova. She began supervising Valentino's pictures and she emphasized the softness of his character, putting him into foppish films like *Monsieur Beaucaire,*
presenting him with a slave bracelet that he wore to the great derision
of the masculine American.

It was at this point that the *Chicago Tribune* called him a "pink
powder puff" and suggested that he was setting a terrible example
for American youth. Even the women began to desert him. For what
Natacha didn't realize was that it was essential for Valentino to continue his brave attempts at strongly masculine behavior in his films.
They served to remind his audience that there was a man within, a
man waiting for release through love. The obligatory moment in his
films where he threatened to—and sometimes acually did—take his
heroine by force was, for his fans, a moment of high deliciousness.
Beneath his demands, they sensed his gentleness. Once he had
broken down resistance by its use they knew he would be gentle and
kindly, a perfect lover. Without the tension between this fraudulent
force and this real gentleness, Valentino was just a pretty profile,
and that was what Natacha was reducing him to before they sepa-
rated and he began his much publicized affair with Pola Negri.

Valentino himself sensed the discrepancy between his screen
self and his real self, and as false film followed false film he
complained, "I am beginning to look more and more like my misera-
ble imitators." Many of them were indeed better at playing the
Valentino character than was Valentino. Perhaps he so willingly
followed Natacha's suggestions because he could no longer bear his
pretense. He was, in any case, neither a stupid nor an insensitive

man, despite the counter-legend his detractors created in the attempt to debunk him. He came from a relatively prosperous and educated provincial Italian family. He had a diploma from a college of landscape architecture, and he had come to America not as an immigrant seeking relief from oppression, but out of curiosity. He was a natural dancer, danced for pleasure in the hours after work as a gardener, then turned professional, taking over from Clifton Webb as Bonnie Glass's partner, touring with her until the act broke up in Los Angeles, where he found work as a minor movie player. Hollywood screen writer June Mathis sensed his appeal and brought him to Rex Ingram, who took a big chance by putting him into his arty super-production, *The Four Horsemen of the Apocalypse* at Metro, then, with notable lack of foresight, signed him only for that picture. Zukor picked him up before Metro quite realized what it had. The first film was a solid hit; *The Sheik,* made for Paramount, was a sensation, and the mold was cast.

He was born in Castellaneta, Italy on May 10, 1895. His mother was French and his father was a captain in the Italian cavalry. Rudolf's full name was Rodolpho Alfonzo Raffaeli Pierre Filjbert di Valentina d'Antonguolla. His early schooling was in a military academy and finally the Royal Academy of Agriculture.

After a number of scrapes with the Italian police, young Valentino emigrated to America in 1913 and settled in Times Square, New York City, where he became drawn to the hot spots and all-night bars and operated as a dancer and professional gigolo.

Touring with Bonnie Glass on the West Coast, he met an old friend, Norman Kerry, in Hollywood. Kerry helped him get his first part as a walk-on in *Alimony.*

Valentino spent the years 1917-20 playing bit parts—thugs and gangsters—in sixteen films, before he went to Metro for the part of Julio in *The Four Horsemen.* At this time the typical box-office hero was still the all-American boy running wingback for State U. A swarthy actor like Valentino had been decidedly marked un-American; hence the bad-guy roles. The part of Julio, an Argentinian youth, was a step in the right direction for Valentino—the foreign good guy.

Ingram's *The Four Horsemen of the Apocalypse* became one of the greatest box-office smashes of all time, and the young Italian, whom Metro had been skeptical of using, became an overnight hero.

For the next five and half years Valentino made successful pictures and became the biggest box-office draw in the country. Some of his successes after *The Four Horsemen* were *Camille* (1921), *The Conquering Power* (1921—Metro's last picture with him), *The Sheik* (1921—a Paramount throwaway), *Beyond the Rocks* (1922), *Blood and Sand* (1922), *Monsieur Beaucaire* (1924), *Cobra* (1925), *The Eagle* (1925), and *Son of the Sheik* (1926), his last.

In 1922, he shed his first wife, Jean Acker, and married Natacha. His greatest film, *The Sheik,* revolutionized the film business and the American culture. When he rolled his eyes at Agnes Ayres and dragged her headfirst into his pleasure tent, 1921 audiences went wild. It was a total departure from any love scene on film, and to add to the piquancy of the whole thing was the olive skin, oiled hair and sideburns, penciled eyebrows and gigolo's stare. Immediately the hair tonic business became a major industry. Girls called their boy friends "sheiks" and the word became part of the vernacular. The Hollywood hero was transformed into a Latin lover, and it took the movie industry years to shake off the Valentino-Novarro image.

At the height and pinnacle of his success in the year 1926, Valentino was in New York City making public appearances for publicity for his *Son of the Sheik,* when he was seized with a gall stone attack. He was rushed to the Polyclinic Hospital and, after an operation, died from peritonitis. It was August 23, 1926, the final day of five years and five months of glory. His last words, reportedly, were, "Did I behave like a pink powder puff?"

Rudolph Valentino was thirty-one years old.

One hundred and twenty-five thousand people, mostly women lined ten city blocks outside the Gold Room of Frank Campbell's Funeral Parlor in New York City to file past his casket and look upon his powdered features. Women, probably hired by the studio, hurled themselves before the funeral wagon, and a woman with no studio connection shot herself and left word for her husband that she had gone to join Rudy in heaven. Valentino's agent turned the funeral into an extravaganza.

The Associated Press called him, "The greatest lover in the history of motion pictures and the greatest matinee idol the stage has ever known." But some observers who were removed from the immediate hysteria saw the real pathos to be in the drama of a simple and congenial middle-class Italian immigrant who was exploited, swallowed up, and destroyed by mass adulation. H. L. Mencken called him, "A man of relatively civilized feelings thrown into a situation of intolerable vulgarity."

Contemporary Italian-Americans

The following section of contemporary Italian-American profiles is not meant to be a Who's Who. Such a work would require many volumes to include the large number of biographies necessary to do justice to that goal. Nor does this section necessarily include the most successful Americans of Italian origin. Rather it is offered as a cross-section of the Italian-American community to illustrate the breadth of their contributions.

Also, the last profile, that of Frank Sinatra, was chosen because he typifies much of the essence of the Italian-American. Not that Mr. Sinatra is, himself, typical. On the contrary, his approach to living dramatically illustrates the drive for individuality which has been an American trait that dates back before the Revolutionary War.

JOHN DOMINIC AGOSTINI

Born in Ascoli Piceno, Italy, September 19, 1897, John Agostini came to America when he was sixteen years old and became a construction worker in Massachusetts and Rhode Island. After another sixteen years he established his own firm, the New General Cement Company in 1929, which became the Agostini Construction Company in 1935.

The Agostini organization has become one of the leading construction companies in Rhode Island, with an average volume of over $2,000,000 a year and employing about 150 people. They specialize in the construction of schools, churches, factories and commercial buildings.

He married Maria Federighi in 1928. Children: Dominic, George, and twins Donna and Diane. He is a trustee of the Rhode Island Grand Lodge of the Order of Sons of Italy.

LICIA ALBANESE

"The Albanese" came to the United States in 1940, starting her twenty-year career with the Metropolitan Opera Company by playing the title role in *Butterfly,* which she continued to play so convincingly that the Japanese government gave her a ceremonial wedding dress to wear on the stage. Much earlier, when she was a student in Milan, she was summoned from the audience to sub for a *Butterfly* who had fallen ill, and she sang the role in spite of the fact that she didn't know how to put on the wig.

Born July 22, 1913, in Bari, Italy, Licia first studied at the Bari Conservatory, then with Giuseppina Baldassare-Tedeschi, and made her debut in Bari as Mimi in *La Boheme* (1934). By 1935, she was already a much-admired singer at the Arena Festival and later at La Scala, where she was especially popular as a partner to Beniamino Gigli. Her career in Italy continued to spiral for the next five years. Licia's lyric soprano voice, with its great musicality, was especially suited to Puccini and Verdi roles.

In 1942, Miss Albanese had her greatest triumph at the Met as Violetta in *La Traviata.* She became a naturalized citizen and married opera buff and Wall Street broker, Joseph Gimma, in 1945. They have one son, Peppino.

When complimented on her talent, she once said, "It is much easier to sing well than to have to explain why you didn't sing well."

Anna Maria Alberghetti

"I loved Lili," Miss Alberghetti said of her 1961 Tony Award-winning performance in the Broadway production of *Carnival.* "I believed in everything she said. I'm too mature to believe in puppets myself, but if I'd had Lili's life, I'd have believed in them, too."

Miss Alberghetti has had several lives. She was born May 5, 1936, in Pesaro, Italy. Her father was a cellist and sang baritone for a number of Italian opera companies, including La Scala, and was concert master of the Rome Opera Company. Her mother was a pianist with the Scuola Reggia Musicale on the Island of Rhodes.

Anna Maria was singing at the age of six. During World War II, the Governor of Rhodes heard her sing and had her and her parents flown away from that dangerous island by bomber.

She debuted at Carnegie Hall when she was thirteen (1950). "It was just like the story books," she said of her appearance, in which her voice was reviewed to give birth to "some of the purest, loveliest sounds that have been heard all season."

That June, the child coloratura was the solo attraction with the Philharmonic Symphony Orchestra at Lewisohn Stadium, where she sang arias from *Lucia, Traviata,* and *The Barber of Seville* before an audience of thirteen thousand.

She returned to Italy for a role in Gian-Carlo Menotti's film version of his musical play, *The Medium,* for which she received rave reviews. Returning to the United States, she went to Hollywood for Frank Capra's *Here Comes The Groom.*

She was devoted to her father until his death in 1957. She once asked him why he worked her so hard, and he replied, "You enjoyed every minute of it."

Don Ameche

Dominic Felix Ameche, to whom many a student has attributed the invention of the telephone when pressed by that question on a test, was born to a saloon operator, May 31, 1908, in Kenosha, Wisconsin.

He became interested in dramatics while attending the University of Wisconsin, toured in vaudeville with Texas Guinan, then appeared on radio serials *(The First Nighter* and *The Chase & Sanborn Hour).* His distinctive voice (also the trademark of brother Jim, radio's original *Jack Armstrong)* attracted millions of fans, mainly girls.

Hollywood discovered that "that voice" belonged to a tall, dark, dapper gentleman with an ingratiating smile; and they gave him enough work to frighten a long-distance runner. From frothy roles in the 1930's with such hardy perennials as Constance Bennett and Janet Gaynor, he moved on to the *Story of Alexander Graham Bell* (1941), starred on Broadway in Cole Porter's *Silk Stockings* (1955), *Goldilocks* (1957), and *13 Daughters* (1960).

Married in 1932 and the father of six (Donnie, Ronnie, Lonnie, Bonnie, Connie and Tommie), he switched to television in 1961, playing the ringmaster of NBC's *International Showtime*, and describing his duties on that show as those of a "tanbark Ed Sullivan."

MARIO ANDRETTI

Mario Andretti may be the best race-car driver in the world. He has certainly proved himself to be the man to beat in any race held in the United States. In 1969, after three abortive attempts to take the biggest American prize, the Indianapolis 500, he pushed Andy Granitelli's turbo-powered Ford across the finish line, establishing a 156.867 m.p.h. speed record for that event.

Born February 28, 1940, in Montona near Trieste, Italy, Andretti and his twin brother, Aldo, also a race car driver, were taken to see the 1,000-mile cross-country road race in Florence, where former great Italian racer Alberto Ascari was driving. "He was my idol," Andretti recalls, "and I guess that's when my love of racing first started."

Mario and his brother studied auto mechanics in Lucca and had to do their racing on the sly because of their father's opposition. "None of my relatives even knew . . . except my old priest uncle, and . . . I told him in confession so he couldn't tell."

The family moved to Nazareth, Pennsylvania in 1955, and the father took a job as a textile worker. Mario worked in a garage as a welder. He and Aldo saved their money and rebuilt an old Hudson, with which Mario won over twenty stock-car events. They continued to keep their racing from their father, but he found out in 1959 when Aldo was seriously injured in a crash. His wrath was so great, Mario ran away from home in order to pursue his driving career. Father and son were eventually reconciled.

He married Dee Ann Beverly Hoch in 1961, quit his job at the garage, and became a full-time driver. "My wife was willing to take the chance, so I gambled." He joined the United Racing Club and raced sprint cars for a year. Then, racing midgets for the American Race Drivers Club, he won eleven races in 1963.

Moving up to bigger cars, Andretti joined the United States Auto Club in 1964, won one race and finished in the top ten six times.

In 1965 he won the USAC national championship over such established drivers as A. J. Foyt, Rodger Ward, Jim Clark, and Parnelli Jones. His third-place finish in the Indianapolis won him the Wetzel Rookie-of-the-Year award and $40,000.

The veteran drivers were skeptical until 1966. Andretti won eight of fifteen championship races and his second straight USAC title. Jones said he had "incredible ability" and Foyt called him "the one to beat."

Even before winning the big race at Indianapolis, Andretti was earning about $300,000 a year in Ford and Firestone Tire contracts. He has never entered the European Grand Prix competition. "Sure, I've always dreamed of driving for Ferrari, and he's asked me. It would be a great honor, but . . . Ferrari can't put bread on the table."

Racing is his life. He is nicknamed "the Tiger" because of his aggressive driving. He tries to jump into first place and hold it.

PAUL ANKA

Though he insists he wrote *My Way* for friend Frank Sinatra, one would be hard pressed to find a prototype for this consistently popular singer-composer-actor-businessman. Not one to waste a lot of time, Paul Anka became a millionaire and reached puberty at about the same time.

Born in Ottawa, Canada, July 3, 1941, he was thrown out of the stage doors of the very theaters in which he would later come back and headline. In 1956, he won a contest that awarded him a week's vacation in New York City. He crashed the offices of ABC-Paramount, auditioned a song, and was ignored. Then the fifteen year-old singer performed *Diana*, his own composition. Everyone noticed, and Paul was signed on the spot.

Before his sixteenth birthday, Paul watched his *Diana*—a teenage lament about loving an older woman of seventeen—become a hit. By early 1959, sixteen year-old Paul had three gold records and was the composer of singer Buddy Holly's smash posthumous hit, *It Doesn't Matter Anymore*. Paul garnered his first million dollars, and a year later he made his nightclub debut. By twenty-one he was an international star with 200 songs to his writing credit.

He married Anne de Zogheb in 1963. They have one daughter, Alexandra. In addition to a string of world tours and fifteen gold records, he acted in *The Longest day* (for which he also wrote the title song) and has appeared on most TV variety shows, including the *Tonight Show,* for which he wrote the theme music.

LUIGI ANTONINI

Born at Vallata Irpina, Avellino, Italy, September 11, 1883, the son of Pietro Antonini, a school teacher and poet from Milan, Luigi Antonini served in the Italian Army before coming to America in 1908.

He worked as a waistmaker and became active in the Italian-American labor movement. In 1916 Antonini became editor of the labor magazine *L'Operaia* which laid the foundations for Local 89, I.L.G.W.U. in 1919. This union now has 30,000 members.

A first vice-president of I.L.G.W.U. since 1934, Antonini represented the American Labor Movement at the Bruxelles Congress in 1935. He was one of the founders and New York State Chairman of the American Labor Party.

Antonini has raised hundreds of thousands of dollars and thousands of cases of goods for Italian relief. He made possible the establishment of the F.D. Roosevelt vocational school at Mondello, Palermo, Italy. For years past he has conducted a weekly radio program on labor problems.

EDDIE ARCARO

How big can a little man get? "I feel like I'm leaving on top," said Eddie Arcaro, when he retired in 1962. "Maybe not for three, four years but for ten years (1948-58) I don't think anybody could touch me." The record bears out his claim as America's jockey king. He has ridden more winners (4,779, including five Kentucky Derbies, six Preaknesses, six Belmonts and two Triple Crowns— Whirlaway in 1941 and Citation in 1948), and brought home more money ($30,039,543) than any other jockey in history.

George Edward Arcaro, the son of a Cincinnati taxi owner, was born February 19, 1916. He quit school at fourteen and paid his track dues for three years before bringing home his first winner (unprophetically named "No More") in Chicago, in 1933. He suffered a fractured skull that same year when his mount threw and trampled him.

Arcaro was given a one-year suspension in 1942 for fighting Cuban jockey Vincent Nodarse, who had almost knocked Arcaro out of his saddle.

Married and the father of two sons, a golfer in the 70's, he refuses to name his best horse: "Nashua, Citation, Kelso and Assault could beat each other on any given day."

GIOVANNI ARCIERI

Born in Castrovillari, Cosenza, Italy, January 30, 1897, Giovanni Arcieri came to America in 1923 and has been a U.S. citizen since 1928. He received his Doctor of Medicine degree from the University of Rome.

A specialist in chest diseases, Dr. Arcieri has served on the staffs of the International Medical Center, Parkway Hospital, Bellevue Hospital, and several hospitals in Italy. He has also served on the faculties of the University of Rome and the New York Post-Graduate Medical School.

Dr. Arcieri has authored several books and many medical tracts, including *The Italian-English Medical Dictionary*.

He served in the Italian Army in World War I and is a knight in the Order of the Crown of Italy.

MARIO ARCIOLI

Born in the province of Novara, Italy, in 1885, Mario Arcioli came to the United States in 1927. He was educated at the Seminary of Novara, where he was ordained a priest in 1918.

Father Arcioli served as assistant pastor in Newark, New Jersey for five years and at our Lady of Loretto's Church in Brooklyn from 1932 to 1950. He has served as pastor of Our Lady of Miracle Church in Brooklyn since 1950.

Awarded a gold medal and the Grand Cross of Saint Conrad for his many activities for youth welfare, he has also organized numerous choirs both in Italy and in the United States.

HENRY ARMETTA

One of the greatest Italian comedians of the American screen was born at Palermo, Italy on July 4, 1888. After his education at local public schools, Armetta, an adventurous youth, made his way aboard a ship at the age of fourteen as a stowaway and wasn't discovered until he and the ship landed at Boston.

Young Henry was turned over to the police. A barber, John Armato, guaranteed to give the boy a home if they would release him. A few days later Henry was learning the barber's trade.

During his second year in a New York shop, his jovial disposition and eagerness attracted a customer, Raymond Hitchcock, who offered the Italian a small part in his production of *Yankee Consul.*

After many years in legitimate theater Armetta landed a part in *Littlest Rebel,* and for months afterward worked at the Fox East Coast Studios.

Armetta went to Hollywood in 1932. As an Italian character comedian his services were in great demand in films. He worked for all the major studios. His screen credits include *Farewell to Arms, Seventh Heaven, Winner Take All* and others. His last film was *A Bell for Adano,* made in 1946, which starred John Hodiak and Gene Tierney.

GERALD ARPINO

By blending modern dance and theatrical techniques with the rigid form of classical ballet, Gerald Arpino, chief choreographer of the City Center Joffrey Ballet, has sometimes been charged with gimmickry, faddism, and a Broadway showmanship. But most critics agree with the statement made by Jean Battey of the Washington *Post* on Arpino's occasional experimental miscalculations: his "failures are more wondrous than the successes of other choreographers."

Gerald Peter Arpino was born January 14, 1928, in Staten Island, New York City. His father, Luigi, had emigrated to the United States from Italy and was engaged in the real estate business. An honor student in high school, Gerald enlisted in the Coast Guard in 1945.

Stationed in Seattle, he called on the son of an old friend of his mother's. He was Robert Joffrey, then a dancing student. Arpino became interested and attended class whenever he could get time off from his Coast Guard duties. Out of the service, he studied many styles of dance for the next few years. After studying and performing with the modern dancers, May O'Donnell and Gertrude Shurr, in New York City, he toured South America with the Ballet Russe in 1951-52 and appeared on television and in Broadway musicals.

Arpino then joined Robert Joffrey in 1953, when the latter founded his company. Arpino became one of the six dancers who made up the original Robert Joffrey Ballet, and made many outside appearances to help finance the company.

He made his transition to choreographer in the early 1960's. Mrs. Rebekah Harkness assumed financial responsibility for the company in 1962. In her workshop, Arpino created *Incubus,* a nightmarish fantasy set to music of Anton Webern. This was added to the repertory which included two other Arpino works: *Ropes* (music of Charles Ives) and *Sea Shadows* (music of Ravel).

The company toured Russia in 1963 and performed at the White House for the President, Mrs. Kennedy and Emperor Haile Selassie. Arpino's *Partita for 4* was shown, along with a new work, *The Palace,* a nostalgic view of vaudeville.

Joffrey and Arpino broke away from the company, which is now the Harkness Ballet, and formed a new company partially funded by the Ford Foundation. The new Robert Joffrey Ballet went on tour in 1965 and became the resident dance company of City Center in 1966.

Among Arpino's more successful recent ballets are: *Viva Vivaldi; Olympics; Nightwings; Secret Places; The Clowns; Cello Concerto;* and *The Poppet. Trinity,* a rock ballet, premiered in the 1970 season.

MAX ASCOLI

As an educator and editor Max Ascoli has tried to live by the theory that the American's "capacity to grasp facts and ideas is crudely underestimated by most of the existing media of information."

From 1949 to 1958, Dr. Ascoli was editor and publisher of *The Reporter,* a fortnightly magazine known for interpreting national and international news along liberal and literate lines. In 1960, he edited an anthology of fellow scribes (A. A. Berle, Jr., Marya Mannes, Theodore White, et al) in *The Best from The Reporter.*

He was born in Ferrara, Italy, June 25, 1898, and received his LL.D. from the Universita Statale de Ferrara in 1920. While getting his Ph.D. from the University of Rome in 1928, he was arrested for his outspoken anti-Mussolini sentiments; and his writings were suppressed after his release. He taught jurisprudence at Italian universities from 1926-31.

Coming to the United States in 1931 (naturalized in 1939), he has been on the graduate faculty of the New School of Social Research since 1933. Author: *Intelligence in Politics* (1936); *Fascism for Whom?* (with Arthur Feiler) (1938); *The Power of Freedom* (1948).

Dr. Ascoli married Marion Rosenwald in 1940, after his divorce from poetess Anna Maria Armi. They have one son, Peter. He believes "in America, a nation whose freedom and well-being are inseparably tied to the freedom and well-being of other nations".

Charles Atlas

Body builder Angelo Siciliano migrated to Brooklyn with his family in 1904 from the farm in Acri, Italy, where he was born. Angelo was a weak, sickly boy. One night, when he was fifteen years old, while returning home he was attacked and severely beaten by a larger boy. He never forgot the experience nor has anyone else.

The ninety-seven pound teenager brooded over the incident, and after being impressed by a statue of Hercules he set about exercising at a local gym. The more he lifted the more tired he got.

While visiting the zoo one day, Angelo noticed the lion's muscles and wondered how it could be so powerful with no room to exercise in that small cage. As he stared at the animal, it got up and stretched. Seeing the beast pit one muscle against the other gave the boy the idea for what was to change his life and the lives of many others around the world. It was the basis for the system he called "dynamic tension."

Employing his techniques on himself, he built his body, adding muscles, and then adding muscles to the muscles. In 1922, he won a national contest and was named the "World's Most Perfectly Developed Man." He also won the award the following year.

When someone remarked how much he looked like a statue of Atlas that stood at a local bank, Angelo was flattered. The young Coney Island janitor changed his name to Charles Atlas.

In the early 1920's he became a model for artists. By the time he was earning $100 a week, he figured that if people liked his body so much, why not show them how they could have such a physique. In 1929 he began a correspondence course. He met a young promoter named Charles Roman, who owned an advertising firm, and Roman gave him a few ideas for a promotional campaign.

In 1942 Atlas publicized his system by pulling six cars chained together for a distance of a mile, while the press and public looked on in awe. His imaginative advertising ran in comic books, Sunday supplements and magazines. It was simple and well understood by American men who sought the national ideal: the he-man. A series of drawings any man could identify with showed a ninety-seven pound weakling getting sand kicked in his face and then losing his girl to the bully who did it. Months later, after taking a Charles Atlas course, the weakling comes back to the beach and sees the bully with his girl. But this time the weakling looks like a killer. He slugs the bully and retrieves his girl. "My hero," she sighs, with admiration.

Charles Atlas lived near an abandoned Coast Guard station on Point Lookout where his house was furnished by furniture he built himself from driftwood until his death in 1972. His wife died in 1965.

Richard R. Aurelio

Richard R. Aurelio was appointed Deputy Mayor of New York City by Mayor John V. Lindsay on January 1, 1970, a post he resigned in 1972.

Deputy Mayor Aurelio had been active in the city, state and national politics in recent years, and was campaign manager for Mayor Lindsay in 1969 in his successful bid for reelection.

A resident of New York since 1951, Mr. Aurelio, 44, is a native of North Providence, Rhode Island. He was graduated from Boston University's School of Public Relations in 1949.

In 1954, he was a member of the reportorial staff of Newsday Magazine which won a 1954 Pulitizer Prize for its expose of the harness racing scandals.

In 1961, Mr. Aurelio joined the staff of Senator Jacob K. Javits as his Press Secretary. He was in charge of press and communications for Senator Javits' successful 1962 campaign for reelection. Following that campaign, he became the senator's administrative assistant in Washington. He took leaves of absence to work in New York as a Special Assistant in the campaigns of Senator Kenneth B. Keating in 1964, Mayor Lindsay in 1965, and Governor Nelson A. Rockefeller in 1966. He also assisted in the national presidental campaigns of William Scranton in 1964 and Governor Rockefeller in 1968.

Mr. Aurelio lives in New York City with his wife, the former Suzanne Berger of New York, and his son, Marco.

FRANKIE AVALON

Riding through the crest and fall of the mighty wave of teenage idols, Frank (no longer Frankie) did not lose his following, as many of his contemporaries did. He has proven that he has the talent for durability.

A Philadelphia product, he was born September 8, 1940. He was a prodigy with the trumpet, organized his own teenage night club when he was fifteen, then came to national attention with his early hits, *De De Dinah* and *Teacher's Pet*.

He was one of the boy wonders of pre-Beatle-post-Buddy Holly rock and roll, one of many Italian lads, most from Philadelphia—Bobby Rydell, Dion DiMucci, Fabian—who took over pop music and slowed it down after Elvis Presley was drafted and Buddy Holly was killed in an airplane crash. In 1959, at age seventeen, Frankie recorded *Venus,* a million seller twice-over that stayed number one on the top-forty record charts for five weeks.

In the early sixties he teamed up with Annette Funicello for a series of B-movies (the B stands interchangeably for Beach and Bad) —*Muscle Beach, Beach Party, Beach Blanket Bingo*—all of which would be best forgotten.

When he was "buried" in the new wave of rock and roll that immigrated to America from England in 1964, Frank Avalon dropped the "ie" from his name and went on the cabaret circuit as an adult entertainer, where he found new success reviving old prom memories for his generation, which had grown up.

He married a former Miss Rheingold contestant, Kathryn Diebel, in 1963.

KAYE BALLARD

A top favorite in television and night clubs, as well as the Broadway stage, Kaye Ballard has been singing and playing comedy since the late 1940's. Currently doing guest shots and club dates, Kaye's own television series, *The Mother-in-Laws,* in which she co-starred with Eve Arden, had a successful two-year run on NBC-TV from 1967 to 1969.

Born Catherine Gloria Balotta, November 20, 1926, in Cleveland, Ohio, she persisted against family pressure in her early ambitions to become an actress. Her high school drama teacher wouldn't let her into class because she wasn't pretty enough, so she turned to comedy.

After graduation, she turned down an art scholarship and joined a burlesque show as a straight woman. Soon she was on the road with her own act of songs and comedy. She joined the Spike Jones band of musical madmen in 1945 and toured the RKO vaudeville circuit throughout the United States and Canada.

Miss Ballard landed a small part in the Broadway production of *Three to Make Ready* in 1946, and toured with the national company of *Touch and Go* and *Top Banana*. Her first featured role came in 1954, in *The Golden Apple*.

After a few more road tours with her own act and a tour of the *Ziegfeld Follies,* her next memorable role was as the incomparable Rosalie in *Carnival!* in 1961. She continued to work both on and Off-Broadway while doing guest appearances on all the major television shows (fifty times with Johnny Carson) before her own series came along. In 1965, she did impersonations of Mabel Mercer, Sophie Tucker, and Beatrice Lillie for eight months to a sold-out house at the Square East Theatre Off Broadway. The revue was made up of over thirty of Cole Porter's lesser-known songs. It was called *The Decline and Fall of the Entire World As Seen Through the Eyes of Cole Porter, Revisited.*

GIUSEPPE BAMBOSCHEK

Born in Trieste, Italy, conductor, opera coach and composer Giuseppe Bamboschek studied at Trieste Conservatory and directed his first concert at the age of sixteen.

Bamboschek came to the United States in 1913 as accompanist and assisting artist with Pasquale Amato. He was conductor and general musical secretary with the Metropolitan Opera Company from 1913 to 1930 and was the musical director of the Philadelphia La Scala Opera Company from 1939 to 1946.

He married Carolina Ghidoni and since 1933 he has appeared in concerts with Martinelli, Lily Pons, Grace Moore, Edward Johnson and Jeanette MacDonald, among many others. He has appeared as conductor all over the world, is past president, Lega Musicale Italiana, and Knight, Order of the Crown of Italy.

ANNE BANCROFT

When asked what was the most thrilling moment of her spectacular performance in *The Miracle Worker,* Anne Bancroft replied, "When my parents came backstage to congratulate me." Having been typed as a B-actress for six years in Hollywood, she returned to New York, determined to work in her chosen craft.

After a successful stint in *Two for the Seesaw,* she really put it all together in *Miracle*, winning every dramatic award in sight, including the Oscar for the film version in 1962.

Born Anne Marie Italiano, September 17, 1931, in the Bronx, New York, she has always been aware of the acting drive within her. "When I was two, I could sing *Under a Blanket of Blue*. And the quality of the voice was never as good as lots of other kids; but I was so willing, so wanting, that nobody had to coax me for long."

She married comic genius Mel Brooks in 1964. Movies: *Don't Bother to Knock, Tonight We Sing, Demetrius and the Gladiators, The Pumpkin Eater,* and *The Graduate* (for which she won the Golden Globe Award in 1968.)

BRUNO BEGHÉ

Painter, sculptor and violinist Bruno Beghé was born at Carrara, Italy, March 11, 1892. Educated at the Royal Academy of Fine Arts and the Musical Institute of Carrara, Beghé spent several years as violinist at Teatro Reale of Rome, Colon Opera House of Buenos Aires, and Teatro Regio of Parma.

In America since 1923, Beghé spent nine years as a violinist with the Chicago Civic Opera Company while continuing to work as a free lance artist. From 1937 to 1954 he was on the music staff of C.B.S. in Chicago.

Beghé's works of art have won many prizes and have been exhibited in Europe as well as the United States. He was awarded a cross in the Order of the Crown of Italy.

He married Emmavve Freimeyer in 1932 (deceased, 1952). They had two sons, Renato and Gino. He remarried, 1960, Theo Liddell. He is past president of the Italian Musicians Club and is a member of the Italo-American National Union and the Sons of Italy.

MELVIN BELLI

The list of Melvin Mouron Belli's clients, past and present, is as varied as it is illustrious. It includes Errol Flynn, Tony Curtis, Mae West, Mickey Cohen, Marie MacDonald, and both Lee Harvey Oswald and his assassin, Jack Ruby.

Though he mainly works out of the law offices of Belli, Ashe & Gerry, San Francisco, he has won decisions in six states, including a record $225,000 personal injury award. He has been counsel in over a hundred court cases in which the award exceeded $100,000.

Author of thirty volumes and an active member in as many professional clubs and organizations, Belli was born July 29, 1907, at Sonora, California. Educated at the University of California at Berkeley and Boalt Hall, he has been married twice and has five children.

PIETRO BELLUSCHI

"Coming to America," recalls Pietro Belluschi, renowned architect, "changed my life to a greater extent than I thought possible. From a dreamy, lazy boy, I became almost overnight an aggressive and determined man - determined to succeed."

He was a young man of twenty-five when he left his native Italy (born August 18, 1899 in Ancona). The Juilliard School at Lincoln Center in New York City and the Art Museum in Portland, Oregon are but two concrete examples that his dream has been realized.

He works in an "international" style ("Architecture is, and always has been, an expression of the human spirit").

Former dean of architecture at MIT (1951-1965), he is married to his second wife, Marjorie Bruckner, and has two boys, Peter and Anthony.

TONY BENNETT

Not possessed of the best voice in the business, Tony Bennett is a top-notch performer with a thoroughly professional style. He learns his songs so well that when he sings them to an audience, they seem to be a part of him.

Born Anthony Benedetto in Long Island City, New York, August 3, 1926, he was discovered by Bob Hope in 1949. After serving in the army during World War Two, he had studied at the American Wing Theater.

His sincere approach to his songs comes off particularly well in front of live audiences; hence his success as one of the all-time top nightclub performers in the country. He frequently appears at Las Vegas and on nation-wide television.

Perhaps his best known and most requested songs are *Because of You* and (I left my heart in) *San Francisco,* a million seller.

BRUNO BERNABÓ

General manager of Mamma Leone's Restaurant, Bruno Bernabó was born in New York City, January 1, 1911. He was taken back to Italy, at the age of three, returned to New York when he was sixteen and began his restaurant apprenticeship under his father, the well-known Bernabó of the Plaza Hotel.

Under his management Mamma Leone's Restaurant has grown until today it is able to serve as many as 4,500 meals a day and employs 350 people.

Bernabó served in the U.S. Army during World War II. He was awarded the Star of Solidarity by the President of the Italian Republic for his outstanding contribution to the betterment of the Italian-American community.

He has promoted many benefits, including the Carnevale of Italy, a festival for the "Children's City" of Rome and others for the Orphanage of Bedonia.

YOGI BERRA

Finding Leonard Bernstein sitting next to him at dinner, Lawrence Peter Berra (nicknamed "Yogi" by boyhood friends who compared him to a fakir they had seen in a movie) told the famed conductor-composer that he had been given a piano and asked him, "Would you mind coming over to my place and show me how it works?" Another time he said, "Mickey Mantle hits right-handed and left-handed—he's naturally amphibious." When Yogi's looks were criticized, he said, "No one ever won a ball game with his face."

For nearly thirty years Yogi's malapropisms added a lot of color to baseball, sometimes at the risk of overshadowing what a great catcher he was. His Boswell, Joe Garagiola, has captured most of them in his book, *Baseball Is a Funny Game;* and Yogi co-authored his own autobiography (*Yogi*, 1961).

In his seventeen years as a player for the New York Yankees, he set and still holds many World Series records. A notorious bad-ball hitter, he was particularly dangerous in the clutch.

The son of an immigrant brickmaker, Yogi was born in St. Louis, May 12, 1925. The Yankees brought him up to the majors in 1946. Under his management the Yankees won the American League pennant in 1964. From 1972 to 1975 Yogi managed the New York Mets. He is vice president of the Yoo-Hoo Beverage Company, married to Carmen Short, and has three sons.

Mario Biaggi

Mario Biaggi is the representative from the 24th Congressional District, Bronx and Yonkers, New York. He was born in New York City on October 26, 1917. A graduate of the New York Law School, he was admitted to the State Bar in 1963.

Biaggi was elected to the 91st Congress on November 5, 1968, where he served on the Committee on Science and Astronautics. He was reelected to the 92nd Congress by an overwhelming majority.

From 1942 to 1965, he was a member of the New York City Police Department. Wounded eleven times in the line of duty, he retired with a disability as Detective Lieutenant, holding the police department's Medal of Honor and twenty-seven other decorations. In 1967 he was elected president of the National Police Officers Association of America and is a member of its Hall of Fame and winner of its Medal of Honor for Valor. As the most decorated policeman in the United States, he has also received honors from Canada and Italy. The President of the Republic of Italy knighted Mario Biaggi with the Order of Merit in the grade of Cavaliere.

A resident of Bronx, he is married and has four children.

Joseph F. Blasi

Lawyer and former judge Joseph Blasi was born in Brooklyn, New York, January 18, 1908. A graduate of Loyola University, New Orleans, Louisiana, he has been in general practice of law since 1931.

Blasi has served as member of the Louisiana House of Representatives for four terms and Judge of the Civil District Court for the Parish of Orleans in 1948.

He married Agnes MacGrath in 1934 and they have four children: James, Agnes Belle, Edward and Thomas. He is a member of several civic organizations including, the New Orleans Chamber of Commerce and the Knights of Columbus.

Sonny Bono

The husband-wife, singing and comedy team of Sonny and Cher have been breaking records since they made their first one in 1964. Good response to their television show, which began in 1971, added a new dimension to their success as recording and concert artists.

Born Sonny Salvatore Bono, February 16, 1940, he has composed many songs, including the theme for the movie, *Good Times,* in which he starred with Cher in 1966. Other compositions are "Koko Joe," "You Bug Me Baby," "Needles and Pins," "Baby Don't Go," and "Dream Baby".

Perhaps his biggest hit was "I Got You, Babe". In the mid sixties, he and Cher had one hit after another and were at the top of pop music. In 1969, they financed and starred in their own film, *Chastity*.

The Bonos were married in 1964 and have one daughter — Chastity.

Blase A. Bonpane

Born in Curwensville, Pennsylvania, December 16, 1892, Superior Court Judge Blase Bonpane served in both World Wars, leaving the Army in 1946 with the rank of Lieutenant Colonel.

Educated at Ohio State and Ohio Northern University, Bonpane was admitted to the Ohio Bar in 1916 and to the California Bar in 1938. He was president of the Los Angeles City Public Utilities and Transportation Commission from 1955 to 1961.

Bonpane was appointed by the President to the Conference of the Inter-Governmental Committee for European Migration in 1956 and was appointed to the Superior Court of California for the County of Los Angeles in 1966. He was Assistant Prosecuting

Attorney in Cleveland, Ohio, 1921-1922; editor and publisher of *The Tribune* in Cleveland; and Republican Congressional nominee in Ohio in 1936.

He married Florence Marco in 1918 and they have three children: Betty Jane, Margie Ann, and Blase, Jr.

Very active in California politics and Italian-American, as well as other civic affairs, Bonpane has received many commendations, including the Star of Solidarity from the Republic of Italy.

ERNEST BORGNINE

"What do you want to do tonight, Marty?"

"I don't know. What do you want to do?"

With those words, Ernest Borgnine dispelled the rumor that he could only play a "heavy who dies well." His gentle and sensitive portrayal of the fat and lonely Bronx butcher won him an Oscar and opened up many avenues in which he could apply his talent. Unlike *Marty*, Borgnine is a gregarious, fun-oriented guy who is seldom seen without his winning grin.

Born Ermes Effron Borgnino, January 24, 1915, in Hamden, Connecticut, he spent ten years in the Navy, experience which did him no harm in the long-running *McHale's Navy* television series. He studied drama on the GI Bill and appeared in *Harvey* and *Mrs. McThing* before moving on to Hollywood.

After doing *The Mob*, he landed the juicy role of the sadistic Sergeant Fatso Judson in *From Here to Eternity* and played it to the hilt. More heavy roles followed: *Bad Day at Black Rock, Demetrius and the Gladiators, Violent Saturday*, then *Marty* (1956), *Square Jungle, The Catered Affair, The Best Things in Life Are Free, Three Brave Men, Hell Below, Badlanders, Rabbit Trap, Man on a String, Barabbas, Flight of the Phoenix, The Oscar* (1966), *The Dirty Dozen*, and *Willard*, which was 1971's top box-office attraction. More recently, he has played in *Hannie Caulder* with Raquel Welch.

Married to his fourth wife, Donna Rancourt, they have one daughter. He also has a daughter from his first marriage.

GIOVANNI BUITONI

Giulia Buitoni started a small macaroni business in San Sepolcro, Italy, in 1827. Each generation of Buitonis added to the pasta and chocolate empire, but great-grandson Giovanni is credited with building it into an international complex with pasta plants in Rome, San Sepolcro, Paris, and South Hackensack, New Jersey; a candy installation and a lithography plant in Perugia, Italy; several American subsidiary corporations; and many retail stores.

Born November 6, 1891 in Perugia, Italy, Giovanni received good gradés in school. While getting his doctor of laws degree at the University of Perugia, he took over the family's ailing chocolate company and enlarged it from a staff of fifteen workers in a basement to hundreds of workers in a large factory.

In the early 1930's he became intrigued with advertising and was the first Italian to use a contest to sell a Buitoni product. Pictures of figurines were placed in Buitoni and Perugina products. Cars, motorcycles, refrigerators, etc. could be won by gathering a complete set of these cards. This campaign, launched during the Depression, led to widespread bartering, and eventually the figures were quoted like stocks and bonds on the business pages of newspapers.

After World War II, which left Giovanni without funds, he came to the United States and opened a Buitoni restaurant at the New York World's Fair and a Perugina store on Fifth Avenue. Mrs. Buitoni pawned her jewels (ironically Giulia's wife had done the same thing to start the first business) and her husband established a modest branch of the Buitoni business in Jersey City, followed by two Buitoni restaurants on Broadway, which featured all the spaghetti diners could eat for twenty-five cents.

In 1952 a modern two-million-dollar plant was opened in South Hackensack. A plaque in its entrance hall reads: "In fond memory of my beloved and unforgettable parents who taught me the religion of God and the religion of work, I dedicate this Buitoni enterprise in the New World. Giovanni Buitoni."

Buitoni speaks four languages and his biggest avocation is opera. He once hired Carnegie Hall and the services of Anselmo Colzani and Licia Albanese for an evening in 1961. With them he sang arias from *Rigoletto, Ernani,* and *Don Giovanni.* The *Life* review read: "As a tribute to Verdi, pasta, and Walter Mittyism, it couldn't have been better."

He married opera singer Letizia Cairone in 1936.

FRANK CANTELMO

Born in New York City, May 30, 1902, journalist and editor Frank Cantelmo followed in the profession of his father, Ercole.

A graduate of New York University, Cantelmo was an associate editor and treasurer of *The New American* (monthly) before joining the staff of *Corriere D'America* where he was managing editor from 1929 to 1940. He has been managing editor of *Il Progresso* since 1940. A radio commentator and lecturer, Cantelmo wrote *Sanctions of Love, Heart News,* and *Dictator of Your Heart.*

He married Frances Costabile in 1924. They have two daughters: Patricia and Joan.

Frank Capra

Frank Capra's incurable optimism (branded Capra-corn by some critics) provides the track on which his twenty-plus feature films run. His sentimental approach works. Many of his films [*Arsenic and Old Lace* (1944) is an excellent example] never lose their freshness or become attached to the period in which they were made.

His biggest sleeper was *It Happened One Night* (1934), a film about which no one was enthusiastic about making. The Columbia studio did the film practically as a throwaway, and Clark Gable was on loan from MGM and assigned to the film as punishment. As it happened, *It Happened One Night* won the four top Oscars—Gable, Best Actor; Claudette Colbert, Best Actress; Best Film; and the first of three Oscars for Best Director to Capra (the others were *Mr. Deeds Goes to Town* and *You Can't Take It With You).*

Born in Palermo, Sicily, May 18, 1897, he came to America at the age of six. His career started in 1921, when he directed *Screen Snap Shorts.* He was also a gagman for the *Our Gang* comedies.

Four-time president of the Academy of Motion Pictures and three-time president of the Screen Directors Guild, he has added his particularly human touch to such classics as *Lost Horizon* (1937), *Mr. Smith Goes To Washington* (1939), and *It's a Wonderful Life.* In 1953, he directed the television films *Our Mr. Sun, Hemo the Magnificent* and *The Unchained Goddess,* discovering that educational films are harder than those which flow from his imagination.

He married Lucille Rayburn in 1932 and they have two sons and a daughter. His autobiography, *The Name Above the Title,* was published in 1971.

Pasquale Carone

Psychiatrist Pasquale Carone was born in Brooklyn, New York, June 26, 1914. A graduate of New York University and Creighton

University, Dr. Carone interned at St. Vincent Hospital in Staten Island and was resident in psychiatry at Colorado Hospital in 1942.

He was chief neuropsychiatrist at the Army and Navy General Hospital from 1944 to 1946, then became resident psychiatrist at Lyons V.A. Hospital and the New York State Psychiatric Institute. He has since been associated with many hospitals and mental health associations.

Dr. Carone married Jacqueline Bruno in 1940. They have two children: Patrick Francis and Jacqueline Susan.

OLEG CASSINI

A world-renowned dress designer and older brother to Igor ("Our survival was due to a collective effort. . .It's the only old-fashioned thing about us"), Oleg Cassini was born in Paris, April 11, 1913. He graduated from the Academia Belle Arti, Florence, Italy in 1934, worked as a free lance designer in Paris, and owned his own studio in Rome before coming to America in 1936.

He struggled in New York City for a few years, then moved to Hollywood where he became a noted designer for Paramount Pictures and Twentieth Century Fox and married screen star Gene Tierney in 1941 (divorced 1952 - two daughters).

After returning to New York, he established Oleg Cassini Incorporated in 1950. His national prominence gained extra publicity when he designed clothes for Jacqueline Kennedy. He has worked as costume designer on *As the Girls Go* and other Broadway shows.

MICHAEL CATALANO

A Supreme Court Justice of New York State, Michael Catalano was born December 27, 1907 in Buffalo, New York. His father, Pietro, founded the first macaroni factory in Buffalo in the 1890's. Catalano was educated at Cornell University, Harvard and the University of Buffalo Law School.

Elected Judge of the New York State Supreme Court in 1957, Catalano served as a lecturer and faculty member of the University of Buffalo before taking that position. He is the author of *The Solution of Legal Problems*.

Carmen Cavallaro

Carmen Cavallaro's parents arranged formal piano lessons for him when he was five, and he was an accomplished pianist by the time he reached high school. Best known for his classical adaptions, he recorded: *Full Moon and Empty Arms* (Rachmaninoff); *My Reverie* (Debussy); and *Tonight We Love* (Tschaikovsky).

Born in New York City, he joined the Rudy Vallee orchestra. His popularity zoomed with the release of his album, *Dancing in the Dark.* He has appeared in several movies and made the sound track for *The Eddy Duchin Story.*

Anthony Celebrezze

Now a member of the Sixth Circuit Court of Appeals, the post he has held since 1965, Judge Celebrezze seemed settled in his job as Mayor of Cleveland, Ohio (winning his fifth election with almost seventy-five per cent of the popular vote) when President Kennedy called him to Washington to become Secretary of Health, Education, and Welfare in 1962.

Born September 4, 1919, in Anzi, Italy, he was the ninth of twelve children of Dorothy and Rocco Cilibrizzi. He grew up in Cleveland, worked his way through college, and received his LL. B. from Ohio Northern University in 1936, adding three doctor's degrees to his credit over the following years.

A successful lawyer, he was elected Ohio State Senator in 1952. He served in the Navy in World War II and has won many humanitarian awards.

Judge Celebrezze married Anne Marco in 1938, and they have three children.

Francis Cerbini

Biochemist Francis Cerbini was born in Saracena, Cosenza, Italy, July 24, 1902. A pioneer in biochemical research work on cancer and allied diseases, Cerbini came to the United States in 1921 as assistant to Dr. Ralph Romer.

He was research director for the American Chemical Products Company, Cerbiniol Laboratories, Westbury Chemical Company, and since 1947 has been the President and Research Director of Cerbini Research Corporation.

Cerbini's sons, Achilles and Innocenzo, are both associated with their father's laboratory, from which have been developed several well known drugs such as *Acerbine* and *Cerbartrol.*

GIUSEPPE CERVETTO

Born in Varazze, Savona, Italy, June 13, 1909, businessman Giuseppe Cervetto went to sea at the age of nineteen. After a hitch in the Italian Navy, he joined the Italian Merchant Marines. After five years of seeing the world, he settled in San Francisco.

Two years later he established the Cervetto Building Maintenance Company, a firm that now employs over 100 people. An avid civic leader, Cervetto has served as an officer or member with twenty-four civic organizations over the years.

He married Esther Mae in 1949. There are two children: Charlene Louise and Joseph Maria. Among his many awards are the Italian Star of Solidarity and a resolution of commendation from the Board of Supervisors of San Francisco.

CARLO CIANCI

Father Carlo Cianci was born in Castelgrande, Potenza, Italy, December 2, 1881. He came to America in 1909 and has been Pastor of St. Michael's Church in Paterson, New Jersey since 1919.

In 1928 Father Cianci built the new St. Michael's Church. He built the new St. Michael's School in 1949 and established the St. Joseph Rest Home for the Aged in 1955.

For his untiring assistance to Italian immigrants, he has been awarded the Cross of Knight of the Order of the Italian Crown and the Star of Solidarity. Pope Pius XII elevated him to Domestic Prelate in 1941 and to Protonotary Apostolic in 1960.

JOHN CIARDI

Currently the poetry editor of *The Saturday Review,* John Ciardi (pronounced Chardy) has greatly increased the popularity of his art form through his writings and criticism. He has written twenty-seven books, including criticism, poetry, children's books, and translations. His translation of Dante's *Inferno* sold over half a million copies.

Born in Boston, June 24, 1916, he was three when his father died and left four children. Though she could hardly speak a word of English, John's mother managed, by working day and night, to support and educate her family.

Ciardi is a burly fellow and hardly has the effete appearance generally associated with the professional poet. He married Myra Judith Hostetter in 1946, and they have three children.

Dr. Ciardi attended Tufts College, The University of Michigan, Wayne University, Ursinus College, and Kalamazoo College. He taught at Harvard and has been a staff lecturer and director of the Bread Loaf Writers Conference since 1947.

Raphael Cilento

One of six practicing physicians in the family, Dr. Cilento, a surgeon specializing in neurology, was born in Telokanson, Malaya, February 19, 1921. He was educated at the University of Queensland, Brisbane, Australia and came to the United States in 1961.

His father, Sir Raphael, was knighted by King George VI for his outstanding work in tropical diseases. His mother, Lady Phyllis is famous for her work in natural childbirth. His sister Diane is a leading stage actress and the wife of actor Sean Connery.

In addition to his achievements as a surgeon, Dr. Cilento holds amateur fishing, boxing and fencing championships in Australia. He married Mavis Ross in 1958 and they have seven children: Adrienne, Julienne, Vivienne, Raphael IV, Penelope, Giovanna, and Abigail.

Joseph Coletti

Joseph Arthur Coletti was a pupil of painter John Singer Sargent and later became his assistant. He has become one of the world's leading sculptors, contributing importantly to church and historical sculpture in the last 50 years.

Born November 5, 1898, in San Donato, Italy, Coletti was brought to the United States when he was two years old. He studied at the Massachusetts Art School from 1915-1917 and graduated from Harvard University in 1923. He married Miriam Kerruish Whitney in 1929, and they have two daughters.

His American statuary and other works include: the baptismal font at St. John's Episcopal Church in Westwood, Massachusetts; the Henry B. Washburn Memorial in Cambridge, Massachusetts; Gagnon statue, Manchester, New Hampshire; Senator David I. Walsh Statue in Boston; and the Father Michael Joseph McGivney statue in Waterbury, Connecticut.

He is represented abroad by the statue of Saint George, Florence, Italy; the Admiral Samuel Eliot Morison medallion in the Vatican Collection; and the Paderewski Centennial medal in Cracow, Poland. Recipient of countless awards, Mr. Coletti has written *Aristide Maillol* and many articles for the *Encyclopaedia Britannica*.

PERRY COMO

"Have a drink and make yourself comfortable before you ask me if I'm really 'that relaxed'," Mr. "C" once told an interviewer. "And the answer is 'No'." After Perry signed his record (at that time) twenty-five million dollar contract with NBC-TV, he went on a seventy-two-hour work week to give the show its easy-going atmosphere.

Born Pierino Roland Como, May 18, 1913, in Cannonsburg, Pennsylvania, the seventh son of a seventh son, he eventually had six children of his own. "Pop raised thirteen children on thirty-five dollars a week and taught us we were our brothers' keepers." Hurrying through school, Perry owned a three-chair barber shop by the time he was fourteen. He met his future wife, Roselle Beline, two years later.

In 1934, he retired his razor and went on tour with the Ted Weems band. Having read reports about how rough it was for him during those days, he said, "Imagine being twenty-one and in love, with your own wife and car and baby, and making twenty-eight dollars a week *steady! Hardship!* I only wish it could happen to our kids!"

The trail led to Hollywood where he found work in the movies. Among them: *Something for the Boys; Doll Face;* and *If I'm Lucky*. Mr. Como has won an Emmy Award and the *Motion Picture Daily TV* Poll for Best Vocalist, 1952-1953.

Tony Conigliaro

The 1965 American League home-run king, Tony Conigliaro, was hit in the face with a pitched ball in 1967. The retina of his left eye was seriously damaged and he was told he would never play again. Almost miraculously the eye healed and Tony "C" was back in the Boston Red Sox lineup in 1969. He tells his story in *Seeing It Through* (1970), his autobiography, written with the late Jack Zanger.

Born January 7, 1945, in Revere, Massachusetts, Anthony Richard Conigliaro was introduced to baseball by his father Salvatore, a plant manager, at the age of four. He showed talent in the Little League, and by his junior year in high school he was hitting .600.

The Boston Red Sox signed him to a twenty thousand dollar contract in 1962 and sent him to spring training where he discovered he was much lighter than the other players (six-feet-three, one-hundred-seventy pounds). "I worked on a weight-lifting campaign," he recalled in his book. "I worked and worked and worked. I knew what I had to do to improve myself and did it." After two years of minor league ball, he went to Boston.

In the middle of Boston's pennant race in 1967, Tony was hit. "We were playing a night game with the California Angels . . . I came to bat in the fourth inning . . . Jack Hamilton was pitching . . . When the ball was about four feet from my head I knew it was going to get me. And I knew it was going to hurt because Hamilton was such a hard thrower. I was frightened. I threw up my hands in front of my face and saw the ball follow me back and hit me square on the left side of my head . . . Just before everything went dark, I saw the ball bounce straight down on home plate. It was the last thing I saw for several days."

Returning to Boston in 1969, Conigliaro hit .225, slammed twenty home-runs, and batted in eighty-two runs. In 1970 he hit thirty-six home-runs and batted in one-hundred-sixteen runs. After he was traded to the Angels in 1971, Conigliaro announced his retirement later that same year.

Richard Conte

"It was a lucky accident that I got to be an actor," said Nick Conte. "I had no ambitions as a kid. I was a kind of drifter, a guy who hung out on street corners."

In the summer of 1935, while working as a waiter in a Connecticut country club, Conte was called upon to help stage an amateur theatrical show. Robert Lewis and Sanford Meisner, leaders of the Group Theatre, were watching and helped him get into the Neighborhood Playhouse as a scholarship student.

Born March 24, 1914, in Jersey City, New Jersey, Nicholas Conte attended Dickinson High School ("It took me five years to finish the four-year course"). He married actress Ruth Frome in 1943.

He was typed as a dashing villain in his early career ("I got one of Barbara Stanwyck's earrings in my mouth and almost swallowed it during a love scene."), then went on to distinguish himself as a comedian in *Full of Life*.

He made *Oceans Eleven* and *Assault on a Queen* with Sinatra, Martin, Davis, Lawford, et al. Other films are: *Guadalcanal Diary, The Purple Heart, Call Northside 777, Cry of the City, House of Strangers, Thieves Highway, I'll Cry Tomorrow, Brothers Rico, They Came to Condura,* and *The Greatest Story Ever Told,* among others.

Franco Corelli

This radiant tenor turned down a civil service career after vocal studies at the Conservatories of Pesaro and Milan. He won a singing contest in Florence in 1950 and sang on provincial stages and Italian radio for three years, then moved on to La Scala. He quickly achieved stardom on the more important stages in Italy and at the Magio Musical and Arena Festivals.

Born in Ancona, Italy, in 1925, he came to the United States in 1960 to make a very well received debut at the Metropolitan Opera Company as Manrico in *Il Trovatore*. He sang the same role at the Salzburg Festival in 1962.

Married to the soprano Loretta di Lelio, Mr. Corelli has made guest appearances at the Vienna State Opera, Covent Garden, the Paris Opera, and the Chicago and San Francisco Operas.

Michele Corino

Musician, composer, and orchestra leader Michele Corino was born in Cuneo, Italy, April 27, 1918. At the age of ten he was playing the accordion professionally. He made over fifty records in Italy and formed his own orchestra in 1940.

Corino came to the United States in 1947. Some of his noted compositions are *Fisarmonica Impazzita, Fisarmonica Allegra, Dallape* and *Polca Moderna.*

He married Gloria Campanelli in 1948. They have two children, Jeffrey Joseph and Glenn Mario.

ANN CORIO

At a time when theatre audiences would rather pause and reflect on the past than venture forward into uncharted territory, stripper Ann Corio rescued her "lost art form" in an Off-Broadway revue called *This Was Burlesque.* The show was a big smash and has gone on to gross millions with touring companies all over the world.

Born in Hartford, Connecticut, Miss Corio won a dance contest at the age of fifteen and joined a burlesque troupe. Her mother "had never heard of burlesque" and, as Ann recalls, her "great line" that showed her approval of her daughter's chosen profession was: "They look, but no touch."

Some of her Harvard fans who attended her early engagements at Boston's Old Howard (which has since burned down) "are now in very high places in Washington. Green Harvard men were told they couldn't graduate until they had seen Ann Corio."

QUINTIN CRISTY

Born in Brockton, Massachusetts, November 16, 1909, chemical manufacturer Quintin Cristy went to Hollywood at an early age, appearing as a tenor in films, including *Delicious* with Janet Gaynor and sang on the N.B.C. radio network.

Then in 1946, he started his present firm, the Cristy Chemical Corporation, manufacturers of automotive chemicals, with a volume of business in excess of $1,000,000 a year.

Cristy married Helen Alzapiede in 1954. They have two sons: Kevin and Brian.

VIC DAMONE

Heralded as the "world's greatest singer" by Frank Sinatra, Vito Farinola Damone's ups and downs in show business have rarely, if ever, had anything to do with his singing talent. "Success came too early, too fast, and there was too much," admits the disarmingly handsome tenor. "I went from coffee money to five-thousand dollars a week before I was twenty, and I didn't handle it very well."

Born in Brooklyn June 12, 1928, he got his start by singing *There Must Be a Way* to Perry Como between floors on an elevator. With Perry's encouragement, he won a first-place tie on Arthur Godfrey's *Talent Scout* show, which led to a booking arranged by Milton Berle.

After the breakup of his marriage to Pier Angeli (one son, Perry, named after Como), he said, "I want nothing out of life that is not granted to every man. To love and be loved." Now married to Judy Rawlins (one daughter), Damone continues to captivate night club and television audiences.

BOBBY DARIN

Songwriter, actor, singer and television and nightclub entertainer, Bobby Darin combined the clean-cut look of the Sixties with the casual, with-it look of the Seventies. Once called the "angry young man" of show business, he mellowed in his last years without losing any of his dynamic flair for the business.

Walden Robert Cassotto was born May 14, 1936, in the Italian section of East Harlem, New York City. Bobby's father, a cabinet-maker, died shortly before his birth. Bobby's mother, his older sister Vania, and her husband, Charles Maffia, saw him through a series of painful rheumatic fever attacks that continued until he was thirteen years old. For most of this time, the family was on relief or Charles Maffia was working at two jobs to pay the high medical bills.

Unable to attend grammar school, his mother taught him well enough for him to be accepted at the Bronx High School of Science. But the curriculum was difficult, and he was disparaged for his flashy dress and drum playing. "All the arrogance you read about," he once said, "stems from those days in high school. It all stems from a desire to be nobody's fool again."

He became interested in acting at Hunter College, but he was in a hurry. He left college and took odd jobs. "I would work for a month or two, then quit and make the rounds, trying to get something in the theater. But nothing happened."

He took a job as a drummer for a dancer, only to wind up broke and unemployed several months later. He took the name "Darin" from the phone book, got together with another young hopeful, Don Kirshner, and they raised the money to cut two demonstration records by singing radio commercials. Out of that came a contract with Decca Records in 1956, and a spot on the Tommy Dorsey television show, but still nothing happened. He made several unsuccessful records and his contract expired.

Two years later, Atlantic Records signed him and released his own tongue-in-cheek rock and roll number, *Splish Splash*. It was a hit. This was followed by another composition, *Dream Lover*, which established him. Wanting to avoid the fickle tastes of the kids, Darin financed his album, *That's All,* which appealed to a wider market. One of the songs on the album was *Mack the Knife,* taken from Brecht and Weill's *Threepenny Opera*. The album sold almost a half-million copies. *Mack* was released as a single and sold two million. Now Bobby was an "adult" entertainer.

Darin married Sandra Dee in 1961, when he started getting movie roles. They later divorced. Among his movies are: *Come September, Too Late Blues,* and *State Fair*.

Darin died December 20, 1973.

VITTORIO DE FIORI

Born in Venice, Italy, author-journalist Vittorio De Fiori was educated at Tito Livio College and at the Universities of Padua and Zurick. He was an instructor of modern languages before joining the staff of *II Popolo d'Italia* in Milan in 1914.

He then came to New York and founded and edited the Italian publication, *Rinascenza Italica*. He taught Italian at Cornell University in 1943 and now publishes and is editor of *Italamerican*. Among his books are *The Man of Destiny* (1928) and *Italia Incandescente* (1937).

De Fiori married Enrica Laglia in 1947. They have one son, Victor Donatello.

GEORGE DELACORTE

Dell Publishing Company, Dell Books, Laurel Books, Delacorte Press Books, and twenty-five magazines list George Delacorte as Chairman of the Board.

He is the largest comic book publisher in the country, owning, at one time or another, over two hundred magazines, including *Modern Screen, Modern Romance, Inside Detective,* etc.

Born in New York City, June 20, 1894, he was educated at Columbia University and was married to the late Margarita von Doenhoff (six children). He married Valerie Hoecker in 1959.

He is responsible for the Delacorte Theatre, which shows free presentations of Shakespeare in Central Park.

NORMAN DELLO JOIO

It is not a coincidence that Norman Dello Joio's compositions for ballet, opera, symphony and choral groups sound as though they might be influenced by church music. They were. A descendant of three generations of Italian organists, and a student of his godfather, who was the organist at St. Patrick's Cathedral, he became organist and choir director for a church on City Island when he was fourteen years old.

Among his best-known operas is *Triumph of St. Joan,* of which he writes: "Insofar as the little warrior from Lorraine is a symbol for ultimate courage, I feel impelled in this disjointed time to find in her some needed illumination to my own problems."

Born January 24, 1913, in New York City, Mr. Dello Joio attended All Hallows Institute and City College before becoming an instructor at Juilliard Graduate School of Music in 1939. He is married to Grayce Baumgold (four children).

The recipient of many foundation grants, he joined Samuel Barber and Aaron Copland in a tour of Poland in 1947. Among his many and varied compositions are the opera *Blood Moon,* a suite *Meditations on Ecclesiastes,* and *Magnificat.*

MARIO DEL MONACO

Devoted to painting and sculpture, Mario Del Monaco studied at the Conservatory of Pesaro, Italy, to learn those crafts. At the age of twenty he won a prize in a singing contest arranged by the conductor Tullio Serafin in Rome.

He obtained a leave from the army during World War II to make his debut at the Teatro Puccini. After the war (1946), he created a sensation as Radames in *Aida* at the Arena Festival, and in the same year he sang the title role in *Andrea Chénier* at Trieste. A tour with the ensemble of the Teatro San Carlo made him internationally known in 1948.

His career then took him to La Scala, London, Paris, and Vienna. In the summer of 1950, he was applauded at the Teatro Colon and at the San Francisco Opera.

Born in Florence, May 27, 1915, he has been a member of the Metropolitan Opera Company since 1951. His subsequent tours have brought him great acclaim all over the world. He toured the Soviet Union in 1960 and Germany in 1961-1962.

He is one of the finest heroic tenors Italy has produced in the twentieth century, with an elemental power of expression and glowing brightness in the high register. He is especially known for his interpretations of Verdi and Puccini roles.

CHRISTOPHER DEL SESTO

Former Governor Christopher Del Sesto was born in Providence, Rhode Island March 10, 1907. Educated at Boston University and Georgetown University Law School, Del Sesto was admitted to the bar in Washington, D.C. in 1937.

He was an instructor at Boston University and Northeastern University, served on the staff of the U.S. Securities and Exchange Commission, and was special assistant to the Attorney General from 1938 to 1940. He served as Governor of Rhode Island from 1958 to 1960.

Del Sesto married Lola Elda Faraone in 1933. They have two children: Christopher and Ronald.

JOHN DEMARCO

Perhaps one of the most extraordinary careers is that of John De Marco, jack of all trades and master of many. Novelist, businessman, screen writer, poet, musician and actor are but a few skills in his repertoire.

Born of Italian immigrant parents in Welch, West Virginia, September 10, 1934, he showed an early flair for playing guitar and singing. Rather than staying and working in the coal mines with his father and seven brothers, John finished high school and won a scholarship at Morris Harvey College in Charleston. To augment his small income, he began playing in the local night spots, singing country music.

In 1952, he was signed to a contract with Sun Record Company and called immediately to Nashville, Tennessee to make four records. When Sun's president, Simon Judd Phillips, impressed with his musical talents, offered him a job as a session man, or company musician, John decided to forget about college and stay in Nashville.

Though he made an appearance on the Grand Ole Opry and his first record, *Coal Tipple Blues,* made a stir on the country charts because his style resembled that of Hank Williams, John's musical career nonetheless floundered. After cutting several demonstration records for Starway Recording Company, which were never released, De Marco decided to open his own nightclub in Nashville. By featuring such greats as Marty Robbins and Chet Atkins, his venture proved successful, but in 1954 the club was destroyed by fire.

Sun Records re-hired him as a back-up musician, and he played with such country stars as Carl Perkins, Johnny Cash and the "Hillbilly Cat"—Elvis Presley. Presley's first five records were cut at Sun's studios, with John behind him, playing guitar.

In 1956, De Marco left Nashville and toured with top country singer Gene Vincent, who was cashing in on the recent rock and roll popularity. John was instrumental in Vincent's number-one hit—"Be-Bop-A-Lula." "It went higher on the charts than Doris Day," he said smiling.

While recovering from a severe case of mononucleosis, he found time to write a novel about his musical experiences. Called *The Circuit Gods,* it was adapted for NBC's Kraft Theater and televised in 1958 as *The Singing Idol,* starring Tommy Sands.

John resumed his education at West Virginia University and graduated in 1962. Four years later, his first film script, a satire called *Alice in Bongoland,* was produced by London-based Hammer Films. De Marco auditioned for the lead male role and got it.

While staying in London, De Marco joined a theater guild and developed his acting skills. Though Hammer rejected his next script, which he had written especially for Boris Karloff, one of its directors, Freddie Francis, suggested to De Marco that he play a minor role in Hammer's newest picture, *Dracula Has Risen From The Grave* (1968). After that came *The Anniversary* (1968), with Bette Davis, and Terence Fisher's *Frankenstein Must Be Destroyed* (1969), with Peter Cushing.

John De Marco currently lives in New York City, where he

writes and acts. Married to former actress Jill Entsminger, he has finished a novel called *The Morgantown Conspiracy*.

A book of his poetry, *Tides,* won the Dorothy Kendrick Mentor Award for 1971, putting yet another feather in his diverse, almost bizarre hat.

Johnny Desmond

A familiar face in Las Vegas, as well as night clubs all over the country, Johnny Desmond refuses to join the current rock craze ("I can't see myself getting stuck with all that noise").

Born Giovanni Alfredo de Simone, November, 14, 1921, in Detroit, he attended the Conservatory of Music there, later got a job with Gene Krupa, and was "discovered" by Glenn Miller during his Air Force tour.

He is married to Ruth Keddinton (two girls). A star of *Say Darling,* the 1958 musical, he enjoys working in stock.

Fileno Di Gregorio

Industrialist Fileno Di Gregorio was born in Bolognano, Pescara, Italy, January 6, 1885. He came to America in 1912. Determined to get into his own business, he formed the United Lens Company in 1916 on a capital investment of $500. His firm now employs 140 people and is the largest independent manufacturer of lens blanks for the optical industry in the world. His products are used in cameras, projectors, telescopes, microscopes, riflescopes, fire control instruments, binoculars, copy machines, and for space projects.

Di Gregorio has been very active in Massachusetts charitable and civic affairs over the years and has received many honors over the years, including the *Enrico Fermi Award of Merit - Man of the Year*. He married Maria Sonsini in 1911. They have seven children: Conceta, Albert, Richard, Ronald, William, Raymond, and Leonard.

JOE DI MAGGIO

Recently named the "Greatest Living Player" of the game, Joe Di Maggio, the Yankee Clipper, still draws standing ovations from baseball fans all over the country.

Leaving the game with a .325 lifetime batting average, Di Maggio led the Yankees to ten World Championships in the fifteen years he played (1936-1951). His record of hitting safely in fifty-six consecutive games will most probably never be topped.

Fireballer Bobby Feller once said of the shy Yankee, "Maybe Joe has an inferiority complex, but not when he's in uniform."

Born Joseph Paul Di Maggio, November 25, 1914, the eighth of nine children of a San Francisco fisherman, he first married starlet Dorothy Arnold (one son). His second marriage was to Marilyn Monroe.

A fierce competitor, he was awarded the Most Valuable Player trophy three times.

MICHAEL DISALLE

A relentless campaigner and outspoken ex-Governor of Ohio, Michael Di Salle currently makes his home in Washington, D.C., where he works with the law firm of Chapman, Di Salle, & Friedman. But he didn't leave Ohio quietly. "I have less respect for him," Di Salle said of Governor Rhodes, who beat him in 1962, "than for any opponent in my career."

Born January 6, 1908, in New York City, Michael Vincent Di Salle grew up in Toledo, and attended Georgetown University. He married Myrtle England (five children) in 1929 and began his law practice in Toledo in 1932. After becoming mayor of Toledo and balancing the city budget, he was called to Washington to head the Price Stabilization Office in 1950. "I couldn't get elected dog catcher," he said when he left. FDR had once called that post, "the worst job in Washington, next to mine".

Before moving to Washington, he taught history at The University of Massachusetts.

PETER DOMINICK

How does a Yale grad from New England get to be a United States Senator from Colorado? Senator Dominick, while serving his tenth year in that capacity, attributed this act of magic to "the thousands of independents, Republicans and volunteers who did a special job on my behalf."

Born July 7, 1915, in Stamford, Connecticut, Senator Dominick is married to socialite Nancy Parks (four children). Shortly after his admission to the New York Bar, he served in the Air Force (1942-1946), receiving promotions from aviation cadet to captain.

After the war, he settled in Denver and entered politics in the successful senatorial campaign of John Love.

ALFRED DRAKE

"The audience always confuses the actor and his roles," Alfred Drake once told Maurice Zolotow. "An actor begins worrying, *Who am I? What is this acting self? Does society really respect me?* You lose hold of your own ego, then. You feel you've got to find your true identity."

Born Alfred Capurro, October 7, 1914, in the Bronx, New York, he studied under Bernard Grebanier, a Shakespearean scholar, at Brooklyn College. Drake never liked doing Broadway musicals (*Kiss Me Kate* was the exception), and preferred doing straight non-musical Shakespeare and directing classical plays. In 1961 he rejected eight starring roles.

His great success as Curly in *Oklahoma* (1943) was followed by *Kate* (1949), *Kismet* (1953) and *Kean* (1961). In his favorite element, he did an English version of *Rugantino* in 1964.

"I am a little stolid," he declares, smiling. "I don't ride on motorcycles at ninety m.p.h., grow orchids or smoke marijuana."

Divorced from Alma Tollefsen, he is married to Esther Harvey Brown (two daughters).

PETER DUCHIN

"Even if I could play like my father, I wouldn't want to. We belong to different times, and jazz is the language now." Son Peter may not imitate his late father's (Eddy Duchin) great piano style, but he plays some of the same rooms like the St. Regis Hotel.

Born July 29, 1937 (his mother died six days after his birth), Peter was raised by the Averell Harrimans, his godparents. Eddy Duchin was in the Navy at the time.

"I learned to play much against my wishes," he said of his career which began at the age of five. "I would have rather played ball and gone fishing. My father didn't want me to become an orchestra leader . . . he said it was a hard life."

Peter has recorded two albums and looks forward to writing a Broadway musical. "When I've investigated all the stages, then I'll become a composer."

JIMMY DURANTE

James Francis Durante is still going like a house afire. It sometimes takes him a couple of beats to catch up with the material but, other than that he is the same all-stops-out song plugger who opened the Club Durant (he couldn't afford to put the "e" in lights) in New York City in 1923, with his lifelong friends, Eddie Jackson and Lou Clayton.

While running the speakeasy, the team appeared in Ziegfeld's *Show Girl, The New Yorkers* and the film *Roadhouse Nights* (1929). The Schnozzola (Lou Clayton's nickname for his nose, which is insured with Lloyd's of London for a million dollars against any possible "catastroscope") left the team to go to Hollywood where he made *Get Rich Wallingford, Irene and Mary, The Passionate Plumber,* and *Sally,* among other films.

Returning to Broadway in 1936, he did the musicals: *Jumbo, Strike Me Pink, Red Hot and Blue, Stars in Your Eyes,* etc. His radio malapropisms became a trademark, as did the "Goodnight, Mrs. Calabash, wherever you are" sign-off of his successful television series. Jimmy came full circle in his career in the movie version of *Jumbo.*

John Barrymore reportedly once remarked, "You know, Jimmy, you should play *Hamlet.*" To which Jimmy replied, "To hell with them small towns. New York is the only place for me."

In 1960 he married his second wife, Margie Little (two adopted daughters). He was born February 10, 1893 in New York City.

VINCENT EDWARDS

Ben Casey put away his scapel in 1966 after five years of stern, no-nonsense bedside manners that captivated as many as thirty-two million television viewers. Vince Edwards is now trying to undo the Casey image by concentrating on feature films.

Born Vincento Eduardo Zoino, July 7, 1928, in Brooklyn, Edwards attended Ohio State University and the University of Hawaii, where he became interested in dramatics. Returning to New York, he studied at the American Academy of Dramatic Arts and made his Broadway debut as a chorus boy in *High Button Shoes.*

Always an excellent athlete, he won the "Mr. Universe" contest and went to Hollywood to make the movie of the same name. Many movies and several television anthology shows *(Alfred Hitchcock Presents, The Untouchables, Studio One,* etc.) later, he was finally "discovered" for the role of Ben Casey. "Big deal. I'm an eleven-year overnight sensation," he said.

Briefly married to Kathy Kersh (one daughter), his second wife is Linda Ann Foster. His motion pictures include: *Rogue Cop, Three Faces of Eve, Night Holds Terror, City of Fear, Murder by Contract, The Killing,* and *Too Late the Blues.*

MEADE HENRY ESPOSITO

When he was chosen as leader of the Democratic Party in Brooklyn, New York, in 1969, Meade Esposito took the reins of the most powerful Democratic organization in the United States with the possible exception of Mayor Richard Daley's position in Chicago. In this age of streamlined politics, former New York City Mayor Robert F. Wagner called Esposito, "a new breed of old line boss".

Born in Brooklyn, he was the son of Giuseppe Esposito, a carpenter who left Italy at the age of eighteen to seek his fortune in America around the turn of the century. Giuseppe managed to save enough money to buy a saloon. Meade (Amadeo) was born and the family lived in the rooms above the saloon. Hard work was the order of the day.

After finishing elementary school, young Meade dropped out and took a job as office boy in an insurance business run by former U.S. Marshal Jim Powers, a local Democratic leader, and the Democratic Party became his life's work.

Realizing he wasn't going to get a formal education, he would read an average of three to four hours every night. "I read everything from Mickey Mouse to Plato."

Aware of the possibility that the Italian-American community had a lot to gain through political activity, he started his own political club at the age of eighteen and merged his club with the regular Democratic organization three years later.

Esposito's political career grew quietly for the next thirty years while he weathered the depression as a wholesale beer salesman. He ran his own surety bond business for twelve years before becoming vice-president of a bank and then vice-president of an insurance brokerage firm.

He never ran for office but worked in many campaigns in local elections, helping to launch the careers of several public figures.

In 1960, at the age of 51, he and Mrs. Shirley Weiner were elected Democratic leader and co-leaders in their district of Carnarsie, with the endorsement of Eleanor Roosevelt and Herbert Lêhman, the totems of the Manhattan reform movement. They have won every year since without opposition.

"I like being part of the scheme of things," he told a *New York Times* reporter in 1972. "Politics is fascinating, vicious, unpredictable, demeaning, and it's very satisfying."

Married to the former Ann De Cunzo, the Espositos have one daughter, Phyllis.

FABIAN

If all the singers from Philadelphia were laid end to end, they would probably reach all the way to Hollywood and Vine. Such a Philadelphian, Fabian Forte attracted the eye of a talent scout and made such a trip to California in 1958. His handsome features, which slightly resembled those of Elvis Presley, and well-edited voice put him briefly on the top of the music heap and made him a bonafide American millionaire by the age of eighteen. He ignored the critics who said he couldn't sing and cried all the way to the bank.

Fabian was an enigma to the music business—a manufactured product, promoted and sold to the public. He arrived after a huge advertising campaign. Lacking a singing voice, his records were composites of many tapes edited together, and even then his hits— *Hound Dog Man, Turn Me Loose* and *Tiger*—sounded less than professional.

He was born February 6, 1943, to Dominic and Josephine Forte.

In the early sixties he bought his way out of the corporation which had formed around him and went to Hollywood. He had a disappointing first outing in the movie *Hound Dog Man,* but bounced back quickly by his excellent portrayals of a psychopathic killer in the television serial *Bus Stop* and as John Wayne's kid brother in *The Sons Of Katy Elder.*

JOHN FANTE

Novelist-screenwriter John Thomas Fante has contributed to the body of Italian-American fiction for over thirty years. His characterization of the immigrant father determined to build his children a fireplace (*Full of Life*) won him an Academy Award nomination in 1957.

A contributor to many national magazines and recipient of the National Catholic Theatre Drama award in 1964, he was born in Denver, Colorado, April 8, 1909. He married Joyce Smart in 1937, and they have four children.

His novels include *Wait Until Spring Bandini* (1938), *Ask The Dust* (1939), and *Full of Life* (1952). Among Fante's screenplays are *Walk on the Wild Side, Reluctant Saint*, and *My Six Loves* (1962).

LAURA FERMI

Author and widow of Enrico Fermi, the Nobel Prize atomic scientist, Laura Fermi found it difficult to hold her esteemed husband in awe. "He is the man I cook and iron shirts for. How can I take him that seriously?"

A celebrity in her own right, she has written *Mussolini, Atoms for the World,* and *Atoms for the Family*. When writing the latter, she confessed, "My Italian had become very rusty. My English, although it was getting good, was not entirely fluent. So here I was torn, or rather stuck, between two languages - one half-learned, the other half-forgotten."

Born in Rome, in 1907, she has two children. She was the winner of the Friends of Literature Prize in 1968.

FRANK FONTAINE

Mr. and Mrs. Frank Fontaine's eleven children have provided them with a way of life. "Success?" Frank asks. "What is it? It's not five million dollars. I'd call it contentment. It's your being contented and your family being contented."

A long-time radio personality, Fontaine had been doing his characterization of "Crazy Googenheim" for twenty-five years before he became a regular on the Jackie Gleason show in 1962. Gleason is to be credited with the discovery of Fontaine's singing voice. He heard him singing in the dressing room and decided to put it in the show.

Born in Haverhill, Massachusetts, in 1920, Fontaine is adamant about not letting any job take him away from his family. "Honest to Pete," says Fontaine's manager, Joe Lyttle, "I've seen him turn down things you wouldn't believe - Hollywood, the Palladium and even Las Vegas. You name it, he won't do it."

Says Fontaine, "When I was a boy, my father was in vaudeville and my mother went with him. Sometimes my brother and I went with them and I went to fifty-three schools. But sometimes we didn't, and we were boarded out. And I don't want my kids ever missing going to the ball game, or being with Dad over any Christmas holidays or birthdays or times like that."

TONY FRANCIOSA

"Okay, so I belonged to the torn T-shirt school of acting," admits Actors Studio grad, Anthony Papaleo, "but I always wore a clean T-shirt under it."

Franciosa is a gut actor, and the audience always knows there is a lot more than a T-shirt under the performances he gives on the stage and screen. His anger used to surface in public until he decided that "a chip on the shoulder can weigh as much as a boulder."

Born October 25, 1928, in East Harlem, the son of a contractor, Franciosa worked as a dishwasher, awning installer, welder, doorman and ship waiter before making his debut on Broadway in *End as a Man* (1953). Then he starred in *A Hatful of Rain* (he later won an Academy Award nomination for the film version), followed by *A Face in the Crowd* (1957). His off-Broadway appearances include *Hamlet* and *Six Characters in Search of an Author*.

Formerly married to Beatrice Bakalyar and Shelly Winters, he married Judy Balaban in 1961. His films include *Long, Hot Summer, Wild Is the Wind* (1958), *Naked Maja* (1959), *Go Naked in the World* (1962), *Senelita* (1962), *Period of Adjustment* (1962); and in 1966 he made *Assault on a Queen, A Man Could Get Killed,* and *The Swinger*.

CONNIE FRANCIS

Concetta Franconero was studying psychology at Rutgers when her father suggested she record the old favorite, "Who's Sorry

Now?'' The psychology worked and the record (1957) sold more than a million copies within six months.

Born December 12, 1938 in Newark, New Jersey, Connie sang and played the accordion at benefits, lodge celebrations, church socials, and other community functions for many of her early years. In 1950 she got a spot on George Scheck's television variety show, *Startime;* Scheck later became her personal manager. After winning Arthur Godfrey's *Talent Scouts* first prize, she began to sing in clubs and cocktail lounges around the country, aided by a doctored identification card. Scheck got her a contract with MGM Records in 1955, and she cut ten singles, none of which was a hit. Rejections from night clubs and television shows followed.

Discouraged, she went on to college, fully prepared to give up show business completely. She made "Who's Sorry Now?" to fulfill the last record on her MGM contract. It was a hit.

Then Miss Francis struck while the iron was hot with such successes as: "My Happiness," "Everybody's Somebody's Fool," "My Heart Has a Mind of Its Own," "Lipstick on Your Collar," "Frankie," "Mama," and "Where the Boys Are."

A big hit in Europe, she has traveled literally all over the world and appeared with such television stars as Jimmie Rodgers, Dick Clark, Perry Como, Jack Benny, and Ed Sullivan. Her first film was *Where the Boys Are* (1960).

Antonio Frasconi

Born in Buenos Aires, Argentina, April 28, 1919, while his parents were en route from Brazil to Uruguay, Antonio Frasconi was moved to Montevideo when he was two weeks old.

The son of a sea cook, he helped his mother run the family restaurant and studied art at night. For years he practiced his art "as something naughty, something hidden."

Now one of the few contemporary artists to achieve an international reputation solely through a graphic medium, Frasconi is largely responsible for setting the character and standards of the current revival of the woodcut in America.

Finding his subject matter in everyday experiences, Frasconi's style is strongly decorative and often humorous. William S. Liebermann, curator of prints and drawings at the Museum of Modern Art, has pointed out: "Whatever his work, he never forgets that, at its best, the woodcut is the most direct of the graphic processes. He always exploits the most obvious virtue of the medium - the very texture of the wood itself."

Frasconi has had more than sixty one-man shows in the United States, Europe, and Latin America. He has illustrated prize-winning books for children and adults, magazine covers, Christmas cards, appointment calendars, record album covers and book jackets. His widest distribution came in 1963, when his design for a United States postage stamp was reprinted 120,000,000 times.

At nineteen Frasconi became a political cartoonist for a satirical newspaper in Montevideo. He came to America to study at the Art Students League in New York City in 1945. After one year of study there, he went to California, working as a gardener, then as a guard at the Santa Barbara Museum of Art, which gave him his first American one-man show in 1946.

Among his books are: *Twelve Fables of Aesop* (1955), *See and Say* (1955), *The House that Jack Built* (1958), *The Snow and the Sun* (1961), *Woodcuts 1957* (1957), *A Whitman Portrait* (1960), *A Vision of Thoreau* (1965), *Unstill Life* (1969), and Melville's *On the Slain Collegians* (1971).

In Art in America, Charlotte Willard wrote of his series of prints, *Oda a Lorca,* (1963), "Frasconi seems to be one of the few artists who have not abdicated their brotherhood with man. He makes us feel that in the death of a poet, we have all died a little."

Married to the former Leona Pierce, also an artist, Frasconi lives in South Norwalk, Connecticut with their two sons, Pablo and Miguel. He believes that "An artist must be aware of the comic strip as well as of the serious side of life."

FOSTER FURCOLO

Ex-Governor of Massachusetts, Foster Furcolo was born in New Haven, Connecticut, July 29, 1911. He received his law degree from Yale in 1937.

After World War II, in which he served in the Navy in the South Pacific, Furcolo was elected to Congress for two terms, 1948 to 1952. He then served as State Treasurer of Massachusetts in 1952, and was elected Governor of that state in 1956. He wrote *Let George Do It* in 1957.

Furcolo married Katheryn Forhan in 1936. They have three children: Charles Mark, David and Foster, Jr.

PAUL GALLICO

It took Paul William Gallico quite a while to learn how to experience life vicariously. As a young sportswriter for the *Daily News,* he went a round with Jack Dempsey ("I know everything I need to know about being hit in the ring"), played golf against Bobby Jones, hit against Dizzy Dean, and even swam against Eleanor Holm.

Not at all pleased with his sports forecasts ("I was usually wrong"), he capped his fourteen-year stay with that newspaper by becoming the assistant managing editor. He served in both World Wars as soldier and correspondent, receiving the Victory Medal (1918) and Ribbon with battle star (1945).

Born July 26, 1897 in a boardinghouse in New York City, Gallico is the son of a Triestian musician who made his first trip to America at the age of fourteen, to become a concert pianist.

Best known for his excellence as a short story writer, Gallico is married to Baroness Virginia Falz-Fein, his fourth wife. His screenplays include *Pride of the Yankees*, *The Clock*, and *Lili*. Among his many published works are: *Adventures With Hiram Holliday*, 1939; *The Snow Goose*, 1941; *The Lonely*, 1947; *Jennie*, 1950; *The Small Miracle*, 1952 (from which he wrote the screenplay *Never Take No for an Answer*); *Love of Seven Dolls*, 1954; *Tomasina*, 1957; *Confessions of a Story-Teller*, 1961; *Love, Let Me Not Hunger*, 1963; *The Man Who Was Magic*, 1966; and *The Poseidon Adventure*, 1969.

JOE GARAGIOLA

"I once played with a baseball team that was so bad, we'd have a victory celebration when the game was rained out." Such quips have caused Joe Garagiola to be called the Will Rogers of baseball. A much better catcher than he would have you believe, he started with the St. Louis Cardinals (1946-1951) and later played for the Pirates, Cubs and Giants. An injury helped him make his decision to switch to broadcasting, where he did double duty for NBC as a regular on the *Today* show and the host of the quiz show *Sale of the Century*.

Born February 12, 1926, in St. Louis, he grew up with Yogi Berra, with whom he was discovered playing sandlot ball. Married to Audrie Ross (three children), he is the author of *Baseball is a Funny Game*.

BEN GAZZARA

An actor since the age of twelve, Ben Gazzara gets his talent from the most natural source possible, "My mother laughs, cries, screams and carries on within five minutes with all the fervor of a real actress. I only need to watch her to get any inspiration I need."

Born August 28, 1930, in New York City, Gazzara has done well in every medium. He is married to his second wife, actress Janice Rule (two stepchildren).

Broadway: *Night Circus* (1955); *End as a Man; Cat on a Hot Tin Roof* (1955); *A Hatful of Rain* (1957); *Strange Interlude* (1963); and *Traveller Without Luggage* (1964).

Television: *Arrest and Trial* (1963-1964) and *Run For Your Life* (1965-1968).

Motion Pictures: *The Strange One* (1957); *Anatomy of a Murder* (1959); *The Young Doctors* (1961); *Convicts Four* (1961); *Captive City* (1962); *A Rage To Live* (1964); *Bridge at Remagen* (1969); and *Husbands* (1970).

PETER GENNARO

In the past ten years Peter Gennaro has displayed his choreographing and dancing talents on the television shows of Perry Como, Polly Bergen, Andy Williams, Bob Crosby, Judy Garland, Bing Crosby, and Ed Sullivan. Ten years before that he was a semi-permanent fixture on Broadway. Among his shows were: *Kiss Me Kate, Guys and Dolls, Pajama Game, Bells Are Ringing, Seventh Heaven, Fiorello,* and *West Side Story.*

Born in New Orleans in 1924, he met wife Jean Kinsella, a former ballet dancer, on his first dancing job with the San Carlo Opera Company. They have two children. Recipient of many awards, he was originally tending bar for his father when he "decided he was better off tapping floors than beer."

DUSOLINA GIANNINI

Soprano Dusolina Giannini was born December 19, 1902 in Philadelphia to the Italian tenor Ferruccio Giannini and the pianist Antonietta Briglia-Giannini. To round out this most talented family, her brother Vittorio became a composer.

After her studies with her parents, she became a pupil of Marcella Sembrich and gave her first concert in Carnegie Hall in 1923, followed by concerts in London and Berlin. In 1925 she made her stage debut at the Hamburg State Opera as *Aida.* She continued making guest appearances all over the world before joining the Metropolitan Opera Company from 1936 to 1941.

She undertook another European tour in 1947. Since 1962 she has conducted an opera studio in Zurich.

ROCKY GRAZIANO

Any legitimate conversation on the subject of boxing will eventually cover the knock-down-drag-out bouts between Rocky Graziano and Tony Zale. The likeable ex-middleweight champion is right at home, whether matching wits with Johnny Carson or trying to figure out which spoon to use at a posh DuPont dinner party.

Born Rocco Barbella, June 7, 1922, in New York City, he left school in the seventh grade, hung around the gym, then returned to boxing after a hitch in the army. "If I hadn't gone back, I would have wound up in jail," he said. "I was a loused-up kid."

About his career in television, he says, "I never knew it could be this way. I get paid because people laugh instead of stand up and scream for me to belt somebody."

Paul Newman starred in the film of Rocky's life, *Somebody Up There Likes Me.*

VINCENT IMPELLITTERI

Born in Palermo, Italy, February 4, 1900, Vincent Impellitteri was brought to the United States when he was one year old. He graduated from Fordham University Law School in 1924, served as Assistant District Attorney from 1929 to 1937 and as secretary to Supreme Court Justices Schmuck and Gavagan.

Impellitteri was elected mayor of New York City in 1950, running on the Experience Party ticket. He defeated the nominees of the Democratic and Republican county organizations, the first such victory in the history of a mayoralty that goes back to 1665.

Very active in Italian-American affairs, he married Elizabeth McLaughlin in 1926.

FRANKIE LAINE

After ten years of singing for spaghetti diners, Frankie Laine recorded *That's My Desire,* which eventually sold two million copies. "Those of us who didn't hit quick with one record," he recalls, "had time to survive a series of misfortunes and starvation. By the time we were lucky and made it, we were pros."

Born Frank Paul Lo Vecchio on March 30, 1913 in Chicago, he was already seasoned when a record company executive heard his restaurant singing. He followed his hit with others (ten records in the million-plus category). Among them are: *Mule Train* (1949); *Jezabel* (1951); *I Believe* (1952); *My Heart Goes Where the Wild Goose Goes;* and *Moonlight Gambler.*

Laine has worked in practically every form of entertainment: nightclubs, movies, stage, and television. He has also composed songs, is the president of five music companies and a personal management firm. He loves golf, horses and sponsors a Little League baseball team. He is married to Nan Gray (two children by her former marriage).

He has been given the dubious compliment of having started the long trail of loud singing and gymnastics. To which he says, "As you get older, you tone down your act. Once you become accepted, it is the singing that you want to be accepted for and not the trappings."

Frankie Laine recently "came back" with a top-seller, *You Gave Me A Mountain.*

ELISSA LANDI

Elissa Landi was born in Venice on December 6, 1904. Her pursuit of a stage career led her to London where she made her debut in *The Storm,* which ran for five months. It was a great success and she followed it with leads in *Lavender Ladies, The Constant Nymph,* and many other stage roles. A beauty with light auburn hair and green eyes, she was immediately snatched up by foreign film companies and starred in eight pictures in two years.

She went to New York to play the role of Catherine Barclay in the stage version of *Farewell to Arms.* The play was not successful, but Elissa received six motion picture offers. Her first Hollywood part was in *Body and Soul,* opposite Charles Farrell.

She made films throughout the thirties for Paramount, Fox and United Artists. Perhaps her most famous roles were in *The Sign of the Cross* (1932), a Cecil B. DeMille spectacular starring Fredric March, Claudette Colbert and Charles Laughton; *Enter Madame* (1935), in which she co-starred with Cary Grant; *The Count of Monte*

Cristo (1934), opposite Robert Donat; and at least twelve other pictures. Aside from the stage and screen, Elissa found success as a writer and poetess. She died in 1948.

MARIO LANZA

History repeated itself! Richard Hageman, who conducted the orchestra while Enrico Caruso sang "Vesti La Giubba" from *Pagliacci* in the 1917 Liberty Bond Drive at the Metropolitan Opera House, directed Mario Lanza in the identical scene for the film, *The Great Caruso*. Like the man he portrayed, Mario Lanza was an Italian and a famous tenor whose career skyrocketed through his short life.

He was born January 31, 1921, in Philadelphia and educated in the Berkshire School of Music. He performed for Victor Recordings and was successful on radio and concert tours.

Lanza's short, tempestuous career embraced radio, concert, opera, recording and motion pictures. He was the first vocalist in the history of Victor Red Seal (his recording company) to receive a golden disc, for *Be My Love*. He was also the first singer in recording history to sell two and a half million albums. He received the greatest royalty check ever given a singer for a ten month period— $746,000 in 1951.

His screen appearances besides *The Great Caruso* include, *That Midnight Kiss, Toast of New Orleans, Because You're Mine* and *Serenade*. He made appearances in *Winged Victory* and *Seven Hills of Rome*. For the first time in motion picture history, the cameras stayed on the close-up of an artist for the full length of an aria when Lanza sang "Celeste Aida" in *That Midnight Kiss*.

His death on October 7, 1959, was a shock to all his admirers and followers. Mario Lanza was only thirty-eight years old.

LIBERACE

Wladziu Valentino Liberace was born in 1919 in Menasha, Wisconsin, son of an Italian-born father and a Polish mother. His father, Salvatore, a musician who played the French horn, taught Wladziu and his older brother George to play musical instruments.

Both Lee (as Liberace was called) and George got their start in show business in Milwaukee theaters, then later went on the road with bands and orchestras. Lee played piano, George violin.

Liberace is basically a showman. To his piano playing, he adds a liberal sprinkling of corn, ham and humor.

When he landed his own television show in 1952, Lee brought his brother George into the act to conduct the orchestra and play violin. The show caught on with viewers all over the country, especially older women, and Liberace skyrocketed to fame.

In 1954, the Liberace syndicated show was carried by 192 stations throughout the country. Throughout the mid-fifties the pianist was one of television's top-paid entertainers. He and George drew top billing at state fairs and in Las Vegas.

The brothers made one film, *Sincerely Yours,* in 1955. Liberace's trademarks are his candelabrum, which is always placed atop his grand piano, his sugary voice, his sequined clothes, and his Mother Liberace ("Mama"), who dotes constantly on her boys. She frequently made guest appearances on the show.

Few acts took more criticism or ridicule from the press. Music critics were particularly contemptuous of Lee's piano and George's violin. Lee frequently made a reply to this, saying he was crying "all the way to the bank."

Though he was the darling of nearly every American woman over forty, Liberace was generally unpopular with male audiences, who objected to his now-famous distinct manner of speech, his gaudy sequined costumes, and his weekly dedications "for Mama."

In 1957, a mutual jealousy, which friends say existed from the beginning in Milwaukee, came to a head, and George left the act. Mother Liberace publicly threatened not to speak to either of them until they made up. George continued on his own, however, entered several business ventures, and conducted his orchestra. He died in the late Sixties.

Liberace now lives in a Hollywood mansion and continually makes appearances around the country and on television.

ROLAND VICTOR LIBONATI

Former Congressman Roland Victor Libonati was born in Chicago, December 29, 1900. A graduate of the University of Michigan and Northwestern Law School, Libonati received his Doctor of Jurisprudence degree in 1924.

After serving as a lieutenant in the Army during World War I, Libonati finished his education and went into politics, serving in

Chicago and the Illinois General Assemblies for thirty years before being elected to the United States Congress in 1957. He was re-elected in 1958, 1960 and 1962.

Libonati married Jeanette Van Hanxleden in 1942. They have one child, Michael Ernest.

FERDINAND LIVA

Violinist, conductor and concert master Ferdinand Liva was born in Naples, Italy, February 8, 1912. He joined the Sacchini Theatre of Pozzuoli, Italy, as a violinist at the age of thirteen, rising to the position of first violin and conductor within three years.

Liva then settled in Scranton, Pennsylvania after studying under Bernard Sinshimer and Theodore Pashkus in New York City from 1931 to 1937. He was musical director of the Italian Radio Hour, Scranton, from 1936 to 1941, organized the Scranton Youth Symphony in 1941, and has been concert master of the Scranton Philharmonic Orchestra and Scranton-Wilkes-Barre Symphonette since 1939.

Liva married Anna Vanko, pianist and teacher, in 1936.

VINCE LOMBARDI

Football fans all over the country were deeply shocked by the passing of Vince Lombardi in 1970. Formerly one of the "Seven Blocks of Granite" at Fordham University and the winningest coach in professional football, Lombardi was the personification of endurance in American sports.

Vincent Thomas Lombardi was born in the Sheepshead Bay section of Brooklyn on June 11, 1913. As a boy he planned to enter the Roman Catholic priesthood, but his love for sports began to show at St. Francis Preparatory School, where he played football, baseball, basketball, and was on the track team.

He earned a B.S. degree in business with honors from Fordham University in 1937. As a scrapping lineman, he won three letters in football and the reputation for violent charges that made him appear twice as large as his 172 pounds.

He worked as an insurance salesman, played professional football on weekends and studied law at night. He took his first coaching job in 1939 at St. Cecilia High School in Englewood, New

Jersey. For an annual salary of $1700 he assisted the football coach, taught physics, chemistry, algebra, and Latin. At one stretch his football team won thirty-six straight games.

He returned to Fordham as freshman coach in 1947 and installed the T formation offense. Then he moved on to the United States Military Academy at West Point in 1949 to coach under Colonel Earl "Red" Blaik. Of Blaik's training Lombardi later said: "The most important thing that ever happened to me in football was the opportunity to coach under Colonel Blaik. Whatever success I have had must be attributed to 'the old man.' He molded my methods and my whole approach to the game. The unqualified superlative is precarious, but if there is a Number One coach of all time, in my opinion it is Colonel Blaik."

He took his knowledge of the T attack to the New York Giants where he was hired as offensive coach in 1954. According to former Giant halfback Frank Gifford: "Vinnie didn't understand our game when he first came here . . . At first, we players were showing him how it went. By the end of the year, though, he was showing us."

Basing his game on defense and making the proper trades to achieve a strong defensive team, Lombardi said, "A good defense will help the club's morale." The Giants finished that season with a seven and five record, having lost nine games the season before. In 1956 the Giants won their first NFL championship since 1938.

Lombardi signed a five-year contract as head coach and general manager of the Green Bay Packers in 1959. The team had been poorly managed by forty-five directors from all over the state and was known as the Siberia of the National Football League, where coaches from other teams threatened to send errant players. Lombardi demanded and got complete control over the team. He realized most of the talent was there and he set out to mold them into a winning team. "Before Lombardi arrived," said Paul Hornung, former Packer halfback, "I was a jumping jack. Once I was a quarterback, then a fullback. I never knew where I might end up. When he came, everything changed. He said, 'You're going to be my left halfback, period.' Having a coach's backing was like coming out of the dark."

And out of the dark they came. The Packers won the Western Conference titles in 1960, 1961, and 1962 and won the NFL championship in 1961 and 1962, beating his old team, the New York Giants. He added three more world titles in 1965, 1966, and 1967.

The miracle man of football moved over to the Washington Redskins shortly before his death. He left a widow, the former Marie Planitz, whom he married in 1940, and two children.

Luigi Lucioni

For over fifty years Luigi Lucioni has been contributing to the rich art history of the United States. His paintings and etchings are represented in many of the country's museums, galleries, and colleges. Among them are: The Metropolitan Museum of Art, Whitney Museum of American Art, Denver Art Museum, the Library of Congress, Carnegie Institute, and Dartmouth College.

Born in Malnate, Italy, November 4, 1900, Lucioni was brought to this country when he was eleven. He became a naturalized citizen in 1922. He studied at the Cooper Union Art School and the National Academy of Design.

Lucioni has been awarded the Tiffany medal, 1928; Allied Artists medal of honor, 1929; the first popular prize at Biennial, Washington, 1939, 1941, 1949; and the Purchase Prize, at the Library of Congress, 1946.

A bachelor, Mr. Lucioni lives and works in Greenwich Village, New York City.

Salvador Luria

Three Italian-Americans have won the Nobel Prize. Enrico Fermi and Emilio Segre were awarded the coveted honor in 1938 and 1959, respectively. In 1969, Salvador Luria became the third, sharing the Nobel Prize with Max Delbruck and Alfred D. Hershey. These three distinguished biologists were honored for "discoveries concerning the replication mechanism and the genetic structure of viruses" that "set the solid foundation on which modern molecular biology rests."

Salvador Edward Luria was born in Turin, Italy, August 13, 1912. He took his M.D. degree with highest honors at the University of Turin in 1935. For the next three years he served as a medical officer in the Italian army, turning his attention to mathematics and physics. His interest in bacteriophages (a virus which infects bacteria) started in 1938, when he struck up a conversation with a fellow sitting next to him on a trolley car in Rome. "He told me he was working with bacteriophages. We became friends, and I started working for him a few weeks later."

As a research assistant at Columbia University from 1940 to 1942, Dr. Luria continued his study of bacteriophages. He went to Vanderbilt University in Nashville, Tennessee on a Guggenheim fellowship and met Delbruck and Hershey there. They were also doing work on the bacteriophages. The three men collaborated at

Vanderbilt and continued to exchange information after going their separate ways.

Giants in the scientific field recognized and respected Luria as a "rare kind of biologist . . . a man of extraordinary scope and flexibility."

The team's first difficulty was to actually see the virus they were trying to isolate. They marked the bacteriophages with a radioactive substance, irradiated them with ultraviolet rays, and picked up the virus' images with the newly invented electron microscope. They discovered that viruses mutate, or change their characteristics from one generation to another.

The team's pioneering work has contributed immeasurably to the fight against virus diseases; their work was the foundation of the success of James Watson, who took his doctorate under Luria, and Francis Crick. In 1953, Watson and Crick succeeded in identifying the structure of the typical DNA molecule, enabling scientists to translate the hereditary process into simple chemical terms. Later breakthroughs have brought us even closer to being able to manipulate man's genetic future. Luria warned, however, that this manipulation would be very dangerous unless present-day society, with its "distorted priorities," is reformed. "Basically we need to create a society in which technology is purposefully directed toward socially chosen goals."

Dr. Luria has written a textbook, *General Virology* (1967, revised), and contributed many articles to scientific journals. He married Zella Hurwitz, now a psychologist at Tufts University. They have one son.

Luria believes the poor in this country are victims of the war in Vietnam and our overgrown defense programs. He donated a large portion of his share of the Nobel Prize to several antiwar groups.

Henry Mancini

Most motion picture theme music lurks in the background, content to fill silence. Not so with Mancini scores. His music is up front, integrated with the pace and emotional level of the story, but never obtrusively detracting from it. The audiences love it, the stars of the films he scores love it, and Mr. Mancini has a lot of money and a brace of Oscars to show for his talent.

This gift expresses itself in bold and unorthodox instrumentation. The cool, driving jazz of a small combo set the mood for the television series *Peter Gunn*. The lush, big sound of strings and organ gave *Mr. Lucky* the music of a winner. And who can forget the marvelous score of the movie, *Breakfast at Tiffany's?*

Born April 16, 1924, in Cleveland, Ohio, Henry started playing the piccolo at the age of eight, quickly switched to the flute, and added the piano when he was twelve. His father forced him to practice until he fell in love with jazz.

In high school he knew every Glenn Miller arrangement by heart (knowledge which would later earn him his first Academy Award nomination for scoring *The Glenn Miller Story*). He studied at the Music School of Carnegie Institute of Technology in Pittsburgh, and then enrolled at the Juilliard School of Music in New York City.

After serving in the Army Infantry, he joined the Glenn Miller band, reorganized under Tex Beneke in 1945, and continued to study under composers Mario Castelnuovo-Tedesco and Ernst Krenek, and with Dr. Alfred Sendry.

He joined the composing staff of Universal-International Pictures in 1952 and contributed to over a hundred films over a period of six years, including: *The Benny Goodman Story* (1956); Orson Welles' *Touch of Evil* (1958); and *Voice in the Mirror* (1958).

A chance meeting with producer-director Blake Edwards outside a barbershop in 1958 became a turning point in Mancini's career. Edwards asked him if he would score *Peter Gunn,* a mystery series he was producing for television. He agreed and Edwards later credited him with half of the success of the series. He teamed with Edwards again for *Mr. Lucky.*

Mancini married Virginia O'Connor, formerly a singer with the Mellolarks, in 1947. They have three children and a mantel cluttered with statuettes representing awards for his albums and film scores: *Hatari, Experiment in Terror, Days of Wine and Roses, Charade, The Pink Panther, Dear Hearts,* and others.

JERRE MANGIONE

Author Jerre Mangione is finding his life at its most productive point at the age when most men retire. He has been a faculty member at the University of Pennsylvania since 1961, where he teaches Contemporary Art, English, and directs the university's writing program. His most recent volumes include: *Night Search,* 1965; *Life Sentences for Everybody,* 1966; *A Passion for Sicilians,* 1968; and *American Is Also Italian,* 1969.

Born March 20, 1909, in Rochester, New York (he received the Key to the City in 1963), he married Patricia Polizzi in 1957. A graduate of Syracuse University, he worked as a writer for *Time Magazine* in 1931. His next post was that of book editor for Robert M. McBride & Company (New York City) from 1934 to 1937. He was national coordinating editor of the Federal Writers' Project (1937-1939) and the special assistant to the U.S. commissioner for immigration and naturalization (1942-1948).

Among Mr. Mangione's earlier works are: *Mount Allegro,* 1943; *Ship and the Flame,* 1948; and *Reunion in Sicily,* 1950.

CHARLIE MANNA

"You guys are in big trouble now," Charles Manna says, playing Julius Caesar in his comedy act. "Here comes my good buddy Brutus."

One of America's most likable comedians, he chooses material with a range wide enough to appeal to all age groups. He is equally at home performing at Radio City Music Hall and at Manhattan's Bon Soir.

Born Charles J. Manna, October 6, 1925, in the Bronx, New York, he showed singing talent at five and had memorized many Italian operatic arias by the time he was twelve. Entering the Army Special Services in 1942, he wrote, produced and appeared in revues. "Once I heard those laughs," he recalls, "I was hooked."

Back in New York in 1950, he attended the Third Street School of Music, still hoping for an operatic career; but he continued to write comedy sketches which he gave at house parties. Carl Reiner heard him and directed him to the William Morris Agency. They gave him his first booking on the Borscht Circuit, and he went on to perform at the top supper clubs in the country. Guest shots on such television shows as Jackie Gleason, Garry Moore, and Ed Sullivan followed. His flair for original comedy received good reviews from such columnists as Dorothy Kilgallen, Lee Mortimer and Walter Winchell.

In 1961 Decca Records released his first album, *Manna Overboard,* which included a sketch about an astronaut who refused to be launched until his box of crayons were returned. The album was released only two weeks before Alan Shepard made his historic ride in space. Shepard's doctor handed him a box of crayons just before takeoff, and he commented, "This was a real tension breaker." Manna's album soared almost as high as Shepard did. He did well with a subsequent album called *Manna Alive!*.

He is married to Florence Post, who sometimes helps her husband in the writing of his material. They have two children. About his art, he says, "Comedy is a subject that everyone feels he can discuss with authority. Yet comedy is the most complex of all the arts, and certainly the most elusive."

ALFRED MARCELLO

Journalist Alfred Marcello was born in Providence, Rhode Island, April 19, 1904. In the newspaper business since 1923, Marcello worked for fourteen years on the News-Tribune of Providence as reporter, drama critic, city editor, and news editor. He has been Day City Editor for the Worcester (Massachusetts) Telegram since 1949.

Among Marcello's many awards are: Outstanding Service Award by President Eisenhower's Committee on Employment of the Physically Handicapped (1956); Pall Mall's "Big Story" award (1953); Italian Star of Solidarity (1957); and the Elks' Most Outstanding Newspaperman Award (1958).

Marcello married Elsie Lynum in 1930.

JOHN J. MARCHI

John J. Marchi, Republican leader of the N.Y. State Senate, was born May 20, 1921 in Staten Island, the son of Louis and Alina Marchi. He received the degree of Juris Doctor from St. Johns University School of Law and the degree of Doctor of Juridical Science from Brooklyn Law School. He was awarded the degree of Doctor of Laws honoris causa, from St. Johns University. He is engaged in the general practice of law with offices in Staten Island.

Senator Marchi was first elected to the New York State Senate in 1956. After service as member and chairman on several standing and joint legislative committees, he was named Chairman of the Senate Standing Committee on the City of New York. In 1966, he was elected as a Delegate to the Constitutional Convention and chaired the Senate Judiciary Subcommittee on Constitutional Issues to assist in research and issue development for the Convention.

In 1969, he was the candidate of the Republican and Conservative parties for the office of Mayor of the City of New York.

On June 2, 1968, he received from the President and Prime Minister of Italy the highest award that nation bestows on a non-resident, the Award of Commander of the Order of Merit of the Republic of Italy.

He and his wife, the former Maria Luisa Davini of Lucca, Italy, have two daughters, Aline, and Mrs. Gabriele Migliori.

ROCKY MARCIANO

In September 1955, Rocky Marciano knocked out Archie Moore in the ninth round of their title bout in Yankee Stadium. A total of 61,574 people witnessed what was to be the champion's last fight. The receipts from all sources amounted to two and a quarter million dollars. Only the second Dempsey-Tunney fight had made more money up to that time.

The following April, Marciano announced his retirement. He had won all of his forty-nine fights, forty-three by knockout, and became the only retired undefeated heavyweight champion in ring history.

Born Rocco Francis Marchegiano, September 1, 1924, in Brockton, Massachusetts, he showed an interest in sports at an early age, setting his sights on becoming a professional baseball player, then shifting his interest to football in high school.

He wanted to enter college but had to go to work to help support the family of eight. Marciano's father had been severely gassed fighting with the American Expeditionary Force in World War I and was able to work in the Brockton shoe factories only intermittently.

Rocky learned to fight in the streets, with coaching from his uncle. When he entered the service in 1943, he fought recreation-period bouts for the three-day passes awarded the winner. Returning to civilian life in 1947, he took a job as a construction worker. The next spring he was given a three-week tryout with a farm team of the Chicago Cubs, but he was rejected because an arm injury he sustained in the war interfered with his fielding.

With his friend Al Colombo as his second and trainer and Gene Caggiano, a Brockton mechanic, as his manager, Rocky started boxing amateur bouts, winning twenty-seven of thirty fights before turning professional in July, 1948.

Under the tutelage of the New York promoter Al Weill, Rocky was brought along slowly through twenty-four "soft" contests. His first big fight was with Roland LaStarza, described as "a clever, cautious fighter," who had remained undefeated in thirty-seven matches. Marciano won by a split decision and the Madison Square Garden fight crowd wasn't impressed by the clumsy brawler. As an underdog in his fight with Rex Layne in 1951, Rocky knocked him out in the sixth round.

In October of that year Marciano boxed Joe Louis, who was on the comeback trail. Rocky connected with a classic right cross that knocked the former champion through the ropes unconscious. Marciano told Bob Brumby of *Sports Stars* "After I knocked Joe down with a left hook I set him up with another one, then I let go with my right. The punch made all my dreams come true. But it was the saddest punch of my life. How else could I feel seeing such a great ex-champion and one of the finest sportsmen that ever lived lying there on the canvas?''

Trailing in points in his title fight with Jersey Joe Walcott in 1952, Marciano backed the champion into the ropes in the thirteenth round and knocked him out. It was one of the greatest fights of all time, and again, Marciano was glad he was champ but sad that Jersey Joe had lost.

The gentlest of men outside the ring, Rocky married his childhood sweetheart, Barbara Cousens, in 1950. One of the reasons he retired was because he could spend only four months out of the year with his family while he was boxing.

Tragedy struck in the form of a plane crash in 1969, and Rocky Marciano was dead at the age of forty-five.

Rosa Zagnoni Marinoni

Poetess, lecturer, writer Rosa Zagnoni Marinoni was born in Bologna, Italy. The Poet Laureate of Arkansas, she first began to write for publication in 1926. She has contributed novels, poetry, short stories and articles to newspapers and magazines in the United States and Europe.

Among her works are: *Behind the Mask* (1926); *Pine Needles* (1927); *Red Kites and Wooden Crosses* (1928); *In Passing* (1929); *North of Laughter* (1930); *Tales of the Setting Sun* (1933); and *Side Show* (1939).

She was married to Professor Antonio Marinoni in 1908.

Dean Martin

When the phenomenal comedy-singing act of Martin and Lewis broke up in 1956, almost every newspaper in the country carried Dean Martin epitaphs. Undaunted by the wave of public opinion against his decision to leave the team, Dino went on to establish himself as a leading recording star, top-drawing night club performer, and star of over a dozen motion pictures. To cap off his attempt to do his own thing, he signed a record thirty-four million dollar contract with NBC for his weekly television show.

Born Dino Crocetti, June 17, 1917, in Steubenville, Ohio, Martin was the son of a barber, who emigrated from Italy. Dean's mother, Angela Barra, was in a convent when she met Guy Crocetti. He couldn't speak English and she couldn't speak Italian. Two weeks later they were married. "Pop got his own barbershop, and then a beauty salon, and so he gave us a beautiful home, a car, good food, good Christmases, and we never were poor, my brother and I. 'Cause my Pop had guts. My Mom, too.''

Martin quit school in the tenth grade "because I thought I was smarter than the teacher." He worked as a shoe-shine boy and as a filling-station attendant. At the age of fourteen he was earning ten dollars a match as boxer. His other early jobs included being a steelworker, cigar-store clerk and croupier. He sang under the name of Dino Martini in Steubenville cafes. "When a Bing Crosby movie came to Steubenville, I would watch all day. That's how I learned to sing, 'cause it's true I don't read a note. I learned from Crosby. So did Sinatra and Perry Como.''

Martin didn't take his singing career seriously until 1946, when he started working clubs in New York City and New Jersey. He was on the same bill with Jerry Lewis at the Glass Hat in New York. Lewis was doing a lip-synchronization act, pantomiming phonograph records. "We started horsing around with each other's acts,'' Martin said. "That's how the team started. We'd do anything that came to our minds.''

They played six weeks at the 500 Club, then Jules Podell hired them for the Copacabana at five-thousand dollars a week. They signed for six weeks and stayed for twelve. After that their manager, Abby Greshler, booked them into Slapsie Maxie Rosenbloom's night club in Beverly Hills, California. As a result of that booking, Joseph Hazen, Hal Wallis' partner, signed them to a long-term contract. Martin and Lewis made sixteen movies for Paramount Pictures. All made money, and at one time, the team was making two million dollars a year. Among their films were: *My Friend Irma* (1949); *At War with the Army* (1951); *That's My Boy* (1951); *Jumping Jacks* (1952); *The Caddy* (1953); *Living it Up* (1954); *Artists and Models* (1955); and *Pardners* (1956).

Martin tired of being constantly pushed into the background, and he claims that the real trouble began when Lewis began to think of himself as a "second Chaplin." He refused to do a picture Jerry had written, *The Delicate Delinquent,* and the team split up.

Martin's future looked doubtful. Of his appearance in his first solo film, *Ten Thousand Bedrooms* (1957), Bosley Crowther of the New York *Times* reported Martin to be "just another nice-looking crooner without his comical pal. Together, the two made a mutually complementary team. Apart, Mr. Martin is a fellow with little humor and a modicum of charm."

The next time out of the chute, for *The Young Lions* (1958), Martin proved he could act, and the critics agreed. He also found a close friend in the late Montgomery Cliff while making *Lions.*

"Nobody wanted him around, nobody would eat with him. So I took him to dinner, or I would have a drink with him, or I would put him to bed 'cause he was always on pills, you know. He was such a sad, sad man, and he was like a boy, so unhappy and rejected, and so I'd say, 'If you don't want him, you don't want me.' And we'd leave the party. But first I'd spit in their faces for him."

Next came *The Dean Martin Show* on NBC-TV in 1959, during which Martin made *Rio Bravo,* playing the alcoholic sidekick to John Wayne. The film was both a critical and financial success. Frank Sinatra got him his co-starring role in *Some Came Running,* the film that firmly established Martin as a motion picture star in his own right. "It was the happiest picture I've ever been in," Martin has recalled. "A part like that will never come my way again. Being with Shirley MacLaine and Frank - I don't know, it was just happy."

To fulfill the old Martin and Lewis contract, he made *Career* for Paramount in 1959. His portrayal of a theatrical opportunist was favorably received by the critics. Among Martin's later films are: *Who Was That Lady* (1959); *Bells Are Ringing* (1960); *Ada* (1961); *Toys in the Attic* (1963); and in the Matt Helm series, *The Silencers* and *Murderer's Row.*

Dean Martin married Elizabeth Ann MacDonald in 1940. Martin was awarded custody of their four children when they divorced. He married Jeanne Biegger, a former model, in 1949, and they had three children before divorcing in 1971.

Most of the swinging done by Dean Martin is with a golf club. He tries to play every day. He admits to stealing Phil Harris' drinking image for comedy purposes.

According to ex-wife Jeanne, "He is one-hundred per cent man, covering the range between eight- and eighty-year-old men."

TONY MARTIN

1976 marks Tony Martin's fortieth anniversary in a show business career that includes movies, night clubs, radio, records, and the stage. "I have had no great disappointments in life. That's because I never build castles in the air. Most disappointments are the results of setting your sights too high."

Passing up the stage role in *Guys and Dolls,* he lost the movie role to Marlon Brando, only to pass up seventy-five thousand dollars worth of bookings to do it in summer stock. "I'm a gambler," he admits. "Once it cost me two thousand dollars to walk across the Sands Hotel casino in Las Vegas to buy a newspaper."

Born Alfred Norris on Christmas Day 1912, in Oakland, California, he played (saxophone and clarinet) in San Francisco's vaudeville theatres when he was twelve. After a period with the Tom Gerun band in Chicago in 1933, he turned to radio and recording. After his divorce from Alice Faye, he married dancer Cyd Charisse in 1948. They have two sons.

Among his films are: *Sing, Baby, Sing; Follow the Fleet; You Can't Have Everything; Music In My Heart; Ziegfield Girl; Till the Clouds Roll By; Two Tickets To Broadway; Here Come The Girls; Easy to Love; Hit the Deck;* and *Let's Be Happy.*

He won a Bronze Star serving with the Air Force from 1942-1945.

Kay Mazzo

Ballerina Kay Mazzo joined the New York City Ballet company when she was fifteen, became the company's youngest principal dancer at twenty-two and the odds-on favorite to succeed Suzanne Farrell, the company's unofficial prima ballerina, until she left the troupe in 1969. Miss Mazzo continues to expand her reputation and dancing prowess in such productions as *Jewels, Dances at a Gathering, Agon, Brahms-Schoenberg Quartet, A Midsummer Night's Dream,* and *Don Quixote.*

Born Catherine Mazzo, January 17, 1947, in Chicago, she took up dancing at the age of six to improve her health. A frail child, she was nicknamed "Peanut." After three years of study with Bernadene Hayes, she was chosen to be one of the children in Balanchine's *The Nutcracker,* during the New York City Ballet's Chicago performances.

When she was thirteen, her family moved to New York and she enrolled in the School of American Ballet, the New York City Ballet's training school. In 1961 Jerome Robbins borrowed her from the company to tour in his Ballets USA company. Her performance in Robbins' duet, *Afternoon of a Faun,* created a sensation in Paris, Copenhagen, Spoleto, London and Berlin.

Of her success she has said, "Success is a public word. No one here thinks, 'Oh, if I do well in this new part it will make me famous or successful.' What we think about is learning it correctly, doing it well, putting yourself into it. Success is just the joy of dancing."

Lately Miss Mazzo has added to her repertoire: the Sugar Plum Fairy in *The Nutcracker,* the sleepwalker in Balanchine's *La Sonnambula,* and leads in Balanchine's *Donizetti Variations, Who Cares?,* and the *Haydn Concerto.*

Of the inevitable comparisons to Miss Farrell, she has said, "It's illogical to dissect an individual's performance with analogies. I am whatever I am at the moment of the ballet. It makes me uncomfortable to be compared with anyone. But more than that, it makes me mad."

Her three-year marriage to Jordan Benedict ended in divorce in 1971.

GIAN-CARLO MENOTTI

The only man to produce opera successfully on Broadway *(The Medium,* 1946, and *The Telephone,* 1947), Gian-Carlo Menotti is not terribly fond of the Broadway musical. "In a musical, the hero talks and talks and finally says, 'Darling, I love you,' and then there is an abrupt transition while he breaks into a song. End of song and the hero starts talking again where he left off. I prefer my dramas to be entirely musical."

Born in Cadegliano, Italy, July 7, 1911, this unique composer came to the United States in 1928 and has since amassed a most impressive list of premieres, including: *Amelia Goes to the Ball* (opera), 1936; *The Old Maid and the Thief* (radio opera), 1939 (later staged); *Sebastian* (ballet), 1944; *Piano Concerto in F,* 1945; *Amahl and the Night Visitors* (television opera, repeated annually since 1951); *The Consul,* 1950, and *The Saint of Bleecker Street,* 1954 (both Pulitzer Prize-winning operas); *The Unicorn, The Gorgon, and the Manticore,* 1957; *The Last Savage* (opera), 1963; and *Martin's Lie* (opera), 1964.

In 1958, Menotti produced *Vanessa* (the opera by Samuel Barber). His major works have been published, and he is the author of all his libretti, most of which have been written in English.

Menotti studied at the Curtis Institute of Music, Philadelphia, where he taught composition from 1948 to 1955.

He originated and helps finance the Festival at Spoleto, Italy, an ambitious project that combines the Old and New Worlds of music.

SAL MINEO

A one-time street fighter himself, Sal Mineo was a natural for his early roles *(Dino, Crime in the Streets,* etc.), culminating with his

Oscar-nomination performance as the underdog in *Rebel Without a Cause*, 1955. "I guess I was still running away from those punks in New York," he said later. "I wasn't really acting."

Born January 10,1939, in the Bronx, New York, the son of a Sicilian casket maker, Mineo was expelled from school at the age of nine. While attending dancing school, he received daily beatings from street associates who were not sympathetic with his theatrical ambitions.

He was spotted for the movies on the stage (*Rose Tattoo, The King and I, Something About a Soldier*).

Though he still would like to star in a gangster film, he has changed his image from an underdog to a winner. Among his films are *Giant, Somebody Up There Likes Me, Exodus, Gene Krupa Story, Greatest Story Ever Told*, and *Cheyenne Autumn*.

LIZA MINNELLI

Any rumors to the effect that Liza Minnelli has been coasting on the reputation of her famous parents were completely shattered by her portrayal of Pookie Adams in the film *The Sterile Cuckoo* (1969). In it she gave a most believable performance of an insecure college coed who turns to kooky flamboyance to cover up the loose ends of her life.

Born March 12, 1946, in Hollywood, the daughter of Judy Garland and film director Vincente Minnelli, Liza grew up with such movie colony children as Mia Farrow, Candice Bergen, and Tish Sterling. She attended about twenty schools both here and abroad. "The kind of childhood I had can make you or break you. I've had knocks, but I'm not sure it's not better to have them when you're young. At least it teaches you how to handle them when they come later."

Miss Minnelli captured an Antoinette Perry Award in 1965 for her title role in the Broadway musical *Flora, the Red Menace* after paying her dues in stock and Off-Broadway. The label, "Judy Garland's daughter," began to peel off as early as her performance in the Off-Broadway production of *Best Foot Forward* in 1963. She recorded the cast album of that show, and her first album, *Liza, Liza*, sold over a half a million copies in 1964.

But it took an off-beat role in *Charlie Bubbles* (1968) and an Oscar nomination for *Cuckoo* before the public was willing to accept her on her own merits. Miss Minnelli has filled engagements at such spots as Coconut Grove, the Sahara Hotel, the Waldorf-Astoria, and the El San Juan Hotel. She has appeared in London, Paris, Monaco, and has toured Australia twice with her nightclub act. She was a critical Broadway success in *Cabaret*.

On television, she appeared on her mother's show, starred with Arthur Godfrey in CBS's *Ice Capades of 1966,* and *The Liza Minnelli Special* on NBC in 1970. Her third film, *Tell Me That You Love Me, Junie Moon,* directed by Otto Preminger, was released in 1970. Among her ambitions is to be directed in a film by her father.

VINCENTE MINNELLI

As a tribute to his directorial talents, the British Film Institute designated March and April, 1962 as Vincente Minnelli Season. An endlessly creative director, he has adapted his talents to all kinds of films, from musicals like *Gigi* (Academy Award, 1958) and *Bells Are Ringing* to dramas like *Lust for Life* and *Tea And Sympathy,* and comedies like *Designing Woman,* and *Father of the Bride.*

"He directs like a madman," said Kirk Douglas. "If you don't know him, he can drive an actor crazy. But what comes out is beautiful." Metro-Goldwyn-Mayer, where Minnelli has been directing since 1940, know that something else comes out of his movies - lots of money.

Born February 28 (year unrecorded) in Chicago, he started acting at the age of three in the Minnelli Brothers Tent Shows, worked as a stage manager and costume designer, became art director of Radio City Music Hall in 1933, and produced *At Home Abroad, Ziegfeld Follies,* and *Very Warm for May* before striking out for Hollywood.

First married to Judy Garland (daughter actress Liza), he married European socialite Denise Gigante in 1960.

He has directed: *Cabin in the Sky, Meet Me in St. Louis, Madame Bovary, An American in Paris, Bad and the Beautiful, The Bandwagon, Long Long Trailer, Brigadoon, Kismet, Reluctant Debutante, Some Came Running, Home from the Hills, Four Horsemen of the Apocalypse, The Courtship of Eddie's Father, Goodbye Charlie,* and *Sandpiper.*

ANNA MOFFO

Possessed of "a lovely voice and one that, considering how high it can soar, is surprisingly velvety in its lower registers," soprano

Anna Moffo has won acclaim in the concert hall as well as the operatic stage.

Born June 27, 1933 in Wayne, Pennsylvania, she chose a musical career over her great interest in sports and studied at the Curtis Institute of Music in Philadelphia before going to Italy to study at the Accademia di Santa Cecilia in Rome. "If you're just a young American singer, you don't get true respect in American opera houses."

After her debut in 1955 at the Rome Opera, she went on to the Teatro San Carlo, La Scala, the Vienna State Opera, Munich, and Paris. She won fame as Ann Ford in *Falstaff* at the Salzburg Festival in 1957, marrying the celebrated Italian television director, Mario Lanfranchi, the same year.

In 1959 she debuted with the Metropolitan Opera Company as Violetta in *La Traviata.* Her performance there in 1962 as Mélisande in *Pelléas et Mélisande,* under Ernest Ansermet, was especially praiseworthy.

She has sung all three soprano roles in Offenbach's *Les Contes d'Hoffman.* "I don't concentrate on projecting a high B with the thought that there's a high D coming right after it. I just sing."

A. J. Montanari

In 1952, three years before he received his college degree, A. J. Montanari founded the Montanari Clinical School for emotionally disturbed children in Hialeah, Florida. He began taking in boys and girls who had been rejected as hopeless elsewhere. By applying unorthodox, permissive techniques based on intuition, understanding and love, he has restored thousands of such children to society, and is, according to child psychiatrist Dr. Povl W. Toussieng, "helping more kids in one year than many of us manage to help in a decade."

"These kids aren't products of hell," Montanari has explained. "They're just sick little kids who need help because somebody let them down or because something they were born with made them different from other kids or maybe because they had a sickness that damaged their brain power. So they're frustrated, mixed up, and act out of their hates and fears. They're hard to handle and hard to teach, but somebody's got to try or they'll end up in straitjackets, or in jail, or as vegetables."

Adelio Joseph Montanari was born Adelio Giuseppe Ambruano Pasquale Antonio Montanare in Winchedon Springs, Massachusetts, May 25, 1917 to immigrant parents who worked at the local cotton mill. He prefers to be called Monty.

His parents, determined to see their son rise above their station, subjected him to nearly impossible standards enforced by heavy discipline. He complied, but as Arthur Henley records in his biography of Montanari, *Demon in My View* (1966), he developed "a fear of policemen and authority in general."

In school, other children called him a "mamma's boy" and he spent most of his time helping classmates make their grades, letting his own classwork slip below a satisfactory level. He did manage to graduate from high school and his father sent him to Antioch College in Yellow Springs, Ohio in 1935.

There he found it impossible to study, and he questioned everything taught him, particularly the theories advanced in abnormal psychology. He was dismissed after three years, and traveled throughout the United States working in cooperative stores. When the war broke out, Montanari flunked out of Officers Candidate School, served as private and later a sergeant in the Army. He was wounded overseas, and received a Purple Heart, a Bronze Star, and a Good Conduct Medal.

He married Ann Belue, a teacher, in 1943. He has two children by that marriage which ended in divorce in 1957. After receiving more college training in North Carolina, he moved his family to Miami, Florida to teach educationally deprived children at the Ingley School.

Montanari cataloged his teaching experience as "the endless array of tests, professional double-talk, and time-consuming red tape. Everybody was too busy keeping records and raising money to help the kids." There he formulated his motto: "First reach them, then teach them."

Unhappy with the routine pedagogy at Ingley School, he set up a day school in his home. His first students were children with hearing problems sent to him by a Miami osteopath. He continued with his studies at night and summers, receiving his B.S. degree in education in 1955. "It didn't mean a damn thing to me," he said, "but it seemed to mean a lot to the people I had to get along with."

The normal fee for a child at the Montanari Clinical School is four-hundred dollars a month, but this is waived or lowered in needy cases to the extent made possible by donations.

Montanari married his second wife, Carol Straus, a widow he met when she brought her daughter Karen to the school. She has two other children.

Montanari says children who need help must be given it. "We can't wait for more psychiatrists, psychologists, and finely-trained social workers . . . We can't wait for the government, the foundations, and private philanthropists to give us what we think is enough money to get started . . . Emotional disturbance is a contagion and it is already spreading through all levels of society."

VINCENT MOTTOLA

Judge Vincent Mottola was born in Grottaminarda, Avellino, Italy, March 29, 1894. He came to America in 1910 and was educated at the New England Conservatory of Music. After teaching violin for five years he decided to study law and took his degree from Suffolk Law School in 1923. Mottola has been a special justice of the Boston Municipal Court since 1953.

The organizer and member of the board of directors of several Massachusetts corporations, Mottola ran for the United States Congress in 1942.

Since 1941 he has composed and recorded more than a dozen songs and other pieces for violin and piano. He married Emilia Romano in 1917 and they have three children: Vincent Jr., Gloria Sanella and Rudolph.

JOSEPH MOZINO

Builder Joseph Mozino was born in Fossato, Reggio Calabria, Italy, August 21, 1897. He came to America in 1913 and attended night school to get his engineering degree.

Mozino formed the J. S. Mozino Company in 1922, which has built over 2,000 homes in suburban Philadelphia, among other commercial buildings. He is also president of several real estate, construction and investment corporations.

Very active in educational, civic and charitable affairs, he established the Mozino Scholarship at Drexel Institute of Technology and supplied the funds to build a school and rebuild a church in his native town in Italy.

Mozino has received many awards over the years, including two Stars of Italian Solidarity and the Cross of Cavaliere Ufficiale. He married Sarah Johnson in 1936 and they have two children, Andrew and Sarah Marie.

MICHAEL A. MUSMANNO

For almost fifty years, lawyer-judge-author Michael Angelo Musmanno's strong voice for justice, particularly in connection with individual rights, was heard in his many posts of authority. Some of the dramatic highlights of his colorful and sometimes controversial crusades include defending Sacco and Vanzetti, campaigning for the abolition of the Coal and Iron Police Laws, presiding at the Nuremberg war crimes trials, and appearing as a witness for the prosecution in the Eichmann trial.

Born in 1897 near Pittsburgh, Pennsylvania, Musmanno began working as a coal loader at the age of fourteen. He acquired a legal training mainly by taking evening classes. He entered Georgetown University in Washington, D.C., where he got his law degree when he resumed his studies after serving as an infantryman in the Army in World War I.

All in all he had seven college degrees and took additional graduate work at Oxford University, Harvard University, and Notre Dame University.

On being admitted to the Pennsylvania Bar in 1923, he assisted John R. K. Scott, a noted Philadelphia lawyer, winning sixty of sixty-five cases. Always a perfectionist, he was haunted by the five he lost as he related in his autobiographical *Verdict! The Adventures of the Young Lawyer in the Brown Suit* (1958).

He went to Rome for study, traveled to Paris and then to London before returning to Pittsburgh in 1925. His first case in private practice was defending a man who had assaulted him. Concentrating on cases which involved the underprivileged, he became a member of the team which unsuccessfully defended Nicola Sacco and Bartolomeo Vanzetti, the anarchists accused of murder in 1927. He wrote a defense for them in his book *After Twelve Years* (1939).

He served in the Pennsylvania General Assembly from 1928 to 1932, having to resort to emotional and dramatic campaigns to overcome prejudice against his Italian name. He was first elected judge, serving the Allegheny County court in 1932. Two years later he received all but twenty thousand of three-hundred-forty thousand votes to win a judgeship in the court of common pleas.

In 1936 he sentenced himself to a three-day prison term "to find out what it really feels like" to be in jail.

He entered World War II as a lieutenant commander in the Navy and rose to rank of rear-admiral. He served in the Adriatic, was a member of the Italian expedition of the European invasion in 1943, aided General Mark Clark, and served as military governor of Italy's Sorrento Peninsula.

In 1946 he was appointed president of the United States Board of Forcible Repatriation in Austria and was able to prevent many refugees from being returned to their Communist-dominated homelands. His decorations included the Purple Heart (with cluster), Bronze Star for Valor, the Legion of Merit, the Army Commendation Ribbon, the Italian Silver Medal of War, the Military Order of Italy, and the Star of Valor Moroccan Expeditionary Force.

Musmanno was a member of a Navy team to determine whether

or not Adolf Hitler was actually dead after the war. His questioning of some two hundred of Hitler's intimates was recounted in his book *Ten Days to Die* (1950). President Truman appointed him one of the judges in the Nuremberg trials. Confronted with the Einsatzgruppen case, which consisted of twenty defendants charged with the murder of over a million Jews, he asked for a world court to try "crimes against humanity". Such a court is yet to be established.

At the time of his recent death he was serving a twenty-one year term on the Pennsylvania Supreme Court, being elected to that post in 1951. He felt Communists should be imprisoned and even suggested that the Cincinnati Reds baseball team change its name.

His testimony in the Eichmann trial in 1961 can be found in his book *The Verdicts Were Just* (1966). He became incensed when Yale University specialists declared that Leif Ericsson and not Christopher Columbus discovered America. His vehement dissent can be found in his book *Columbus WAS First* (1966).

Justice Musmanno remained a bachelor and forsook all but a minimal amount of social life. In *Verdict!* he wrote: "Being a lawyer was not only my occupation - it was my avocation, diversion, and entertainment. It was my wife, children, and grandchildren!"

CHARLES MUZZICATO

Physician and surgeon Charles Muzzicato was born in Nicosia, Enna, Italy, March 1, 1901. Educated at Alfred University, St. Ignatius College and Loyola University, he became a specialist in radiology and gastroenterology. Muzzicato has served in various New York hospitals as roentgenologist, gastroenterologist, and instructor in radiology.

He has served on many boards and was a member of the New York State Senate in 1941. Among his many awards are: Commander, Order Crown of Italy and Republic of San Marino; Knight of Malta; Italian Star of Solidarity; and was awarded citations by Italian Community Appeal for the Stritch School of Medicine, Loyola University and Alfred University Alumni Association for his contributions in the field of medicine.

Muzzicato married Antoinette Bertini in 1928.

BRUNO PAGLIAI

Bruno Pagliai left Italy in 1921 at the age of nineteen, learned every aspect of the banking business in San Francisco, and traveled south to Mexico to apply that knowledge. What he has to show for his efforts are fifty million dollars, a beautiful wife (movie star Merle Oberon), two adopted children, three homes and an outstanding art collection.

"Clipping coupons give you calluses on the brain. I work because I still have the ability to create," says the man who formed his seamless tube company, TAMSA, under the influence of Mexico's Manuel Avila Camacho.

RALPH PALLADINO

Major General Ralph Palladino was born in Monte Mileto, Avellino, Italy, September 1, 1904. Educated at Boston University, he joined the Army during World War II as major, later serving as commander of the 104th Infantry, 26th Division, with the rank of colonel. He became a Brigadier General in 1948 and a Major General in 1951.

Palladino was selected in 1959 for duty with the Department of Defense as the Military Executive of the Reserve Forces Policy Board in the Office of the Secretary of Defense.

Among his many citations are: Silver Star; Bronze Star; French Croix de Guerre; Czech War Cross; and the Russian Order of the Fatherland.

He married Helena D'Amato in 1929. They have one son, Donald.

ALFRED PANEPINTO

Architect Alfred Panepinto was born in Philadelphia, May 3, 1907. Educated at Villanova College and Harvard University, he won Boston Society of Architects Prize in 1930.

Panepinto served with the U.S. Airborne Army in Europe and was awarded seven battle stars and the Bronze Star. He has been chief architect of the Sun Oil Company since 1958 and has designed many college buildings.

As an artist Panepinto has painted many famous portraits and the cover paintings for the *Saturday Evening Post* and other magazines.

He married Miriam Bennett in 1946. They have four children: Linda, Nina, Alfredo and Marco.

JOHN PASTORE

The first Italian-American to be elected to the United States Senate, John Orlando Pastore has served his home state of Rhode Island in that capacity since 1950.

Born November 4, 1912, in Providence, John helped with the housework and cooking and cared for the babies while his mother, who was widowed when John was nine, and his older brother worked to support the family. After he finished high school and got a fifteen-dollar-a-week job as a claims adjuster, he enrolled in an evening law course given by Northeastern University at the Providence YMCA. He got his law degree and was admitted to the bar in 1932.

Suffering from lack of clients, he accosted Tommy Testa, a local political figure whom he had never met, and told him he wanted to go into politics. Testa was impressed by his manner and helped him get the Democratic nomination for the State House of Representatives in 1934. He won the election in a strongly Republican district and was re-elected in 1934.

He became a "tough prosecutor" in 1940 when appointed assistant attorney-general in charge of the criminal calendar. Elected lieutenant-governor in 1944, he became Governor in 1945, holding that office until he ran for the United States Senate. When he won that election by almost a two-to-one ratio, the Associated Press called him "the biggest vote-getter in the history of the nation's smallest State."

As chairman of the Senate Civil Service subcommittee, he pushed legislation which improved conditions for Federal employees. He has served as the chairman of the joint commission on atomic energy, member of the United States delegation to the United Nations, senate designee to the first conference of the International Atomic Energy Agency, and has attended three Geneva Conferences of Peaceful Uses of Atomic Energy. In 1964 he was the keynote speaker at the Democratic National Convention.

The Senator married Elena Elizabeth Caito in 1951; they have three children.

ROCCO A. PETRONE

"A small step for man, a giant step for mankind." With those words, Neil Armstrong became the first man to step upon the Moon in July, 1969. Among the men most responsible for the gigantic task of getting the astronauts to the Moon and home safely was NASA's Apollo program director Rocco Petrone.

Born March 31, 1926 in Amsterdam, New York, Petrone received a degree in mechanical engineering from the Massachusetts Institute of Technology in 1952. He worked on the Redstone Missile Development Project in Huntsville, Alabama, 1952-1955; was a member of the Army general staff in Washington, D. C., 1956-1960; was manager of the Apollo Program at Kennedy Space Center, 1960-1966; became director of launch operations, 1966-1969; and was named Apollo program director in 1969.

Petrone married Ruth Holley in 1955, and they have four children.

CHARLES POLETTI

Now with the law firm of Poletti, Freidin, Prashker, Feldman & Gartner in New York City, Charles Poletti has had enough professional responsibility to be crowded into three lifetimes.

Born July 2, 1903, in Barre, Vermont, he received his law degree (cum laude) from Harvard in 1928, then went to Italy for his LL.D. from the University of Rome.

Admitted to the New York bar in 1930, he married Jean Knox Ellis in 1934 (three children). He was a justice on the New York Supreme Court in 1937, Lieutenant Governor (1939-1942), and Governor in 1942.

He has served on commissions concerned with dams, education, crime, social welfare, the coat and suit industry, foreign relations, and intolerance. In addition to many awards bestowed upon him by this country and Italy, he is an honorary citizen of Naples, Milan and Rome.

CARMELA PONSELLE

The elder sister of Rosa Ponselle, contralto Carmela Ponselle began her serious study of singing before her sister, but continued to study for an additional five years after Rosa made her debut. Carmela appeared as Amneris in *Aida* at the Polo Grounds in New York in the summer of 1923.

She sang at the Metropolitan Opera Company from 1925 to 1934, but did not appear frequently. She sang a duet with her sister at a Sunday Night Concert in 1925 and appeared once in *La Gioconda* in 1932.

Born June 7, 1892, in Schenectady, New York, Miss Ponselle gave concerts on American radio and taught singing in New York after 1934.

ROSA PONSELLE

Soprano Rosa Ponselle's world fame came quickly and in a torrent. William Thorner, the impresario, heard her when she sang in vaudeville with her sister Carmela in an act billed as the Ponzillo Sisters. He got her an audition at the Metropolitan Opera Company. Enrico Caruso took an interest in her and she debuted with him in 1918 as Leonora in *La Forza del Destino.*

She was an instant success and went on to further triumphs in roles such as Rachel in *La Juive* in 1919 and Giulia in Spontini's *La Vestale* in 1925. She sang in *Norma* in 1927, and the title role in *Luisa Miller* in 1929.

Born January 22, 1897, in Meriden, Connecticut, she married American industrialist Carle A. Jackson and withdrew from musical life in 1936.

GREGORIO PRESTOPINO

Gregorio Prestopino likes to paint the common people. He catches their expressions at work and play and records them, mostly in water color in faithful simple lines and lively color.

Born June 21, 1907 in Manhattan's "Little Italy," he studied sign painting at the Murray Hill Vocational School and entered the National Academy of Design in New York City on a scholarship in 1923, where he studied for six years. He traveled to Mexico and then to Europe in 1936. The painters Roualt, Beckmann, and Braque have influenced his work, as have the art of the Orient, Persian miniatures and Hindu sculpture.

The problem of the common man in the 1930's was unemployment. Prestopino captured his plight in an oil called *Portsmouth Street,* which showed groups of idle men on drab streets. *Winter,* 1945, showed working men boarding a streetcar.

He caught the oppressed Negro in a series of paintings he did in Harlem in the mid-1950's. Green Haven Prison was his subject matter in 1957.

Represented in important American museums, "Presto" divides his time between painting and teaching. He is married to Elizabeth Dauber, an illustrator; they have two sons.

Louis Prima

Louis Prima, Keely Smith, Sam Butera, and the Witnesses put together a sound which rocked audiences and set nightclub records all over the country throughout the 1950's. When Miss Smith left the group (and husband Louis) in 1962, he met, hired, and married Gia Mainone. The sound goes on.

Born December 7, 1912, in New Orleans, Louis worked as a singer and trumpet player in local Los Angeles theatres before forming his band, which played major cities all over the country. Las Vegas, Lake Tahoe, and Reno are the principal areas where his band appears.

Among Prima's compositions are: *Sing, Sing, Sing; Brooklyn Boogie; Marguerite; Sunday Kind Of Love; Robinhood; Oh Babe;* and *Las Vegas Woman.*

Mario Procaccino

Judge Mario A. Procaccino is the Academic President of Verrazzano College, which is now being developed in Saratoga, New York. He is a member of the Battery Park City Authority and Hearing Commission for the N.Y.S. Retirement System.

He was formerly Comptroller of New York City, judge of the Civil and Municipal Courts, Chief Law Assistant of the Supreme Court, Bronx, and a member of the faculty of Fordham University.

Procaccino was born in Bisaccia, Italy on September 5, 1912, one of three sons of Angelo and Rose Procaccino. Since his arrival in this country in 1921, he has resided in the Bronx. He is married and has one daughter.

He graduated Fordham Law School in 1939.

In August 1956, he was appointed Director of Mortgage, Banking and Housing for New York City, where he set up a plan for new housing programs. Government housing was then in its infancy, and Procaccino's programs served as prototypes for similar housing programs throughout the United States.

In the Democratic Party primary of 1969, he won the nomination for the Office of Mayor of the City of New York. However, because of a three-way race and a split in the party, he lost the election by a small margin.

During his 25 years of public service, Judge Procaccino received the highest commendations not only from city, state and national leaders, but also from international sources.

Rodolfo Purcelli

Poet, translator, polyglot, philologist and journalist Rodolfo Purcelli was born in Aquileia, Italy, March 15, 1885. Before coming to America in 1928, Purcelli was Professor of French, Italian, English, German and Latin, in Lyceum and Colleges of Trieste.

He has authored twenty-five volumes (prose and poetry) besides poems and translations in eight American anthologies. He has received many awards and was founder and director of "The New Universal Order" for harmony and peace among nations from 1946 to 1952.

Purcelli married Johanna Facchinetti in 1913. They have one daughter, Beatrice.

George Quilici

Judge George Quilici was born in Chicago, Illinois and educated at De Paul University and Northwestern University. He was elected Judge of Municipal Court, Chicago, in 1940 and re-elected in 1942, 1948, 1954 and 1960. He was elected Judge of the Circuit Court of Illinois in 1962.

Quilici served as special prosecutor of election fraud cases in County Court of Cook County from 1935 to 1938. He served on many councils and boards over the years to fight racial and religious discrimination. Among his awards are: Citation of Recognition by the American Legion and the Italian Star of Solidarity.

Paul Rao

Judge Paul Rao was born in Prizzi, Palermo, Italy, June 15, 1899. He came to America in 1904, was educated at Fordham University Law School, and admitted to the New York Bar in 1924.

Rao served in Europe and Africa with the Navy during World War I and also as an official French interpreter with the French cruiser division. He was appointed as Judge of the U.S. Customs Court by President Truman in 1948 and promoted to Chief Judge of that court by President Johnson in 1965.

Among Rao's many awards are: Knight of Malta; Papal Knight of Lateran; Knight of the Order of St. Hubert; Italian Star of Solidarity; Military Order of Lafayette; and the Catholic War Veterans Americanism award.

He married Grace Malatino in 1922. They have three children: Nina, Paul Jr., and Grayce.

Phil Rizzuto

"I thought it would be easy to talk about something I had done all my life," says Phil Rizzuto, former super-shortstop of the New York Yankees, turned sportscaster, "but I just couldn't get the hang of it . . . Both Mel Allen and Red Barber were big helps to me . . . they gave me the same advice - be yourself, don't copy." Now as familiar with a microphone as he used to be with a double-play ball, the Scooter brings an excitement to the Yankee games he announces which is unmatched by any in the business.

Born September 25, 1918 in Brooklyn, he is married to Cora Esselborn, and they have four children.

Albert Rosellini

Albert Rosellini, two-term Democratic Governor of Washington (1957-1965), gives out artificial roses when he campaigns. "He is charming, attentive, warm," said an admirer, "and genuinely concerned with little people."

Born January 21, 1910 in Tacoma, Washington, he worked his way through law school (University of Washington), was county prosecutor, then served in the Washington State Senate for nineteen years.

Married to Ethel McNeil (five children) since 1935, he has served on the National Governor's Council and presided over the Council of State Governments (1962-1963).

He lives in Seattle where he is currently engaged in law practice and public relations.

Frederick Rossini

Born in Monongahela, Pennsylvania, July 18, 1899, scientist Frederick Rossini was educated at Carnegie Institute of Technology and the University of California. He is a scientist in physical chemistry and was chief of the section of Thermochemistry and Hydrocarbons, National Bureau of Standards, to 1950.

A Silliman professor and head of the department of chemistry, and director of the American Petroleum Institute Research Laboratory at Carnegie Tech, he also served as past editor, secretary and president of the Washington Academy of Sciences and as president of the Commission on Thermo-chemistry.

A winner of many awards and member of several professional societies, Rossini has written seven books and about 150 scientific papers.

He married Anne Landgraff in 1932.

PETE ROZELLE

Professional football has come a long way since the days of Jim Thorpe and Red Grange. The average American male (and more and more women every year) have developed an insatiable appetite for that particular form of violence. As commissioner of the National Football League, Pete Rozelle has the responsibility of overseeing what has become one of the biggest businesses in America. He has been "filling the big shoes of Bert Bell" since 1960, and the shoes fit.

Born in South Gate, California, March 1, 1926, Alvin Ray Rozelle was nicknamed "Pete" by an uncle. "Considering my real name," Rozelle has said, "I am forever grateful to him." After a hitch in the Navy, Rozelle enrolled at Compton Junior College where he played forward for the basketball team alongside Duke Snider, who later achieved greatness with the Brooklyn Dodgers.

He received his B.A. from the University of San Francisco in 1950, where he remained for two years as assistant athletic director. He worked for a time as publicity director of the Los Angeles Rams, leaving in 1955 to work for the P.K. Macker public relations firm in San Francisco. His job was to publicize Australian athletes for the 1956 Melbourne Olympic games.

About this time, quarrels started breaking out among the Rams' owners, and commissioner Bell hand-picked Rozelle to ease the tension. Acting on Bell's advice, the Rams rehired Rozelle as general manager in 1957.

Commissioner Bell died October 11, 1959, and the NFL members met in Miami Beach the following January to select a replacement. The new commissioner immediately found himself on the hot seat. The Dallas Cowboys got one of the two coveted NFL franchises in 1960 when the league expanded from twelve to fourteen clubs. The other went to the Minnesota Vikings in 1961. The American Football League, which had been founded in Dallas in 1960, also wanted a team in the Minneapolis-St. Paul area, and immediately sued the NFL for ten million dollars for attempting to stifle an infant competitor. Largely through research into antitrust litigation done by Rozelle and his assistants, a federal judge ruled in favor of the NFL at a hearing in Baltimore, and that decision was upheld by the United States Fourth Circuit Court of Appeals in 1963.

Rozelle was faced by his biggest task in 1963, namely, the disclosure that Paul Hornung, star halfback of the Green Bay Packers, and Alex Karras, lineman for the Detroit Lions, were betting on the games. When the facts were in Rozelle enforced appropriate suspension and fines on the players and clubs involved. According to Texas Schram, general manager of the Dallas Cowboys, Rozelle's handling of the scandal "made everybody accept him as commissioner and no longer a boy playing the part. He gained once and for all everybody's complete respect."

Rozelle married Jane Coupe of Chicago in 1949 (one daughter). He is a disarmingly gentle man while settling the not-so-gentle disputes which come his way. Gone forever are the days when he was referred to as the "junior G-man of the National Football League".

Peter Sammartino

Former college president Peter Sammartino was born in New York City, August 15, 1904. He studied at New York University, Sorbonne (Paris), the University of Liberia, Long Island University and Kyung Hee University (Korea).

After teaching in the New York City public schools, City College, New College, Teachers College and Columbia University, he founded and was president of Fairleigh Dickinson University for almost thirty years.

Among Sammartino's many awards are: Cavaliere, Order Crown of Italy; Chevalier, French Legion of Honor; Italian Star of Solidarity; Grand Commander, Order of the Star of Africa; Commander, Order National, Ivory Coast; Silver Medal, Sons of the American Revolution; and Outstanding Citizen of New Jersey.

The author of fourteen books in the educational field, Sammartino married Sylvia Scaramelli in 1933.

Alfred Santangelo

Lawyer and past congressman Alfred Santangelo was born in New York City, June 4, 1912. He was educated at City College and

Columbia Law School. After serving as Assistant District Attorney and as New York State Senator from 1947 to 1954, Santangelo was elected to the United States Congress in 1956, where he served for twelve years.

Now engaged in private practice, he has received many awards including: Interfaith Award; Lido Civic Club Award; Service-in-Congress Award, Italian-American Federation of Democratic Organizations; and the Brotherhood Award, National Business and Professional Council.

Santangelo married Betty Rao in 1942. They have five children: May Jo, Eileen, Betty Jane, Patricia and Charles.

VINCENT SARDI, JR.

A caricature on Sardi's wall (the original caricaturist was paid in meals) is as important a status symbol to actors as footprints outside Grauman's Chinese Theatre some three thousand miles away from the only restaurant ever to win a Tony.

Vincent Sardi carries on in the tradition of his father, running "one of the few restaurants which has become an actor's club." Both father and son have been generous in allowing actors credit.

Born July 23, 1915 in New York City, he was a pre-med student at Columbia before getting into the family business. "I have more trouble with businessmen than with so-called temperamental stars. The stars don't care where they sit so long as it's near some people they know, some of their friends. The business people care where they sit—to them it's important to be where they think is the right place."

Married to actress Adelle Rasey (two children), he has trouble keeping up with the current marital status of his clientele. "Many times a man has come in saying he's dining with his wife and I take him to his old wife instead of his new one."

JOHN SCALI

Award-winning journalist John Scali has been reporting from Washington, D.C. on ABC-TV and Radio since 1961. Having no more honors left to bestow upon him, his union (A.F.T.R.A.) created the John Scali Award to be given to television reports which approach his degree of excellence.

Born April 27, 1918 in Canton, Ohio, John Alfred Scali attended Boston University and received his B.S. degree in Journalism in 1942. He served as a war correspondent for the Associated Press in Europe in 1944 and continued to work for A P until 1961.

He married Helen Lauinger Glock in 1946; they have three children.

John Scarne

"John Scarne is to games what Dr. Einstein was to advanced physics." This statement has been echoed by most, if not all, gamesmen who have tested the skills of the man who is the greatest gambling expert in the world.

Author of many books on the subject, Scarne was gambling adviser to the Havana Hilton casino before Castro took over, and now watches the nationalized gambling houses of Puerto Rico and Panama.

"Gambling is the leading industry in the United States," Scarne says. He estimates the annual gross of that business at five hundred billion dollars. His personal crusade is to expose the professional hustler. He toured Army camps during World War II to teach soldiers how to keep from being taken.

He is an unwelcome guest in all the Nevada casinos because he knows the odds of all the games, and he has created many of his own (Tecko, Follow the Arrow, Scarne and Scarne's Challenge).

Next to gambling, his major love is magic. "Fooling other magicians is my hobby," he said, further stating that he took up magic at the age of five. He charges two hundred dollars a lesson in magic and has instructed many celebrities such as Orson Welles and the Duke of Windsor.

Victor Schiro

Former Mayor of New Orleans, Victor Schiro was born in Chicago, May 28, 1904 and educated at Tulane University. He served three years in the Coast Guard. The owner of Vic Schiro Insurance Agency, he has been very active in New Orleans civic affairs and was elected mayor of that city in 1962.

Formerly Commissioner of Buildings and Parks, Schiro founded the New Orleans Optimist Club. Among his many awards are: Order

Civil Merit of Spain; Gold Medal, Madrid; Italian Star of Solidarity; Knight Grand Cross, Justice of Malta; and Doctor of Science, National College of Canada.

Schiro married Margaret Mary Gibbes in 1932.

JOHN H. SECONDARI

When he formed his own company in 1968, John Hermes Secondari ended his twelve-year association with the American Broadcasting Company. As the executive producer of special projects for BAC-TV, he is responsible for much of the finest historical biographies and documentaries yet seen on television.

Born November 1, 1919 in Rome, Secondari is a descendant of a long line of Italian physicians. His family moved to the United States in 1924, and he became a naturalized citizen in 1929. He received his B.A. degree from Fordham University in 1939, and his master's in journalism from Columbia University the following year. World War II took him back to Europe where he served in the United States Army, leaving in 1946 with the rank of captain.

He stayed in Europe as a reporter for the Rome *Daily American* and later as a foreign correspondent for the Columbia Broadcasting System. He left CBS in 1948 to become deputy chief to the information division of the Economic Cooperation Administration's Special Mission to Italy in Rome. During his three-year stay with the E.C.A., he produced thirty-seven films and eight weekly radio shows.

Secondari quit E.C.A. in 1951 to write his novel *Coins in the Fountain,* which was filmed as *Three Coins in the Fountain* in 1954. Two other novels followed: *Temptation for a King* (1954) and *Spinner of the Dream* (1955).

He joined ABC in 1956, serving as chief of the Washington news bureau for three years and appearing as moderator of a weekly documentary called *Open Hearing.* His first special as a producer was *Korea - No Parallel,* which he also wrote and narrated. *Close-Up!* was Secondari's first long-term special project. A weekly, one-hour series, the show received many accolades in its three-year run. One of the highlight shows of that series was *Meet Comrade Student,* filmed in Russian schools and homes in 1962.

Among Secondari's more successful productions while at ABC are: *The Vatican; The Saga of Western Man* series which focused on the years 1492, 1776, 1898 and 1964; *I, Leonardo da Vinci; Custer to the Little Big Horn; The Pilgrim Adventure; Beethoven*

Ordeal and Triumph; I Am a Soldier; A Visit to Washington with Mrs. Lyndon B. Johnson; and *The Birth of Christ.*

Helen Jean Rogers was already a producer at ABC-TV when she met Secondari. They married in 1961. He has a son by his late wife, Rita Hume, and a daughter by his second marriage.

CESARE SIEPI

Considered the most famous living interpreter of Mozart in his vocal range, bass Cesare Siepi has been a star at the Metropolitan Opera Company since his debut as King Philip in *Don Carlos* in 1949.

Born February 19, 1923 in Milan, Italy, he wanted to be a boxer and got a teaching degree before studying under Cesare Chiesa. His singing career was interrupted by the war when, in 1943, he fled to Switzerland for political reasons. In 1948 Toscanini chose him for the title role in *Mefistofele* and the role of Simon Magno in *Nerone,* both produced in memory of the fortieth anniversary of the death of Boito.

"The demands of my career come ahead of everything else," he said, in 1962. "I have a violent temper. No woman would put up with that." Later that year he married dancer Louellen Sibley.

JOSEPH SISCO

Assistant Secretary of State Joseph Sisco is currently sitting in a hot seat, for he is the chief American negotiator in the Middle East. Described as "a fantastic salesman", he is respected by Arabs and Israelis alike for his candor, impartiality and his encyclopedic knowledge of Middle Eastern affairs.

Born Joseph John Sisco in Chicago, October 31, 1919, he helped finance his education by working as a newspaper reporter, salesman at Sears Roebuck, bartender, and laborer in a steel mill. After graduating *magna cum laude* from Knox College in Galesburg, Illinois, in 1941, he served as a lieutenant in the Army in the Pacific. His service overseas stimulated his interest in foreign affairs. He obtained his M.A. degree in international relations from the University of Chicago in 1947 and completed his studies with a Ph. D., as a specialist in Soviet affairs, in 1950.

Sisco then served as an officer with the Central Intelligence Agency and joined the State Department staff where he was placed in the division dealing with United Nations affairs, which was largely preoccupied with events in the Middle East.

From 1951 to 1958 Sisco was successively foreign affairs officer, specialist in international organization affairs, officer in charge of General Assembly and Security Council affairs, foreign service officer, and officer in charge of U.N. political affairs. He was appointed deputy director in the Office of U.N. Political and Security Affairs in 1958 and became its director in 1960. From 1963 to 1965 he was deputy assistant secretary of the Bureau of International Organization Affairs.

Dean Rusk named Sisco to succeed Harlan Cleveland as Assistant Secretary of State for International Organization Affairs in 1965. The Senate confirmed the appointment and Sisco became the youngest assistant secretary in the State Department.

When Arthur Goldberg left government service in 1968, the role of chief United States mediator in the Middle East fell to Sisco, who had worked in close harmony with Goldberg. He is one of the few men to serve in the upper echelons of the State Department in the administrations of both Lyndon Johnson and Richard Nixon.

During most of 1969, Sisco was locked in heated discussions with Soviet Ambassador Anatoly Dobrynin. He warned Dobrynin, as reported in *Newsweek* (December 1, 1969), before the talks completely bogged down at one of their last meetings: "The rubber band has stretched to its maximum point. And if I let go, it'll hit you in the nose."

According to a report in *Time* (March 8, 1971): "Largely under the aegis of . . . Sisco, the United States has been moving to repair its badly damaged position in the Arab world. Today United States-Arab relations are better than they have been at any time since the Six-Day War of 1967, and as one American diplomat puts it, 'Joe is there pulling all the strings.' "

In 1960 Sisco received the State Department's Superior Service Award, and in 1966 the Civil Service League presented him with its Top Ten Career Service Award. He married Jean Head in 1946 and they have two daughters, Carol and Jane.

PAOLO SOLERI

Architect and urban planner Paolo Soleri was born in Torino, Italy, June 21, 1919. He came to America to serve as apprentice with Frank Lloyd Wright in 1947, but returned to Italy two years later because of differences of personality and architectural theory between himself and Wright.

On his return to his homeland, he built the Solimene ceramics factory. The building's spiral ramps and curved outline blending with the cliffs of the rugged Amalfi Drive bear the mark of Frank Lloyd Wright.

Since 1956 he has lived near Scottsdale, Arizona in "earth houses" that he has constructed from the materials of the desert itself, wasting nothing, preserving the integrity of the landscape. He stunned the public with his brilliant exhibit at the Corcoran Gallery in Washington, D.C. in 1970. His vision, as predicted by Edward Hibgee, "will be more influential than anything now standing in steel, concrete and glass."

Soleri married Carolyn Woods in 1950 and they have two daughters, Kristine and Daniela.

FRANK STELLA

At the age of thirty-three, when most artists are striving for their first one-man shows, Frank Stella was honored with a retrospective exhibition at the Museum of Modern Art in New York City in the spring of 1970. He is an "old master" in the field of Minimal Art, involved with three-dimensional, "shaped" paintings.

"The idea in being a painter is to declare an identity," Stella has said. "Not just my identity, an identity for me, but an identity big enough for everyone to share in."

Born May 12, 1936 in Malden, Massachusetts; Stella studied with abstractionist Patrick Morgan at Phillips Academy in 1950. After receiving his B.A. degree from Princeton in 1958, he settled in a storefront studio in New York City's Lower East Side, supported himself as a housepainter and created his "black" paintings, which impressed critics with their simplicity and austere aesthetic. "Everybody was tired," Stella explained. "All you had to do was do it." At twenty-three, he was the youngest artist in the Museum of Modern Art's "Sixteen Americans" exhibition. The museum bought his *Marriage of Reason and Squalor*.

Stella's "aluminum" series of paintings came next. Like his "black" series, they consisted of simple stripe patterns. Some of the stripes didn't conform with the rectangular corners of the canvas, so he cut them off, thereby creating the first contemporary "shaped canvases." His "copper" series, in 1960, consisted of L-, U-, and other radically shaped canvases. "The Benjamin Moore series," named for a brand of paint which he used right from the can, was exhibited at the Galerie Lawrence in Paris (1961).

The "purple" series are all polygons - among them a trapezoid, pentagon, hexagon, and triangle. Stella cut a corresponding shape out of the center of these paintings which serve as a framing edge for the internal space.

Other, more ambitious series followed. The retrospective exhibition at the Museum of Modern Art consisted of sixty works—forty-one paintings and nineteen drawings. Of the exhibition, Douglas Davis wrote in *Newsweek* "The retrospective reveals . . . a carefully structured career that has become seduced by the sensuousness of its own medium to the point where it no longer represents the cutting polemic edge of vanguard art. Frank Stella is a painter now. He is no longer a logician."

Stella married Barbara Rose, the art critic, in 1961. The marriage, which ended in divorce, produced two children. Stella also lectures and teaches at universities. He has had nineteen one-man showings to date.

GAY TALESE

Writer Gay Talese was born in Ocean City, New Jersey, February 7, 1932. He graduated from the University of Alabama in 1953 and went to work for the *New York Times* as a copy boy. Two years later he was promoted to reporter. His talents as a human interest writer started to show in a piece called "Then and Now" about silent screen actress Nita Naldi, then living in obscurity in Manhattan. That article had a theme to which Talese would often later return. In his own words, "The impermanence of fame, the way people fade in large cities that once adored them, and how little of what we do survives us."

His first book, *New York: A Serendipiter's Journey* (1961) was written from material in his *Times* articles and was well received by the critics, though not a financial success.

Talese left the *Times* in 1965 and produced a national bestseller four years later in *The Kingdom and the Power*, a book about the history of the *Times*. In 1971 *Honor Thy Father* was published. It sold more than 300,000 copies within four months, and in March 1972 Fawcett purchased the paperback rights for a record $451,000.

Tom Wolfe, considered by many to be the inventor of the "new journalism," has recognized Talese as the real pioneer in that literary genre, in which the techniques of fiction are applied to the craft of nonfiction.

His third collection of articles, *Fame and Obscurity* (1970) covers the new journalism practised by Wolfe, Norman Mailer, Truman Capote, and himself, with emphasis on his own methods.

Talese married Nan Ahearn, a senior editor at Random House, in 1959. They have two daughters, Pamela and Catherine.

RENATA TEBALDI

One of the great sopranos of her time, Renata Tebaldi was stricken with polio when she was a child. Her mother was "my best friend, my adviser, my constant companion, the full partner of my life."

Born January 2, 1922, in Pesaro, Italy, she studied singing at the Parma Conservatory and later with Carmen Melis. She made her debut in Rovigo as Elena in *Mefistofele* (1943). After World War II Toscanini engaged her for La Scala.

She received great acclaim on her tours which had taken her all over the world before she made her debut at the Metropolitan Opera Company as Desdemona in 1955.

Of her rivalry with Maria Callas, she said, "It is against my nature to hate. Perhaps it is Callas who hates me."

GEORGIO TOZZI

His powerful and expressive bass voice has brought Georgio Tozzi applause wherever his world travels have taken him.

Born January 8, 1923, in Chicago, he began as a concert singer, but after further study in Italy and a guest appearance at La Scala he was invited to the Metropolitan Opera Company in 1955. He has had great success as Figaro in *Le Nozze di Figaro,* as Don Basilio in *Il Barbiere di Siviglia,* and in 1958 he sang the part of the Doctor in the world premiere of *Vanessa.*

He has also appeared on Broadway in *South Pacific.* "No real artist can forget that he must convey emotions, not just sing," he said. "You phrase your gestures and body movements within a musical idiom . . . whether it's opera or musical comedy."

He was married to the late Catherine Dieringer.

JACK VALENTI

Jack Valenti's shift from President Johnson's right-hand-man to president of the Motion Picture Association of America came as a surprise in 1966. Perhaps Johnson's most dedicated worker, Valenti fought back the tears when he explained to White House reporters that he was making the move for the financial needs of his growing family. The new post reportedly carried a salary of over a hundred thousand dollars a year plus expenses, compared to the thirty thousand he was earning in Washington, D.C.

Born in Houston, Texas, September 5, 1921, Valenti is the son of a clerk in the county tax office of that city. He was the youngest graduate of Sam Houston High School at the age of fifteen. He became an office boy for the Humble Oil Company while studying at the University of Houston.

Valenti became a bomber pilot in World War II, flying fifty-one missions in Europe. His war decorations include the Distinguished Flying Cross, the Air Medal, the Distinguished Unit Citation, and the European Theatre Ribbon. Returning to Houston, he graduated from the University of Houston with a degree in business and earned his master's degree from the Harvard Graduate School of Business Administration in 1948. He then returned to Humble as head of advertising and promotion.

In 1952 Valenti left Humble to form the advertising agency of Weekley and Valenti, Inc. with classmate Weldon Weekley. The agency handled the campaign advertising for a succession of political candidates, including the state Eisenhower campaign in 1952.

Valenti met Lyndon Johnson, then a United States Senator, at a business gathering where Johnson gave a speech, which impressed Valenti greatly. He worked for Johnson in his unsuccessful bid for the Presidential nomination at the Democratic National Convention in Los Angeles and joined his staff when President Kennedy was assassinated.

He became Johnson's trouble-shooter and constant companion in Washington. He once described his post as that of the "roving line-backer" of the White House staff. He read everything before it crossed the President's desk, edited his speeches, and provided social relaxation for the President.

In his new position as head of Hollywood's self-censorship body, Valenti wrote a new code which reflected the reality of a more liberal public morality than existed when the original code was written in the early 1930's. He proposed a rating system to protect the public from films they didn't want to see or have their children see, rather than attempt to tell movie-makers what they should or should not film. The rating system has worked well as a means of preventing public censorship crusades, while increasing the artistic scope of the filmmaker.

Valenti married Mary Margaret Wiley, former secretary to President Johnson, in 1962. They have three children.

HENRY VISCARDI, JR.

In his book *The Abilities Story* (1967), Henry Viscardi tells of his experiences in rehabilitating handicapped people to lead useful, joyful, and dignified lives through self-support. Severely handicapped himself, before being fitted with artificial legs at the age of twenty-six, Viscardi has dedicated his life to the cause of the disabled.

Born May 12, 1912 in New York City, Viscardi has described the disability with which he was born: "What should have been legs were half-formed deformities, stumps, like somebody's unfinished statue." On his first day at school in New York City's Upper West Side (after spending his first six years in hospitals), some of his classmates beat him up and called him "Ape Man."

After finishing school, he became manager of the basketball team at Newtown High School (though only three feet, eight inches tall) and reported the outcome of the games to the New York *Times*. After working his way through three years at Fordham University, he was hired as a clerk in the law firm of Gellman and Gellman in Corona, Queens. Then he became supervisor of the taxation division of the Home Owners Loan Corporation.

In 1936 Manhattan limbmaker, George Dorsch, designed a pair of artificial legs for him which other limbmakers said couldn't be made. They increased his height by two feet, and he was able to dance, enjoy his boating hobby and walk with only a trace of a limp.

He includes a letter to Dr. Yanover, the man who treated him and introduced him to George Dorsch, in his autobiography, *A Man's Stature* (1952): "For a time the intoxicating joy of living as a normal man has been so great that all ambition died too, and every hour was the exploration of a new world."

In 1941 the Red Cross accepted Viscardi as a special field service officer in rehabilitation of amputees. From 1943-1945 he held the posts of adviser on the employment of disabled veterans to the surgeon general of the Air Forces and to the director of the War Production Board.

After the war he covered sports events for the Mutual Broadcasting Company and became director of personnel of Burlington Mills in 1947. He left Burlington Mills in 1949 to become executive director of JOB (Just One Break, Inc.), set up an office at Bellevue Hospital, and created a program to change the attitude of prejudiced leaders in industry and labor so that the handicapped person could find employment.

Thousands of blind persons, amputees, and victims of polio and cerebral palsy have found suitable work through JOB. Viscardi then started another pilot project, Abilities, Inc., in 1952. Begun on "a shoestring and a dream" in a vacant garage, the program trains handicapped people to serve in the electronics industry. Within a decade Abilities, Inc. set the pattern for plants in more than thirty countries abroad.

Since 1955 Viscardi has been president and chairman of the board of the Human Resources Foundation. Its purpose is to study the physiological and psychological changes taking place in Abilities, Inc. employees as a result of their work.

Viscardi has received numerous awards and citizenship citations for his work. Among his books are: *Give Us the Tools* (1959); *A Laughter in the Lonely Night* (1961); *A Letter to Jimmy* (1962); and *The School* (1964).

Viscardi married Lucille Darracq in 1946 while both were working for the Mutual Broadcasting System. They have four daughters.

FRANK VITTOR

Sculptor Frank Vittor was born in Como, Italy, January 6, 1888. He studied art at the Brera Academy and under sculptor Bazzaro in Milan. His works range from tablets, plaques and bronze portrait busts of famous personalities to monuments, statues, war memorials, and fountains.

Especially notable are his busts of Presidents Theodore Roosevelt, Wilson and Coolidge, all of whom posed for him and the statue of George Washington at Braddock, Pennsylvania, which was used as model for a U.S. postage stamp.

Vittor has received many honors, including the Grand Prize and Gold Medal at the Bologna Art Shows in 1932 and 1934. He married Adda Mae Humphreys in 1917. They have five children: Frank Jr., Gloria, Phoebe, Carla, and Anthonym.

JOHN A. VOLPE

As Secretary of Transportation in President Nixon's cabinet, John Volpe had the job of turning off the tide of air pollution caused by the internal combustion engine. He concluded the answer lay in cleaner, more efficient, public transportation and fewer private cars on the road.

Born December 8, 1908 in Wakefield, Massachusetts, John Anthony Volpe was the eldest of four sons. He had hoped to enter the Massachusetts Institute of Technology upon graduation from high school, but his father's plastering business failed, and he worked as a plasterer for two years before entering the Wentworth Institute at Boston in 1928. He majored in architectural construction, continuing to work as a plasterer and dress salesman to finance his education. He went to work for a construction company after graduation, but the Depression cost him his job.

In 1933, with money he saved from selling clothes, he won a bid to build a boiler-room and formed the John A. Volpe Construction Company, with himself as president.

He closed his prospering business during the war years, joined the Civil Engineer Corps of the Navy, trained Seabees, and was discharged in 1946, having reached the rank of lieutenant commander. Volpe then reactivated his construction company, and for the next fifteen years built hospitals, schools, shopping centers, public buildings, and military installations along the Eastern seaboard and in other parts of the country.

Never having engaged in highway construction, Volpe was named Federal Highway Administrator by President Eisenhower in 1957 to fill an interim term. He was elected Governor of Massachusetts in 1961, defeated in 1963, then reelected in 1965. He is an officer of five banks and the publisher of two suburban newspapers, the Malden *News* and the Medford *Daily Mercury.*

He married Jennie Benedetto in 1934, and they have two children.

FRANCES WINWAR

Francesca Vinciguerra has been writing novels, biographies, and literary criticism since 1923. She co-founded the Leonardo da Vinci Art School in New York City, lectured on Victorian literary figures, and taught at the University of Kansas City (Missouri).

Born in Taormina, Sicily, May 3, 1900, her parents brought her to the United States when she was seven years old, and she became naturalized in 1929. In 1933 she was awarded the *Atlantic Monthly* $5,000 prize in biography for *Poor Splendid Wings.* She translated *Don Carlo, Lucia di Lammermoor,* and *La Traviata* in 1950.

Her novels and biographies include: *The Immortal Lovers: Elizabeth Barrett and Robert Browning,* 1950; *The Eagle and The*

Rock, 1953; *The Last Love of Camille,* 1954; *Wingless Victory,* 1956; *The Haunted Palace: Edgar Allan Poe,* 1959; *Jean Jacques Rousseau: Conscience of an Era,* 1961; and *Up from Caesar,* 1965.

She is divorced from Bernard Grebanier and has one son, Francis.

Frank Zappa

All the strange rock groups of the late Sixties seem pale when compared to Frank Zappa and his group, the Mothers of Invention. What's more, Frank Zappa will be around when the others are long forgotten.

Although trained in classical music, Frank started his musical career in a high school band in California. In the Sixties, when the Beatles' English invasion was in full force and it still wasn't yet fashionable to be freaky, he and several other musicians organized a freaky group called Captain Glasspack and his Magic Mufflers, which later evolved into the Mothers of Invention. When they rose to prominence in 1966 they were bizarre and shocking; in 1968 they barely raised an eyebrow. On the surface they were ugly—bearded and menacing like rogues out of an old pirate movie—and their music was ugly. The music was satire, all done with almost classical sophistication.

The Mothers were as fascinating as a monster movie. Their first album, *Freak Out,* was unlike anything that was happening at the time (1966). It was not only social and musical satire, but also the first rock album produced as if it were a single piece of music.

The group's style and technique borrowed very cleverly from everything—early rock and roll, modern classical composers, jazz, Rudy Vallee megaphone crooning. They used props and visual aids to bring to rock a whole new element of art, theater and audience participation. Zappa satirized everything from hippies to the middle-class. Even his song titles carry his message: *Chrome Plated Megaphone of Destiny* and *Nasal Retentive Calliope Music.* In the late Sixties the Mothers of Invention broke up, but their albums are still being released. Their legend grows every year.

The Chairman of the Board

Frank Sinatra retired officially from show business at a Los Angeles benefit which netted eight-hundred-thousand dollars for the Motion Picture and Television Relief Fund in June, 1971. Among the celebrities who openly wept as he sang his swan songs were Rosalind Russell and Barbra Streisand, thus illustrating the scope of a following which has applauded his talents for thirty-five years.

The sadness of the occasion was rooted in the feeling that this was not simply the end of a career, but the end of a love affair between an exceptional talent and the American people. Like all great romances the road was often rocky; but when future historians decide who has been the finest entertainer of the Twentieth Century, Frank Sinatra will surely be among the nominees.

Perhaps the most maligned man of his time by the American press, Sinatra has had to fight for every inch of his success. When one hack falsely accused him of carrying two million dollars in small bills from Lucky Luciano to a Hollywood hood, Sinatra dryly pointed out that such a sum would weigh five thousand pounds. The most recent slur came shortly after his farewell performance. It was reported that he had been admitted to a Santa Monica hospital for treatment for throat cancer. He was vacationing in Europe when the story broke.

Perhaps blinded by sour grapes, the press has never focused its attention on the single ingredient most responsible for the fruition of Frank Sinatra's dreams, namely, work.

Hard, constant work. This was evident on a cold Sunday in Hoboken, New Jersey. It was December 12, 1915, and Francis Albert Sinatra had to work to be born. Scaling in at thirteen-and-a-half pounds, the contender was permanently scarred on the left side of his head and neck by a forceps delivery and almost lost his left ear in the process.

Martin and Natalie Sinatra had emigrated from Italy. Both had blue eyes, which served to their advantage in their new Irish-dominated city. Martin worked as a boilermaker and had fought as a bantamweight under the Irish alias of Marty O'Brien. Natalie "Dolly" Sinatra became deeply involved in local politics and left most of Frank's upbringing to an aunt, her mother, and a Jewish neighbor. Martin wanted his son to become a fighter. Dolly wanted him to go to college and make something of himself. When she found a picture of Bing Crosby in Frank's bedroom, and he told her he wanted to become a singer, she threw a shoe at him.

In the early 1920's Hoboken was a rough port and railroad town, often visited by rum-runners. A man's fists generally determined his worth. A draft deferment due to a punctured eardrum bears out Frank's stories about his experiences in gang wars.

If he inherited his "Sicilian temper" from his father, his mother bestowed upon him her fetish for cleanliness. His incessant hand-washing was later dubbed "the Lady Macbeth bit" by members of the Tommy Dorsey band. "I am a symmetrical man, almost to a fault," Sinatra said recently. "I demand everything in its place. My clothing must hang just so . . ."

Dolly had worked herself up to the position of Democratic ward leader and made enough money to buy a bar which Martin tended. Young Frank's needs transcended those satisfied by money. "I'll never forget that kid," said a Hoboken neighbor. "He'd just lean against his grandmother's door and stare into space." He was engrossed by the gangster movies of that time, and was already gaining a reputation for picking up his friend's tabs.

In 1933 the biggest vocalist in the country was Bing Crosby. Frankie took his girl, Nancy Barbato, to hear Bing at Loew's Journal Square Theatre in Jersey City; and after the performance, he vowed to become a singer. For the next six years he ground through a maze of singing jobs which brought in little money, but eventually landed him a job with the Harry James band. "In Nancy," Frank has said, "I found beauty, warmth, and understanding. Being with her was my only escape from what seemed a grim world. All I knew up to that time were tough kids on street corners, gang fights, and parents who were always busy trying to make money . . ."

He sang as an amateur in movie-vaudeville theatres, and his quartet won a Major Bowes Amateur contest. The group was then named the Hoboken Four and went on tour. They traveled to Hollywood. But dissension broke up the group and Frankie came back to New Jersey.

Early in 1936 Frank continued to entertain in local clubs armed with his public address system. He was also getting radio work. He sang on station WAAT in Newark for carfare. The station accompanist at WNEW in New York City was Jimmy Rich, who recalled, "I'd come out of my office, and he'd be standing there to see me or anybody who would listen to him. Somehow he'd get past the receptionist . . . He was a pusher but polite."

For a year and a half Frank sang at the Rustic Cabin, a roadhouse near Alpine, New Jersey for fifteen dollars a week. He married Nancy in February, 1939, and a few months later Harry James signed him to a two-year contract at five times that amount. They played Baltimore, New York and Atlantic City. During their two-and-a-half-month stay at the Panther Room in Chicago's Hotel Sherman, a *Downbeat* reporter complimented Frank's singing to the bandleader. Said Mr. James, "Not so loud. The kid's name is Sinatra. He considers himself the greatest vocalist in the business. Get that! Not even one hit record. No one ever heard of him. He looks like a wet rag. But he says he is the greatest. If he hears you compliment him, he'll demand a raise tonight . . ."

From Chicago, the band traveled to Los Angeles to play in the Palomar Ballroom, but the dance hall had burned down. James took an alternate date at Victor Hugo's, but the band was neither well received nor paid. The disappointed group headed back to New

York. James couldn't afford two vocalists due to this setback and had to fire Connie Haines.

Tommy Dorsey secretly auditioned Sinatra and made him an offer. With mixed emotions Frank asked Harry James to be released. It was January, 1939, and Frank needed more money because Nancy was expecting a baby. He described the break: "It was after midnight. There was nobody around and I stood alone with my suitcase in the snow and watched the tail lights of the bus disappear. Then the tears started and I tried to run after the bus."

The Dorsey band crowded in as many one-night stands as possible between engagements at the Meadowbrook, the Astor Roof, and the Hollywood Palladium. The pace was grueling, traveling in a bus all day, performing at night, then back on the bus to the next town.

Frank's early vocals were "My Prayer," "Careless," "All the Things You Are," and "South of the Border." "Marie" was a production number in which Frank was joined by the Pied Pipers, three men and Jo Stafford. Dorsey's quick temper created an atmosphere of tension in the band, and Sinatra's fighting instinct erupted several times under those tense conditions. "Once in Omaha," Jo Stafford recalls, "a man in the audience threw some popcorn while I was singing. Frank flew off the bandstand in a rage. Fortunately, he couldn't pick the man out of the sea of faces. But he was ready to tear him to pieces."

Showing the stamina of a workhorse, Sinatra polished "I'll Never Smile Again" which became his first hit record in the summer of 1940, an event which coincided with the birth of Nancy, Jr.

During the next two years Frank recorded with Dorsey such classics as "This Love of Mine," "Night and Day," "Stardust," "The Song Is You," "Lamplighter's Serenade," and "The Night We Called It a Day," which became prophetic as Frank wanted to break away from the band and record as a solo artist. Dorsey balked, then let him go, but not with the handshake with which Harry James had resolved their differences. Frank had to pay heavily for his release. He resented it, but always credited Tommy with helping him become a better musician. "Tommy taught me everything I knew about singing," Frank has said. "He was my real education." He learned breath control from Dorsey and translated the flowing quality Dorsey achieved on his trombone to his voice.

There was a lull just before the storm. A strike of recording musicians in August, 1942, prevented Sinatra from cutting records. He sang "Night and Day" in the movie *Reveille with Beverly*. It was just a three-minute spot, but within a few months Columbia would be giving him star billing in the film. He tried to get a job as staff singer at NBC in Hollywood and was turned down.

Back at the Mosque Theatre in Newark in November, his young screaming followers were creating bedlam. Harry Romm, Sinatra's agent with General Artists Corporation brought Bob Weitman, the managing director of the Paramount Theatre in New York City, to hear him perform. The audience went crazy, and Weitman decided much of their joy was due to the fact that Sinatra was from nearby Hoboken. Nevertheless, he signed Sinatra as an "Extra Added Attraction" to Benny Goodman, Peggy Lee, Jess Stacy and the Benny Goodman Sextet, who were headlining at the Paramount. Weitman told Goodman he had hired Sinatra, and the famous clarinetist said, "Who's he?"

Mr. Goodman and the whole world found out exactly who Frank Sinatra was on the evening of December 30, 1942. Not knowing how to introduce the stranger in their midst, Goodman took the microphone toward the end of the show and simply stated, "And now, Frank Sinatra." The bobby-soxers erupted as the skinny kid with the big bow tie sauntered out of the wings. As Frank has described that moment: "The sound that greeted me was absolutely deafening. It was a tremendous roar . . . I was scared stiff . . . I couldn't move a muscle. Benny froze too . . . He turned around, looked at the audience and asked, 'What the hell is that?' I burst out laughing and gave out with 'For Me and My Gal.' "

The girls screamed and moaned. Many fainted. In a moment Frank Sinatra had taken the place of their boy friends fighting overseas. The crowds became larger and even more hysterical throughout his eight-week engagement at the Paramount. Without knowing it, he had kicked off the age of the popular ballad singer. The swing era, dominated by the big bands, would steadily decline and disappear within three years. *Time* magazine reported, "not since the days of Rudolph Valentino has American womanhood made such unabashed public love to an entertainer."

Within a month the young sensation had a spot on the nationwide radio show "Your Hit Parade" and a RKO picture contract. The sophisticated Park Avenue set was skeptical that he was anything but a fad. The posh Riobamba Club, struggling in wartime, paid him seven-hundred-fifty dollars a week to find out. His run lasted ten weeks, his salary doubled, and the club was in the black once again. Master of ceremonies Walter O'Keefe put it this way: "When I came into this place, I was the star and a kid named Sinatra one of the acts. Then suddenly a steamroller came along and knocked me flat. Ladies and gentlemen, I give you the rightful star-Frank Sinatra!"

That and his next engagement at the Waldorf's Wedgwood Room were the young singer's most emotionally grueling experiences up to that point in his career. Though his nervousness wasn't visible, it kept him from being carried away by the wave of rave notices. But however humbled he may have been by his environment, he stopped hecklers dead in their tracks with a word or a look.

By October 1944, the last Frank Sinatra skeptics threw in the towel. Frank was back at the Paramount and the conditions were nearly impossible. "The Columbus Day Riot" consisted of 30,000 teenagers waiting outside the 3,600-seat theatre. The box office was crushed and shop windows were broken. It took nearly eight hundred policemen to break it up. Inside the theater a teenage boy hit Sinatra with an egg. The girls turned on the egg thrower and nearly killed him. *The New Yorker* wasn't stretching the point when they dubbed him, "an American phenomenon."

Most music reporters were baffled by their inability to define Sinatra's appeal and tended to write him off as a fad or a press agent's fabrication. He didn't *look* like a star to them; but they failed to realize that while the most handsome stars of the period were easy to worship, they were not easy to identify with. He quickly became not just the idol, but the spokesman of the younger generation. Rare was the woman of any age who didn't think that he was singing just to her. The boys would soon forget their wounded pride and accept him as their spokesman too, because he disarmed them with his sincerity. When he sang a lyric he meant it. He believed the words. He didn't add them to the music, he wove them into the fabric of the melody. His piercing peacock blue eyes certainly had a hypnotic quality, and his voice had tonal beauty and good range; but his sincere desire to communicate gave each member of the audience the feeling that he was sharing a deep dark secret with them alone.

* * *

"Frank was born to be a star," publicist George Evans once said, "but he was also born to be a controversial figure, and a star and a controversial figure he will remain until he dies."

Frank Sinatra openly worshipped President Roosevelt, and when he offered his services to help FDR with his fourth campaign, his friends told him it was bad for his career. Republican Senators ranted, and columnist Westbrook Pegler called him the "New Dealing crooner." But Sinatra made it very clear that he would give up his career before compromising a principle, and his following generally applauded his decision not to play it safe.

Out of his association with FDR came his desire to plunge into another frying pan, namely, that of calling attention to the issue of discrimination. Remembering the Hoboken catcalls of "guinea" and "wop," his battle against every form of prejudice was one he had waged throughout his life with his fists, but FDR taught him the final battles would be won through education.

In 1945 he again went against his advisers' wishes and began to speak out on the subject of discrimination at youth rallies and in high school assemblies. The newspapers which cheered him when he slugged a Southern counterman for refusing to serve a black musician in his band touring days suddenly became suspicious of his motives when the point was raised in their back yard. Frank's suggestion that the youth of America should work toward better human understanding through the United Nations was heavily criticized in the press. Even when he was accused of "Communist leanings" by congressmen, he didn't flinch.

He made a short film with Mervyn LeRoy called *The House I Live In* in which he discussed discrimination with young people of various racial and religious backgrounds. He received brickbats and bouquets for putting his ideas on film. In March 1946, he and LeRoy were awarded special Oscars for their contribution to *The House I Live In*. Through the years Sinatra has been a very lively force in fighting discrimination within his own industry.

* * *

The pace Sinatra established for himself from 1943 to 1952 was overwhelming by any standard. During this time he participated in ninety-six recording sessions, cutting 281 songs. He worked to break house records in theaters. To set a $93,000 weekly gross in Chicago he had to do forty-five shows a week, singing eighty to one hundred songs a day. In addition, there were club dates and his weekly radio show. Firmly established as the major vocalist in the country, he wanted to add Hollywood to his list of properties. He made thirteen movies by 1952 and was voted "the most popular screen star of the year" by movie fans as early as 1946.

There was always tension—difficulties with the press, physical exhaustion, and later, tax problems. The money was there and he spent it. He paid other people's hospital bills like a one-man Blue Cross, never seeking any publicity for his charitable acts. The busiest man in town, he could always be counted on for benefit performances.

The public eats up its favorites, and he couldn't keep up with its ravenous appetite. By 1950 his popularity had begun to slip. Fans were turning to Frankie Laine, Hank Williams, Johnny Ray, and Tony Bennett, among many others. He also contributed to bringing disfavor on himself. He had vowed not to let his career interfere with his life style, and when he left Nancy to woo Ava Gardner, he felt public disapproval for the first time. His romantic escapades were overlooked, but he wasn't supposed to let it affect his wife and family. Ava did not have that kind of identification with the fans. She was a Delilah-like creature, who could drive men mad. Declaring his love for one woman temporarily cost Sinatra the love of millions of women, and the trust of a like number of men.

Nancy divorced him in 1950 and he married Ava the following

year. He wanted to own her, and she wanted to change him. They each fought losing battles with love. Frank got the rest he needed from a public which exerted more pressure than he bargained for. The press quit hounding him. They also quit talking about him.

By 1952 his career was in serious jeopardy. His box office appeal had slumped. His record sales were off. His club dates were drawing less and less. His critics were writing his professional obituary.

He went to Africa to be with Ava while she was filming *Magambo* with Clark Gable. Unable to face the possibility of becoming known as Ava Gardner's husband, he was soon a bundle of nerves wanting to return to work, wondering if there would be any work to return to.

He had read James Jones' novel *From Here To Eternity*. "For the first time in my life," Frank has said, "I was reading something I really had to do. I just felt it - I just knew I could do it, and I just couldn't get it out of my head. I knew that if a picture was ever made, I was the only actor to play Private Maggio, the funny and sour Italo-American. I knew Maggio. I went to high school with him in Hoboken. I was beaten up with him. I might have been Maggio." He heard Harry Cohn was making the film for Columbia Pictures and asked to be tested for the picture. Cohn was convinced that Sinatra was only a singer, not an actor, as though the two crafts were mutually exclusive. Frank offered Cohn his services at one thousand dollars a week, taking the chance of losing the part by selling himself so cheaply, but choosing to gamble on his knowledge of Cohn's love of a bargain. He later admitted he would have done the role for nothing.

Cohn agreed to test him, but Sinatra returned to Africa without much hope. He kept hearing of other actors who were being tested for the role, and that didn't help his relations with his wife. The cable for him to appear for a screen test arrived. At his own expense, Frank flew back to Hollywood. Producer Buddy Adler gave him a script, but Frank said he didn't need it. "I didn't intend going down on the stage," Adler later said, "but I got a call from Fred Zinnemann, 'You'd better come down here. You'll see something unbelievable. I already have it in the camera. I'm not using film this time. But I want you to see it.'

"None of us thought Frank had a chance," Adler continued. "But I went down to the stage. Frank thought he was making another take - and he was terrific. I thought to myself, if he's like that in the movie, it's a sure Academy Award."

Adler was right. Frank won the supporting player Oscar in 1953. He began making records again. His voice was different. The bell-clear tones of before were huskier. It was an older voice, one tempered with experience that comes from setback. In today's parlance, he now had "soul."

Just as 1944 had been his year, 1954 was Elvis Presley's year, and 1964 belonged to the Beatles. Yet in 1954, Frank Sinatra swept *Billboard's* annual poll of disk jockeys, scoring as number one male vocalist and having "Young at Heart" picked as the year's top single and his *Swing Easy* album as the best LP of the year. And in 1965, he recorded such hits as "Strangers in the Night," "That's Life," and split a Gold Record with daughter Nancy ("Something Stupid").

* * *

Since 1954, Frank Sinatra has made thirty-one movies, fourteen of which have made the "All-Time Box-Office Champ" list (based on a gross of at least four million dollars); and cut about eight hundred sides in approximately two hundred recording sessions. All this came after "Frankie" had taken a nose dive, and "Frank" emerged to have another go at it.

There were more troubles along the way. After his playboy image cost him his association with President Kennedy, in addition, his short marriage to Mia Farrow ended in divorce.

His life has been one of constant adjustment, perhaps the single most important ingredient of any lasting success. His power as an entertainer was so great he could, and did, change nightclubs from the red to the black with a single performance. Frank Sinatra doesn't go where the action is, he *is* the action.

Continuing to adjust to change, he will work for what he believes in. He hasn't retired; he's shifting gears, looking for the next place to use his energies. The current music scene doesn't interest him. He changed so much of the system he has become a part of it. He is now a man of wealth and great social mobility, and he is still doing his thing his way.

Millions of people all over the world have been touched by the emotions he has communicated through songs and movies over the past thirty-five years. It was inevitable that his last appearance should have a note of sadness about it. The baby spot hit him as he went into the lush, haunting ballad "Angel Eyes". The light narrowed as it moved up to catch just his face. The voice was in fine form as he sang, " 'Scuse me, while I . . . disappear . . ."

And he did.

Societies and Associations

Approximately a quarter of the million members of Knights of Columbus are Italian-Americans. This fraternal society of Catholic men has its home office in New Haven, Connecticut.

Knights of Columbus was founded in 1882 by a priest who organized immigrant workers to establish an insurance fund for the widows of its members. The organization takes part in national, state, and community affairs. It is a separate body from the Roman Catholic Church.

Though their major concerns are with providing services to children, the aged, and the impoverished, their interests extend to many areas such as ecology and problems which arise in the schools.

Transportation Secretary John A. Volpe and Carmen R. Capone are on the Board of Directors of Knights of Columbus. Other prominent Italian-Americans within the organization include: Bishop Charles P. Greco, Supreme Chaplain; Senator John Pastore; and Representatives Frank Annunzio, Peter Rodino, Joseph P. Addabbo, Mario Biaggi, and Frank Borasco.

* * *

The Italian-American Civil Rights League was established in 1970 to fight anti-Italian discrimination in media and education. Its home office is in New York City. Because of its work, President Nixon issued a directive to the Justice Department to cease using such epithets as "Mafia" and "Cosa Nostra" in their releases. Among their supporters are: Frank Sinatra, Enzo Stuarti, Joe Pepitone, Congressman Mario Biaggi, and Mayor Joseph Alioto.

* * *

Among other organizations which have served the Italian-American community as significantly are the Sons of Italy and the Italian-American War Veterans of the United States.

EPILOGUE

There is no profession in America in which Italian-Americans are not employed. They are artists, scientists, university professors, journalists, clergymen, judges, politicians, teachers, lawyers, doctors, social workers, designers, builders, engineers and master craftsmen.

Men from Italian families occupy town halls, governors' mansions, and the legislatures and supreme courts of states; they also sit in the Congress as representatives in the House and Senate. It is very possible that one day a President of the United States will be from an Italian-American background.

If one looks at an Italian-American, one will surely notice a zest for life; a deep love and loyalty for family; pleasure in food, companionship, gayety; robust and honest emotions; gestures that speak as eloquently as the tongue; a love for craftsmanship, be it manual or intellectual.

Italian-Americans have made major contributions in the arts. Among the notable Italian singers have been the incomparable tenor, Enrico Caruso, and also Giovanni Martinelli, Tito Schipa, Beniamino Gigli, Amelita Galli-Curci, Licia Albanese, Ezio Pinza and Mario Lanza. More recently we have Renata Tebaldi, Mario Del Monaco, Franco Corelli, Georgio Tozzi, Cesare Siepi, Giulietta Simonato. Performing in the same area were highly popular orchestra leaders, Eddy Duchin and his son, Peter; Guy Lombardo, Frankie Carle, Carmen Cavallaro and Louis Prima.

Italian-Americans have brought classical music to new heights of public interest. Two of the first music conservatories in this country were opened in the early 1800's by the famed Italian composer and musician, Philip Traetta. One of the most famous Italian-American virtuoso instrumentalists is violinist Ruggiero Ricci.

Fine music has come from Walter Piston, Norman Dello Joio, and Gian-Carlo Menotti. Among his better known music and libretti are: *Amahl and the Night Visitors, The Medium, The Telephone,* and *The Saint of Bleecker Street.*

The acting profession has long known Italians. Titans from the field of drama are Tommaso Salvini, Adelaide Ristori, and Eleonora Duse. Well known Italian-American actors have been Henry Armetta, Eduardo Cianelli, Joseph Callea, and Monty Banks. Ezio Pinza, the handsome basso opera star, also appeared in the stage musicals *South Pacific* and *Fanny* and in several movies. The stage singer-actor Alfred Drake is of Italian stock.

The increasingly international movie industry has brought stars such as Gina Lollobrigida, Sophia Loren, Rossano Brazzi, Vittorio Gassmann and Marcello Mastroianni into American theatres.

Notable Italian-American comedians have been Jimmy Savo, Lou Costello, Jerry Colonna, and Jimmy Durante. Remo Bufano was a great puppeteer whose work delighted children.

America owes much to its Italian sculptors. Among the most important of these being Attilio Piccirilli, who worked on monuments in New York and Washington, D. C. The Rome-born sculptor Beniamino Bufano has given us many ingenious and original sculptures in the San Francisco area, most notably his statue of Peace at the entrance to the International Airport. The Italian-born painter Rico Lebrun is probably the most widely known and respected Italian-American artist.

Italians have also lent their talents to writing and illustrating children's books, some of which are accepted as classics. Valenti Angelo, Leo Politi, and Leo Lionni are among these. Many major advertising agencies have Italian-Americans as art directors. The field of achitecture also attracts many Italian-Americans; most prominent among them are Anthony J. DePace and Pietro Belluschi, head of the Department of Architecture at M.I.T. A Cultural Heritage Monument was the result of the lacy, spiral towers made of steel and concrete, built in Watts by Simon Rodia. In Arizona, Paolo Soleri is famous for his unusual ceramics.

In sports—a corner of the entertainment world—Italian-Americans have flourished. They first made their presence known in prize fighting, an arena where contestants of minority groups have made their mark. Among the early champions were Sam and Vince Lazzaro, brothers using the names Joe and Vince Dundee, who became welterweight and middleweight title-holders. In other areas of sports we have had famed baseball players such as Joe Di Maggio, Phil Rizzuto and Yogi Berra, all perennial stars for the Yankees. Two prominent football players were Frank Carideo and Joe Savoldi of Notre Dame. Italian-Americans have also excelled in golf, horse racing and automobile racing.

Two principal features of Italian life—food and wine—have employed many Italians in America. Italians know and love farming. Many subsequently left farms for careers in shipping or wholesaling of fruits and produce. "Patsy" D'Agostino of New York built a chain of grocery stores. Still others began the manufacture of Italian foods. Buitoni and La Rosa manufacture dozens of quality Italian food products.

Much of the growth of the American wine industry is due to the vigor and motivation of the Italians. Fine wines are made by Louis

Martini and by the Mondavi family of Charles Krug Winery. The biggest holders of vineyard estates are Petri and the Gallo brothers.

In other business ventures Italians have made significant advances. The first Italian-American to become a millionaire was Generoso Pope, who worked his way from waterboy on a road gang to owner of a large and highly profitable sand and gravel contracting business. He also had several other types of businesses, one of which was the publication, *Il Progresso Italo-Americano* of New York, the nation's most widely-read Italian-American newspaper. His son Fortunato Pope continues his enterprises.

Many Italian-Americans became lawyers. The best-known trial lawyer of Italian stock is Melvin Belli, the "king of torts." Many Italians, trained as lawyers, entered politics and the Italian vote helped them win positions in city or state governments, a judgeship, or seats in Congress. Congressmen Fiorello La Guardia and Vito Marcantonio, and elective judges Ferdinand Pecora and Salvatore Cortillo, were consistent and conscientious leaders who fought for the rights and well-being of all Americans.

On the west coast an important politician for many years was Angelo Rossi, one of San Francisco's most popular mayors. For years Albert Rosellini served as governor of the state of Washington. Other state governors have been Massachusetts' Foster Furcolo and John Volpe, New York's Charles Poletti, Ohio's Michael V. Di Salle, Rhode Island's John A. Notte and John O. Pastore. Pastore, a skillful political tactician and one of the finest orators in the country, later became a Senator, the highest elective office yet achieved by anyone of Italian heritage. The highest appointive office held by an Italian-American was the cabinet post of Secretary of Health, Education and Welfare, to which Anthony J. Celebrezze, was appointed. Celebrezze was also the outstanding reform mayor of Cleveland. John F. Kennedy was impressed by his brilliant work and asked him to join his political team. Jack Valenti was a close adviser and aide to former President Lyndon Johnson. Valenti is now the highly paid president of the Motion Picture Association of America.

The Italians were slow in uniting and organizing to upgrade their working conditions. Out of financial desperation, the poor immigrants often worked as "scabs" and strike-breakers during the early years when labor unions were finding the going rough.

However, as they became more familiar with the American way of life, these Italians realized that the Rockefellers, Astors, Carnegies, Morgans and other "robber barons" had been exploiting them mercilessly. Inevitably, union leaders emerged from these oppressed workers—Luigi Antonini of the International Ladies Garment Workers Union, August Bellanca of the Amalgamated

Clothing Workers of America, and James C. Petrillo of the American Federation of Musicians.

Though Italians were not numerous in the galaxy of the intelligentsia which immigrated to this country, some were among the most brilliant. Three won the Nobel Prize—physicists Enrico Fermi and Emilio Segre and virologist Salvador Luria. Other prominent creative minds from Italy included Guglielmo Marconi, conductor Arturo Toscanini, the Harvard historian Gaetano Salvemini, the journalist Max Ascoli, the Johns Hopkins physicist Franco Rasetti, the University of Chicago theoretical physicist, the radiobiologist, and physical chemist Ugo Fano, and the Yale medievalist Robert Lopez. These few examples by no means exhaust the list. In the natural and physical sciences there have been dozens of significant Italian-Americans serving on the faculties of universities, or working on research in industries and for the government. One of the most famous Italian physicians was William Francis Verdi of the Yale University Medical School.

Also included among noteworthy Italian-Americans have been many educators. The first Italian professor in America was Carlo Bellini, a friend of Mazzei and Jefferson, who was Professor of Romance Languages at William and Mary College. Other important Italian educators have been Mario Pei of Columbia University, one of the world's foremost linguistic authorities; the psychologist Leonard Covello; the sociologist Constantine Panunzio; and Angelo Patri, a high school principal in New York City who authored several best selling books on child training.

In the religious orders there have been many famous Italian-American clergymen. The first Italian priest to become widely known for his missionary work in the 1800's was Father Eusabio Chino. Benedict Sestini was a brilliant and highly versatile priest of the nineteenth century.

Through the writings of Italian-Americans themselves, the Italian experience is highlighted and given an intimacy which is difficult to obtain from outsiders. These books and stories express in personal and human terms the struggles of the people to blend the values and memories of Italy with the challenges and opportunities of the United States. The most widely read and moving account of the Italian experience is the autobiography, *Son of Italy,* by the famous poet, Pascal D'Angelo. Another valuable account of the American encounter is *The Soul of an Immigrant* by Constantine Panunzio. *Christ in Concrete* by Pietro Di Donato was a popular selling novel of an immigrant's life in America. Other excellent fiction by Italian-American authors has been the works of Jerre Mangione, Michael Capite, John Fante, Guido D'Agostino, and Jo Pagano. *Immigrant's Return* by Angelo Pellegrini, Professor of

English at the University of Washington, and *Americans by Choice,* are two excellent books.

Well-known Italian-American authors are Paul Gallico, Hamilton Basso, John Ciardi, and Bernard De Voto. Three Italian-born authors who settled in this country are Rodolfo Purcelli, Laura (Mrs. Aldous) Huxley, and novelist-biographer Frances Winwar (pseudonym for Francesca Vinceguerra).

Italian-Americans are also represented in the television industry by Nick Carrado, the well-known television producer. Carrado produces children's educational shows and is also known for his extensive work on the study of primates. His book *From Instinct to Intellect, a Study of Primates,* is considered one of the most comprehensive works on the subject.

The courage and loyalty of Italians during war has been proven innumerable times. Francisco Vigo, the fur trader, became a patriot during the Revolutionary War. Vigo was a giant of a man, standing nearly eight feet tall. Many legends grew up around his fierce fighting ability. He joined with George Rogers Clark to keep the British forces from the western frontier. During the Civil War Italians served the Union as both officers and enlisted men. In both world wars Italian-Americans earned high military honors. One of the most decorated heroes of World War II was Marine Sergeant John Basilone, whom General MacArthur called a "one-man army"; he received the Congressional Medal of Honor and, posthumously, the Navy Cross.

Recent news developments show that Antonio Meucci was probably the real inventor of the first telephone, beating Alexander Graham Bell by several months. E. O. Fenzi, the noted horticulturist, experimented for twenty years in introducing plants from all over the world to the warm and fertile soil of California. Electricity pioneers Peter Bellaschi and Giuseppe Faccioli were chief electrical engineers for many years at Westinghouse and General Electric. And Giuseppe Bellanca, a pioneer aviator, has long been considered the finest designer of early airplanes.

The Italian-Americans continue to represent the full spectrum of American life. Dubbed as an integral part of the silent majority, they also have their share of rebels and political activists like Mario Savio and the Reverend James Groppi. Through the agony of Sacco and Vanzetti, they are credited with two revolutionary martyrs.

It is hoped that the general reader as well as the Italian-American will see that Italian immigrants represent more than an ethnic group who built the New York subway and skyline, and occupy a middle ground in the scale of social acceptance, standing between Indian-Americans, Afro-Americans, Mexican-Americans and Puerto Ricans. Rather, this book shows that Italian-Americans have earned a place of distinction in the United States alongside of

Americans in all fields of endeavor. Mario Puzo believes that Italo-Americans have become "the most unaffectedly human of people." Equally perceptive is the statement by Brinley Thomas: "No one will deny the position occupied by the United States in the world today could never have been attained but for the periodic inflows of population over a long span." The fact that Italians have given the United States the benefit of their genius is a tribute to the integrity and unselfish character of Italians. It is with great and sincere respect for Italian-Americans that this book was born. The Italians have come to America to stay. They are the backbone and bright-hued threads woven firmly in the fabric of America.

It is not the intention of the authors to make a complete and comprehensive listing of the names and professions of Italian-Americans. Rather, we have tried to list a representative group from all of the professions where Italian-Americans have made significant contributions.

If the reader wishes to know the exact background of the persons named here, he may refer to WHO'S WHO ITALIO-AMERICAN, which can be found at most public libraries.

Abbadessa, John P	Controller, Atomic Energy Commission
Abbate, Paolo S.	Sculptor, writer & lecturer
Abbo, J. P.	U.S. Congressman (Dem. N.J.)
Addonizio, Hugh J.	Former Mayor Newark N.J.
Aimi, Dante	Dental Surgeon
Albino, Samuel F.	President, Albino Linoleum & Carpet Co.
Aloi, Thomas	Lawyer
Altiero, Nicholas J.	Dentist
Alvino, G.W.	Physician & Surgeon
Amici, Dominic L.	Business Executive
Amigone, Anthony	Funeral Director
Amendula, Fred H.	Asst. Clinical Professor of Surgery, Columbia University
Andretta, S.A.	Asst. Attorney General, U.S. Dept. Justice
Andriole, Gerald L.	Urologist
Angelo, Frank	Managing editor, Detroit Free Press
Angelucci, Venanzio	Dentist
Annunziata, Michele	Musician
Antonelli, Thomas E.	Lawyer
Ardito, Stefano Emilio	City Official
Argullo, Michael A.	Catholic Priest
Armanetti, Frank	Business Executive
Armani, Frank H.	Attorney
Arpair, Anthony F.	Public Official & Lawyer
Arrigo, Cyrus	Podiatrist

Artioli, Walter P.	Catholic Priest
Artusio, Joseph F.	Professor of Anesthesiology, N.Y. Hospital
Aulisi, Arthur C.	Country Judge of Fulton County
Aulisi, Felix J.	Judge
Michael Avallone	Writer
Ballistreri, Domenic	Magistrate
Balsano, Louis J.	Attorney
Banco, Vincent J.	Businessman
Bandini, Alberto R.	Catholic Priest, Author & Poet
Banino, Charles L.	Hotel Executive
Barba, Philip S.	Asst. Professor Preventive Medicine
Barbieri, Roger J.	Attorney
Barletta, Michael A.	Attorney
Barnabei, Allen	Chief, Office of Radio Frequency, National Bureau of Standards
Beinetti, George S.	President, Rochester Telephone Corporation
Bellanca, August	Labor Leader
Bellino, Vitus G.	Professor of Languages
Bello, Francis C.	Science Editor, Fortune Magazine
Benincasa, Pius A.	Auxiliary Bishop of Buffalo N.Y.
Berardi, Frank	Banker
Bernabel, Bruno P.	Lawyer & Public Official
Bernardi, Eugene D.	Importer
Bernardi, Simon D.	Catholic Priest
Bertoglio, Peter J.	Consulting Engineer
Bertoni, Louis P.	Judge
Bertusi, Armando F.	Importer
Besozzi, Leo	Consulting Engineer
Biaggini, Benjamin F.	President, Southern Pacific Railway Co.
Bianchini, Silvio A.	General Manager & V.P. Peerless Engineering
Bianco, Michele A.	Catholic Priest
Bigami, William N.	Hotel Executive
Bisceglia, John B.	Presbyterian Minister
Bisceglia, Joseph L.	Physician & Surgeon
Bonaccolto, Girolamo	Ophthalmologist
Bonadio, Anthony J.	Public Official & Lawyer
Bonarrigo, Beatrice L.	Dietitian
Bongiovanni, Alfred M.	Professor of Pediatrics Univ. Penn.
Bonidy, Joseph	Lawyer
Bonvini, Roger	Owner, Dental Laboratory
Borrelli, Henry A.	Catholic Priest
Borzone, Enrico M.	Painter, Sculptor
Botta, John Andrews	Financial Expert

Botticelli, William	Catholic Priest
Brusch, Charles A.	Physician & Director of Brusch Medical Center
Buccolo, George	President Utica Foundry
Buffardi, Louis J.	Business Executive & Lawyer
Bumbalo, Thomas S.	Physician & University Professor
Busa, Pierre	Paint Manufacturer
Busco, John J.	Catholic Priest
Cacioppo, Joseph E.	Physician & Surgeon
Calabresse, Joseph V.	Educator & Public Official
Calcaterra, Louis C.	Mortician
Califano, Joseph A. Jr.	Special Assistant to President Nixon
Campana, Jerry J.	Business Executive
Campisi, Rosario A.	President Industrial Enameling Corp.
Campo, Michael R.	College Professor
Campon, Peter T	Former President Binghamton City Council
Canepa, Louis J.	Lawyer & Public Official
Cantini, Raphael S.	Surgeon & Urologist
Capano, Adolph V.	Lawyer & State Representative
Capobianco, John	Builder
Caporale, Philip W.	Lawyer & Prosecuting Attorney
Capurso, Alexander	College President & Musician
Carbonara, Vernon	University Professor
Cardarelli, Michael P.	City Official
Cardone, Leonard P.	Lawyer & Public Official
Carfagno, Edward	Motion Picture Art Director
Cariello, Mario J.	President, Borough of Queens, N.Y.
Carnazzo, Sebastian J.	Surgeon
Carneglia, Vito	Jewelry Manufacturer
Carnicelli, Carlo	Architect & Engineer
Carpino, Simon F.	Lawyer
Carretta, Albert	Educator & Public Official
Carsello, Anthony D.	General Contractor
Carusi, Ugo	U.S. Government Official
Caruso, Mario	Manufacturer
Casassa, Charles S.	Catholic Priest & Educator
Casella, Louis J.	Attorney
Cassiol, Elvio J.	General Building Contractor
Castano, Giovanni	Artist
Castiglione, Salvatore J.	Professor of Italian, Georgetown Univ.
Catelli, Bianchini, E.	Educator
Cavallucci, Peter J.	Catholic Priest
Cavicchia, Dominic A.	Lawyer & Past Deputy Attorney General for N.J. & Speaker of House N.J.

Cavicchia, Peter A.	Lawyer & Former U.S. Congressman
Cecere, Gaetano	Sculptor & Teacher
Cella, Francis R.	Economist
Cenci, Novello N.	Dental Surgeon
Cerulli, Dorando J.	Attorney
Cerulli, Raffaele	Mason Contractor
Cervino, Anthony L.	Surgeon
Chiara, Anthony R.	Attorney
Chiarello, Joseph	Manufacturer of Therapeutic lamps
Chiodo, Vincent	Insurance Executive
Christiano, Frank P.	Business Executive
Ciaccio, Paul	Catholic Priest
Cianciosi, Leo A.	Attorney
Ciardi, Joseph	Dress Manufacturer
Ciarlo, Anthony	Town Attorney
Cinelli, Joseph	Realtor
Cipolla, Carl J.	Attorney
Cipolla, Carlo M.	Professor of Economics, Univ. of Calif.
Cipollaro, Anthony C.	Clinical Professor of Dermatology, Cornell
Cirillo, Frank A.	Chief, Technical Program, Div. Area Redevelopment Administration, U.S. Dept. Commerce
Cislini, Francis H.	Publisher of *The Californian*
Clavelli, Alfred M.	Regional Manager, U.S. General Acct. Office
Coccia, Frank D.	Supreme Secretary, Italo-American National Union
Cocco, Domenico	Civic Leader
Colapietro, Bruno	Attorney
Comito, Vinzo	Journalist
Constantino, Americo	Catholic Priest
Contiguglia, Anthony J.	City Official & Lawyer
Corgiat, Peter P.	Bank Executive & City Official
Corleto, Fred T.	Management Director City of Philadelphia
Corradi, P.	Rear Admiral
Corrado, Nick Jr.	T.V. Producer, Business Executive
Corrado, Pietro	Surgeon
Correnti, Nicholas A.	Physician & Surgeon
Corriere, Joseph	Univ. Instructor & Surgeon
Corso, Gaspare A.	Insurance Executive
Corso, Joseph R.	Public Official & Attorney
Cortese, Ralph	Electrode Manufacturer
Corvese, Anthony	Physician
Corvino, Rudolph	Assistant Professor, Industrial Relations, Cornell University

Coscia, Dominic	Bishop of Jalai, Brazil
Cosenza, Michael A.	Journalist
Costabile, Hugo	Pharmacist
Costabile, Vincenzo	Surgeon
Costagliola, F.	Assistant Secretary of Defense
Costanzo, Henry J.	Director, Office of Latin America U.S. Dept. of Treasury
Costanzo, Thomas J.	Funeral Director
Costanzo, Vincent A.	Surgeon
Crippa, Edward D.	Former U.S. Senator
Crisculol, Anthony J.	Attorney
Cupelli, Albert	Italian Consular Agent
D'Addario, E.Q.	U.S. Congressman
Daleo, James	Lawyer
Dalelio, Gaetano F.	Research Professor, Chemistry
D'Alesandro, Thomas Jr.	Political Leader
D'Alesandro, Clelia	Lawyer
D'Alfonso, Alexander C.	Builder
D'Ambra, Giuseppina	Business Executive
Damia, Peter A.	Attorney
Damiano, Celestino J.	Bishop of Camden N.J.
DaParma, Ulysses E.	V.P. Sperry-Gyroscope Co.
D'Aquila, Joseph	Excavation Contractor
Dardano, Nicholas S.	Pharmacist
Davito, Silvio	Surgeon
DeAngelis, Roger	Photographer
De Bartolo, Hansel M.	Surgeon
De Benedictis, Matthew M.	Catholic Priest
De Capite, Raymond	Novelist
De Carlo, Charles A.	Director of Education, I.B.M. Corp.
Dc Ciantis, Michael	Lawyer
De Cillis, Joseph A.	Hotel Executive
De Dominicis, Rocco N.	County Official
De Falice, Richard A.	Assistant Administrator of Trade, U.S. Dept. of Agriculture
De Ferrari, Roy F.	University Secretary General
De Francisci, Anthony	Sculptor
De Furia, James H.	Industrialist
De Grazia, Sebastian	Educator
Del Bello, Sylvester	Attorney
Del Bene, Donald	Attorney
Del Brusco, Gaetano	Catholic Priest
Delegge, Henry	Funeral Director
D'Elia, Paul	General Broker
Della Badia, Leonard	Catholic Priest
Della Pietra, Alfonso	Orthopedic Surgeon
Del Monaco, Mario	Opera Singer

Del Multolo, M.C.	Judge, Superior Court
Delorenzo, Anthony G.	V.P. General Motors Corp.
Del Sasso, Leo	Professor Emeritus Physics, Univ. Calif.
Del Sesto, Angelo	Jewelry Manufacturer
Del Sesto, John	Baker
Del Terzo, Robert	Surgeon
De Luca, Pino	Art Dealer
De Luccia, Emil	Engineer Chief & V.P. Pacific Power & Light
De Majoribus, A.L.	Business Executive
De Marco, Angelo	General Contractor
De Marco, Anthony R.	Farmer & County Official
De Marco F.	President, South African Marine Corp.
De Marco, Roland	College Professor
De Marieo, Ignatius M.	Surgeon
De Novellis, Fileno	Labor Leader
Dent, John H.	U.S. Congressman
De Palma, Anthony	Orthopedist
De Palma, Samuel	Chief, Political Affairs, Division of U.S. Arms Control Agency
De Pastino, John	President Columbia Insurance Co.
De Petra, Giolio	Public Educator & Professor
De Pilla, Albert T.	Horticulturist
De Prenda, Salvator	Chief, Senate Staff, Veterans Administration
De Prophetis, Rocco	Physician
De Rossi, Domenich	Clothing Manufacturer
De Santillana, Giorgio	Professor, History & Philosophy, M.I.T.
De Sapio, Carmine	Former Leader Tammany Hall
D'Esopo, Anthony	Professor, Clinical Obstetrics, Columbia University
De Stefano, Ettore	Publisher
De Stio, Daniel	Physician
Di Censo, Alfred A.	Manufacturer of Acetate Rayon
Di Dio, Frank P.	Surgeon
Di George, Angelo	Assistant Professor of Pediatrics
Di Giantomasso, Ettore	Methodist Minister
Di Giovanni, Mariano	General Contractor
Di Grazia, Anthony	Attorney
Di Gregorio, Sabantino	Manufacturer of Optical Glass specialties
Di Lello, Francesco P.	Restauranteur
Di Leone, Ralph	Surgeon
Di Lisio, Joseph	Banker

Di Luzio, Frank C.	Assistant Secretary of Interior
Di Lorenzo, Jack T.	Assistant General Counsel, Opinion Div. U.S. Post Office Dept.
Di Meglio, Francis A.	Director, Reactor Operations, R.I. Nuclear Science Center
Di Meo, Anthony L.	Catholic Priest
Di Michael, Salvatore	Psychologist
Di Nardo, Romeo	General Contractor
Di Nicola, Louis F.	Lawyer
Di Palma, Joseph	Professor & Chairman of Department of Pharmacology, Hahneman Medical College
Di Saia, Oresto	Architect
Di Silvestro, Anthony J.	State Senator & Publisher
Di Somma, August H.	Assistant Professor, Organic Chemistry, Columbia Univ.
Di Stefano, Leo	Journalist
Di Vesta, Francis J.	Professor, Psychology, Syracuse Univ.
Donadio, Vincent J.	Lawyer
Dorzaio, Arthur	News Editor, Detroit Free Press
D'Orsa, Charles S.	Major General of Berlin Command
D'Urso, John J.	Dermatologist
Durso, J.P.	Head of City Desk, New York Times
Einaudi, Mario	Professor, Government, Cornell Univ.
Emma, Frank A.	Assemblyman
Errigo, Joseph A.	Lawyer
Fabbri, Remo	Physician
Falbo, Ernest S.	College Professor
Falcone, Anthony T.	Insurance Executive
Falcone, Leonard	Professor of Music, Michigan State Univ.
Falvello, Conrad	Lawyer
Fanelli, Michael A.	Mason Contractor
Farbo, Joseph	Lawyer
Farina, Andrew P.	Catholic Priest
Fazio, Carl	Business Executive
Ferrara, Carl	Florist
Ferrara, Vincent E.	Supreme Treasurer, Italo-American National Union
Ferrazzi, Thomas	Catholic Priest
Ferri, Antonio	Physicist
Ferri, Nicholas A.	Physician
Finelli, Henry N.	Dentist
Finelli, Anthony	Lawyer & College Professor
Fleri, Paul C.	Urologist
Franchino, Luigi C.	Catholic Priest

Frasca, William R.	Chairman, Dept. Political Science, Fordham Univ.
Funaro, James V.	Writer
Fusco, James E.	Insurance Executive
Fusco, John H.	Banker
Galante, Thomas A.	Manufacturer of Paper Products
Galli, Cesare J.	Attorney
Gallo, Anthony J.	Judge
Gallo, Fortunato	President of San Carlo Grand Opera Co.
Gallo, Paul S.	Candle Manufacturer
Garbarino, Joseph W.	Professor of Business Administration, & Economic Research, Univ. of California
Garbin, Arthur L.	Catholic Priest
Gardella, Louis	Photographer
Garofalo, Mauro J.	Business Executive
Gasbarro, Ugo	Lawyer
Gelormini, Otto	Physician & Chemist
Gentile, G.	Deputy Assistant Secretary of State
Gerbino, A. R.	Catholic Priest
Giaimo, R.N.	U.S. Congressman
Giannini, Claire	Bank Executive
Gillette, Henry E.	Mayor of Rochester New York
Giordano, Anthony	Dean, Graduate School of Brooklyn Polytechnic Institute
Giordano, John C.	Ex-Judge
Giunta, Joseph	Business Executive
Gobatti, John	Manufacturer
Gorino, Luigi	Lecturer on Bacteriology at Harvard Univ.
Grandi, Louis L.	Professor of Engineering, Univ. of Calif.
Grasso, Ella T.	Governor of Conn.
Graziano, Charles C.	Labor Leader
Greco, Charles P.	Bishop of Alexandrea, La.
Grieco, Reynold M.	Proctologist & Physicist
Grillo, Elmer V.	Professor of Business Administration, N.Y.U.
Grillo, Hermes C.	Professor, Clinical Surgery, Harvard University
Grillo, Nicholas	Floriculturist
Grippo, Dan	Business Executive
Grossi, Olindo	Dean, School of Architecture, Pratt Institute
Gualillo, Nicholas D.	Orchestra & Opera Conductor
Guarnieri, Lewis L.	Lawyer
Gubellini, Carlo	Assistant Dean of College of Business Adm. Northeastern Univ.
Gugino, Anthony S.	Dentist & Professor

Iacchia, Luigi	Research Assistant, Harvard College Observatory
Iacocca, Lee A.	V.P. Divisional Manager of Ford Motor Co.
Infante, Anthony	Sculptor & Painter
Ingrassia, Anthony	Lawyer
Italia, Gabriel	Catholic Priest
Jackvony, Louis	Lawyer
Julian, Anthony	Lawyer
La Fauci, Horatio	Dean, College of Basic Studies Boston University
Lama, Alfred A.	Architect & Assemblyman
Lamanna, John	Florist
Lamberti, Nicholas J.	Physiotherapist
Lambiase, Charles	Judge
Lanza, George V.	Lawyer
Lanzo, Samuel	Mason Contractor
La Piana, George	Professor Emeritus of Church History, Harvard Univ.
Lascari, Salvatore	Artist
Lasgna, Louis C.	Assistant Professor of Medicine & Pharmacology, Johns Hopkins Univerisity
Latona, Jacob A.	Lawyer
Lavalle, Paul	Musician, & Composer
Laverne, Thomas	Lawyer
Lavrelli, Robert C.	President, National Plumbing Corp.
Lazzaro, Ralph	Director of Languages Studies, Harvard
Leone, John P.	Financial Executive
Liberatore, N.A.	V.P. Raymond Corp.
Ligutti, Luigi G.	Executive Director National Catholic Rural Life Conference
Lo Franco, Ari J.	Publisher & Lawyer
Longarini, Graziano N.	Editor, Publisher
Lo Presti, Salvatore	Protestant Minister
Lo Sasso, D. E.	Ophthalmologist
Lovbet, Francis	Voice Specialist
Mago, Francesco S.	Creator & Designer of Jewelry
Majno, Guido	Assistant Professor of Pathology, Harvard
Mancino, Sabato	Fraternal Leader
Manfredi, Opilio	Restauranteur
Mangone, Gerard J.	Professor of Political Science & Assistant Dean of Graduate School in Public Affairs, Syracuse Univ.
Marchetta, Francis J.	Chiropractor

Marchisio, Juvenal	Judge
Marimpietri, Anzuimo D.	Banker & Labor Leader
Marinaccio, Anthony	Educator
Marinaro, Enzo	Publisher, Editor
Marni, Archimede	College Professor
Marolla, Ed	Writer & Journalist
Marranzino, Pasquale	Editorial Writer
Marsello, Alfred	Jewelry Manufacturer
Martinelli, Giovanni	Tenor
Martino, Alfredo	Singing Teacher
Martino, Joseph A.	President, National Lead Co.
Marto, Joseph	Investment Banker
Massari, Philip	State Representative
Massari, Vincenzo	State Senator
Matacena, Nicola	Civic Leader
Matrumalo, Anthony F.	Architect
Mattiello, Joseph	Chemist
Mazzarella, Bernardino	Roman Catholic Bishop
Mazzitella, William F.	Assistant Professor of Medicine, Univ. Minn.
Merlini, Charles G.	Production Manager
Merlino, Camillo P.	University Professor
Merolle, Augustus	Manufacturer
Miceli, F.P.	Writer & Poet
Miller, George	U.S. Congressman
Millonzi, Robert	Lawyer
Mirabella, Rosamond	Civic Leader
Mirabelli, Eugene	College Professor
Modesti, John	General Contractor
Molino, Francis F.	Catholic Priest
Mondolfo, L.P.	Educator
Montana, Pietro	Sculptor
Montana, Vanni	Journalist
Morreale, Paul	Judge
Muccio, John J.	Diplomat
Mugnano, Pasquale	Catholic Priest
Mussio, John King	Bishop of Steubenville, Ohio
Nestico, Julie A.	Restauranteur
Nicastro, Louis	Business Executive
Orfei, Felix	General Contractor
Ortale, Anthony S.	Director of Italian-American Radio
Pace, Antonio	Professor of Romance Languages, Syracuse U.
Pace, Charles	Pharmacist
Palermo, Nicholos	Business Executive

Panarese, Nicholos	Coal Merchant
Panigrosso, Louis	Surgeon
Paolantonio, Fortunato	President, Colonial Knife Company
Papale, Antonio E.	Dean and Professor of Law, Catholic Univ.
Pappano, Joseph E.	Deputy Attorney General, U.S.A.
Paradiso, Louis J.	Assistant Director, Office of Business Economics, U.S. Department of Commerce
Parisi, Paolo	Journalist
Pasquariello, Patrick	Gynecologist
Pasquariello, Peter C.	Textile Manufacturer
Pasto, Michael	Catholic Priest
Pecora, Ferdinand	Judge
Pei, Mario A.	Professor, Romance Philology, Columbia Univ.
Pellegrini, Casimir	Architect
Pernicone, Joseph	Episcopal Vicar
Perona, Paul D.	Past Assistant Attorney General, U.S.A.
Perrone, Joseph	Surgeon
Petrossi, John	Industrialist
Picciano, Dominic	Manufacture of Perfume
Pierotti, John	Cartoonist, New York Post Newspaper
Pirri, Angelo	Banker
Pirrotta, Nino	Professor of Music, Harvard
Piston, Walter	Composer
Pizzeglio, William	Catholic Priest
Pomponio, Michael	State Senator
Pope, Robert Fortune	Publisher and Business Executive
Potenza, Austin	Chief, Walter Reed Army Institute of Research
Privitera, Santi	Catholic Priest
Provenzano, Patrick	State Official
Pucci, Dominic	College Professor
Raffetto, Edward	Rear Admiral & Dental Inspector, U.S. Navy
Raffi, Charles	Manufacturer
Ragazzini, John	Educator
Raiffo, Howard	Professor of Business Administration, Harvard
Rano, Michael	Attorney
Renze, Nicholas R.	Cigar Manufacture
Reviglio, Peter	Owner of a supermarket chain
Richardi, R.	General Contractor
Rodino, Peter W., Jr.	U.S. Congressman

Romano, Jerame	Physician
Rossetti, John	Judge
Rossi, Bruno	Physicist
Rossi, Mario	Managing editor, Post-Standard Newspaper
Rossi, Robert	Wine Specialist
Rossotti, Alfred	Lithographer
Rota, Gian	Assistant Professor of Math, M.I.T.
Rotondi, Joseph	Department Head of Music, Combs College
Rubba, John	Catholic Priest
Rubino, Pasquale	Conductor
Russo, Joseph	City Official
Salanitro, Alfredo	Pharmacist
Salerni, Guerino	Architect
Sandula, A.	State Official
Santarsiero, D.	Ophthalmologist
Santosuosso, Principio	Journalist
Saponaro, John	Chief Engineer
Sardi, Melchiorre	Restauranteur
Scalapino, Robert	Professor and Past Chairman of Department Political Science, Univ. Calif.
Scicchitano, Romualdo	Surgeon
Scileppi, John	Judge
Scordo, Jack	Attorney
Screnci, Salvatore	Catholic Priest
Scrivane, Paul	Deputy Mayor & Past President New York City Council
Sculco, L.	Judge
Sedita, Frank	Mayor of Buffalo, New York
Shangher, Charles	Judge
Sica, Albert	Dean, College of Pharmacy, Fordham University
Simonetti, Albert	Catholic Priest
Sirayusa, Ross	Chairman of Board, Admiral Corporation
Sirica, John	U.S. District Court Judge
Sisti, Anthony	City Official
Sisto, Louis	V.P. & Director United Fruit Co.
Sorrentino, Anthony	Sociologist
Sperrazzo, Gerald	Clinical Psychologist
Sperti, George	Vice President, N.B.C.
Tagiuri, Renato	Professor of Social Sciences, Harvard
Tasca, Henry	Diplomat
Taurasi, Anthony	Home Builder

Tauro, G.	Chief Justice, Mass. Superior Court
Tedesco, Samuel	Lieutenant Governor of Conn.
Teresi, Matteo	Editor, New York Post Newspaper
Toigo, Adolph	President, Lennen & Newell Advertising Agency
Tomas, Carmelo	Journalist
Tomasello, Samuel	General Contractor
Turilli, Nicholas	Sculptor
Urbani, Robert	Business Executive
Valenti, John	Surgeon
Valeo, Francis	Assistant to Mike Mansfield
Vannelli, Ronald	Director of Chemistry Laboratory, Harvard
Vecoli, Rudolf J.	University Professor
Viglione, Amy A.	Dean, School of Nursing, Univ. South Carolina
Vitale, Joseph J.	Assistant Professor, Nutrition
Viviano, Bartholomew J.	Railroad Executive
Votolato, Arthur N.	Judge
Warren, Harry	Composer
Young, Fred A.	Chairman, N.Y. Republican State Committee
Zappulla, Giuseppe	Journalist, Poet
Zecca, Anthony P.	Deputy Mayor of Philadelphia

BIBLIOGRAPHY

BOOKS

Amory, Cleveland, *The Celebrity Register*, Harper & Row 1963.

Bacci, Massimo Livi. *L'emigrazione e l'assimilazione degli italiani negli Stati Uniti secondo le statistiche demografiche* 1961.

Baltzell, E. Digby. *The Protestant Establishment*. N.Y. 1964.

Barker, Virgil. *Am. Painting History and Interpretation*, N.Y. 1960.

Barzini, Luigi. *The Italians*. N.Y. Atheneum 1964.

Burckhardt, Jakob. *The Civilization of the Renaissance in Italy*. London: 1937.

Carpenter, Niles. *Immigrants and Their Children*. Washington, 1927.

Clark, Francis E. *Our Italian Fellow Citizens*. Boston, 1919.

Cole, Donald B. *Immigrant City, Lawrence, Mass. 1845-1921*. Chapel Hill, 1963.

Corsi, Edward. *In the Shadow of Liberty, The Chronicle of Ellis Island*. N.Y., 1937

Covello, Leonard. *The Social Background of the Italo-American School Child*. N.Y., 1967

Davie, Maurice R. *World Immigration with Special Reference to the United States*. N.Y., 1936

De Latil, Pierre. *Enrico Fermi, The Man and His Theories*. N.Y. 1966

Di Donato, Pietro. *Christ in Concrete*. N.Y. 1939.

Federal Writers Project. *The Italians of New York*. N.Y., 1938.

Fermi, Laura. *Atoms in the Family: My Life with Enrico Fermi*. Chicago, 1954.

————. *Mussolini*. Chicago, 1961.

Fleming, Donald and Bernard Bailyn. *The Intellectual Migration Europe and America*. Cambridge, 1969.

Foerster, Robert F. *The Italian Emigration of Our Times*. London, 1919.

Garlick, Richard C., Jr. *Italy and the Italians in Washington's Time*, N.Y., 1933.

Groce, George C. and David H. Wallace. *The New York His-*

torical Society's Dictionary of Artists in America. 1564-1860. New Haven, 1957.

Hansen, Marcus Lee. *The Atlantic Migration, 1607-1860.* Cambridge, 1940.

Hibbert, Christopher. *Garibaldi and His Enemies.* Boston, 1966.

Hutchinson, E. P. *Immigrants and Their Children, 1850-1950.* N.Y. 1956.

Immigration Saint - The Life of Mother Cabrini N.Y., 1960. 1930-1941. Chicago, 1968.

Italians in Chicago, Chicago, 1928. *Italians in America before the Civil War,.* N.Y. 1952.

Kennedy, John F. *A Nation of Immigrants.* N.Y. 1964.

Kubly, Herbert. *American in Italy.* N.Y. 1954.

La Gumina, Salvatore J. *Vito Marcantonio, The People's Politician.* Dubuque, 1969.

Lonn, Ella. *Foreigners in the Union Army and Navy.* Louisiana, 1951.

Lord, Eliot, J.D. Trenor, Samuel J. Barrows. *The Italian in America* N.Y., 1905

Mangano, Antonio. *Sons of Italy: A Social and Religious Study of the Italians in America.* Boston, 1917.

Mangione, Jerre. *America Is Also Italian.* N.Y., 1969.

Mann, Arthur. *La Guardia A Fighter Against His Times, 1882-1933.* Philadelphia, 1959.

Mariano, John Horace. *The Italian Contribution to American Democracy.* Boston, 1921.

Musmanno, Michael A. *The Story of the Italians in America.* N.Y., 1965.

Neidle, Cecyle S. *The New Americans.* N.Y., 1967.

Pei, Mario. *The Story of Language.* Philadelphia, 1949.

Phillips, John. *Face of a Nation: The Italians.* N.Y., 1965.

Pisani, Lawrence Frank. *The Italian in America: A Social Study and History.* N.Y. 1957.

Puzo, Mario. *The Godfather.* N.Y., 1969.

Rolle, Andrew. *The Immigrant Upraised.* N.Y., 1968.

Rose, Philip M. *The Italians in America.* N.Y., 1922.

Sartorio, Enrico C. *Social and Religious Life of Italians in America.* Boston, 1918.

Schiavo, Giovanni E. *Four Centuries of Italian-American History.* N.Y., 1952.

Shaw, Arnold. *Sinatra: Twentieth Century Romantic,* NY. 1968.

Smith, Denis. *Italy.* Mich., 1959.

Steiner, Edward A. *On the Trail of the Immigrant.* N.Y., 1906.

Stella, Antonio. *Some Aspects of Italian Immigration to the United States.* N.Y., 1924.

Suttles, Gerald D. *The Social Order of the Slum: Ethnicity and Territory in the Inner City.* Chicago, 1968.

Torrielli, Andrew J. *Italian Opinion on America as Revealed by Italian Travelers 1850-1900.* Cambridge, 1941.

Trauth, Sister Mary Philip. *Italo-American Diplomatic Relations, 1861-1882.* Washington, 1958.

Trevelyan, Janet Penrose. *A Short History of the Italian People.* N.Y., 1920.

Wittke, Carl. *We Who Built America: The Saga of the Immigrant.* Western Reserve, 1964.

ARTICLES

Baily, Samuel L. "The Italians and Organized Labor in the United States and Argentina, 1880-1910" *The International Migration Review,* I Summer, 1967. 56-66

Berthoff, Rowland T. "Southern Attitudes Toward Immigration 1865-1914," *The Journal of Southern History,* XVI August, 1951 328-60.

Carter, Hugh "Reappraising our Immigration Policy," *The annals of the American Academy of Political and Social Science,* CCLXII March, 1949, entire issue.

Cassels, Alan. "Fascism for Export: Italy and the United States in the Twenties," *The American Historical Review,* LXIX April, 1964.

Ciolli, Dominic T. "The Wop in the Track Gang." *The Immigrants in America Review,* II July, 1916, 61-64.

Claghorn, Kate Holladay, "The Italian Under Economic Stress," *Charities,* May 7, 1904, 501-04.

Duff, John. "The Italians," in Joseph P. O'Grady, ed. *The Immigrants' Influence on Wilson's Peace Policies.* Lexington, 1967.

Fante, J. "Odyssey of a Wop," *The American Mercury,* XXX September 1933, 89-97.

Fenton, Edwin. "Italians in the Labor Movement," *Pennsylvania History,* XXVI April, 1959, 133-48.

Lodge, Henry Cabot. "Efforts to Restrict Undesirable Immigration," *The Century Magazine,* LXVII January, 1904, 466-69.

Mangano, Antonio. "The Associated Life of the Italians in New York City," *Charities,* XII June, 1953, 203-14.

Mondello, Salvatore. "Italian Migration to the U.S. as Reported in American Magazines, 1880-1920." *Social Science,* XLI April, 1966.

Pecorini, Alberto. "The Italians in the United States," *The Forum,* XLV January, 1911, 15-19.

Puzo, Mario. "The Italians, American Style," *The New York Times Magazine,* August 6, 1967.

Walsh, James J. "An Apostle of the Italians," *The Catholic World,* CVII April, 1918, 64-71.

ITALIAN-AMERICAN AUTOBIOGRAPHIES AND BIOGRAPHIES

Constantino Brumidi

Brown, Gen. *History of the U.S. Capitol.* Washington, D.C., 1900.

Fairman, Charles E. *Our Debt to Italy. The Art of the Italian Artists in the U.S. Capitol.* Washington, D.C., 1930.

Hazelton, George C. *Our National Capitol: Its Architecture, Art and History.* N.Y. 1914.

Herron, Paul. *The Story of Capitol Hill.* N.Y. 1963.

Life Magazine. *The Capitol: A Picture Tour.* July 2, 1951.

Saint Frances Xavier Cabrini

Borden, Lucille Papin. *Francesca Cabrini: Without Staff or Scrip.* N.Y. 1945.

Cabrini, Francesca Xavier. *Travels of Mother Frances Xavier Cabrini.* N.Y., 1944.

Di Donato, Pietro. *Immigrant Saint: The Life of Mother Cabrini.* N.Y. 1960.

Maynard, Theodore. *Great Catholics in American History.* N.Y. 1957.

Caruso, Dorothy, *Enrico Caruso: His Life and Death.* N.Y., 1945.

Luigi Palma Di Cesnola

Cesnola, General Louis Palma di. *Cyprus: Its Ancient Cities, Tombs and Temples.* N.Y. 1878. *The Metropolitan Museum of Art.* N.Y. 1882.

Howe, Winifred E. *A History of the Metropolitan Museum of Art.* N.Y. 1913.

Myres, J. L. *Handbook of the Cesnola Collection of Antiquities from Cyprus.* 1914. .

Preyer, David C *The Art of the Metropolitan Museum of New York.* Boston, 1913.

Corsi, Edward. *In the Shadow of Liberty*. N.Y. 1935.
D'Angelo, Pascal. *Son of Italy*. N.Y. 1924.

Enrico Fermi
Amrine, Michael. *The Great Decision*. N.Y. 1959.
Compton, Arthur H. *Atomic Quest*. N.Y. 1956.
Fermi, Laura. *Atoms in the Family*. Chicago. 1954.
Groves, Leslie R. *Now It Can Be Told*. N.Y. 1962.
Jungk, Robert. *Brighter Than a Thousand Suns*. N.Y. 1958.
Lang, Daniel. *From Hiroshima to the Moon*. N.Y. 1959.
Laurence, William L. *Dawn Over Zero*. N.Y. 1946.
Purcell, John. *The Best Kept Secret*. N.Y. 1963.
Rasetti, Franco. *Enrico Fermi*. N.Y. 1955.

A. P. Giannini
Dana, Julian. *A. P. Giannini: Giant in the West*. N.Y. 1947.
Forber, B. C. *America's Fifty Foremost Business Leaders*. N.Y. 1948.
James, Marquis Rowland. *Biography of a Bank*. N.Y. 1954.
Nicosia, Francesco M. *Italian Pioneers of California*. San Francisco, 1960.
Rink, Paul, *A. P. Giannini: Building the Bank of America*. Chicago. 1963.

Fiorello H. La Guardia
Cuneo, Ernest. *Life with Fiorello*. N.Y. 1955.
Franklin, Jay. *La Guardia: A Biography*. N.Y. 1937.
Gluck, Gemma. *La Guardia: My Story*. N.Y. 1961.
La Guardia, Fiorello H. *The Making of an Insurgent, 1882-1919*. Phila. 1948.
Limpus, Lowell and Leyson, Burr. *This Man La Guardia*. N.Y. 1938.
Mann, Arthur. *La Guardia: A Fighter Against His Times, 1882-1933*. Phila. 1959.
Moses, Robert. *La Guardia: A Salute and a Memoir*. N.Y. 1957.
Rodman, Bella. *Fiorello La Guardia*. N.Y. 1962.
Tugwell, Rexford Guy. *The Art of Politics*. N.Y. 1958.
Weston, Paul B. *A Hammer in the City*. N.Y. 1962.

Philip Mazzei
Bowers, Claude. *The Young Jefferson*. Boston. 1945.
Boyd, Julia P. *The Papers of Thomas Jefferson*. N.J. 1952.
Garlick, Julian C., Jr. *Philip Mazzei, Friend of Jefferson: His Life and Letters*. Md., 1933.
Marraro, Howard R. *Unpublished Mazzei Letters to Jefferson*. N.C. 1945.

Philip Mazzei *(cont.)*
   Schiavo, Giovanni. *One of America's Founding Fathers.* N.Y. 1951.
   Wilstach, Paul. *Jefferson and Monticello.* N.Y. 1925.

   Panunzio, Constantine. *The Soul of an Immigrant.* N.Y. 1937.
   Patri, Angelo. *A Schoolmaster of the Great City.* N.Y. 1928.
   Pinza, Ezio. *Ezio Pinza: An Autobiography.* N.Y., 1958.
   Russell, Francis. *Tragedy of Dedham: The Story of the Sacco-Vanzetti Case.* N.Y. 1962.

Arturo Toscanini
   Antek, Samuel. *This Was Toscanini.* N.Y. 1963.
   Chotzinoff, Samuel. *Toscanini: An Intimate Portrait.* N.Y. 1956.
   Ewen, David. *The Story of Arturo Toscanini.* N.Y. 1951.
   Gatti-Casazza, Giulio. *Memories of the Opera.* N.Y. 1941.
   Gilaman, Lawrence. *Toscanini and Great Music.* N.Y. 1938.
   Haggin, B. H. *Conversations with Toscanini.* N.Y. 1959.
   Hughes, Spike. *The Toscanini Legacy.* London 1959.
   Kolodin, Irving. *The Story of the Metropolitan Opera, 1883-1950.* N.Y. 1953.
   Sacchi, Filippo. *The Magic Baton.* N.Y. 1957.
   Sargent, Winthrop. *Geniuses, Goddesses and People.* N.Y. 1949.
   Schickel, Richard. *The World of Carnegie Hall.* N.Y. 1960.
   Stefan-Gruenfeldt, Paul. *Arturo Toscanini.* N.Y. 1936.
   Taubman, Howard. *The Maestro.* N.Y. 1951.

   Ventresca, Francesco. *Personal Reminiscences of a Naturalized American.* N.Y. 1937.

INDEX